SUPPLY CHAINS IN EXPORT AGRICULTURE, COMPETITION, AND POVERTY IN SUB-SAHARAN AFRICA

Supply Chains in Export Agriculture, Competition, and Poverty in Sub-Saharan Africa

Copyright © 2011 by
The International Bank for Reconstruction and Development/The World Bank
1818 H Street, NW, Washington, DC 20433, USA

ISBN: 978-1-907142-20-8

Typeset by T&T Productions Ltd, London

Published in association with the London Publishing Partnership
www.londonpublishingpartnership.co.uk

Centre for Economic Policy Research

The Centre for Economic Policy Research is a network of over 700 Research Fellows and Affiliates, based primarily in European universities. The Centre coordinates the research activities of its Fellows and Affiliates and communicates the results to the public and private sectors. CEPR is an entrepreneur, developing research initiatives with the producers, consumers and sponsors of research. Established in 1983, CEPR is a European economics research organization with uniquely wide-ranging scope and activities.

The Centre is pluralist and non-partisan, bringing economic research to bear on the analysis of medium- and long-run policy questions. CEPR research may include views on policy, but the Executive Committee of the Centre does not give prior review to its publications, and the Centre takes no institutional policy positions. The opinions expressed in this report are those of the authors and not those of the Centre for Economic Policy Research.

CEPR is a registered charity (No. 287287) and a company limited by guarantee and registered in England (No. 1727026).

The World Bank

The World Bank Group is a major source of financial and technical assistance to developing countries around the world, providing low-interest loans, interest-free credits and grants for investments and projects in areas such as education, health, public administration, infrastructure, trade, financial and private sector development, agriculture, and environmental and natural resource management. Established in 1944 and headquartered in Washington, DC, the Group has over 100 offices worldwide. The World Bank's mission is to fight poverty with passion and professionalism for lasting results and to help people help themselves and their environment by providing resources, sharing knowledge, building capacity and forging partnerships in the public and private sectors.

Supply Chains in Export Agriculture, Competition, and Poverty in Sub-Saharan Africa

GUIDO PORTO, NICOLAS DEPETRIS CHAUVIN
AND MARCELO OLARREAGA

Contents

List of Figures

List of Tables

About the Authors

Guido Porto is a Professor of Economics at the University of La Plata in Argentina. Before joining the University of La Plata, he was an economist in the Research Department of the World Bank. He has taught at Universidad and Instituto Di Tella in Argentina and at the University of Maryland as an invited lecturer. He received a BA in Economics from the University of La Plata in Argentina, a Master's degree in Economics from Instituto Di Tella in Argentina, and a PhD in Economics from Princeton University. His research focuses on the econometric estimation of the impacts of trade policies in developing countries, including impacts on poverty, household welfare, wages, and the distribution of income as well as on firm behavior. His latest work investigates how economic agents (households and firms) adjust to trade reform.

Nicolas Depetris Chauvin is Assistant Professor of Public Policy at Dubai School of Government and a Research Fellow at the Oxford Centre for the Analysis of Resource Rich Economies in the Department of Economics at the University of Oxford. Previously he worked as a policy specialist in the Office of Development Studies at the United Nations Development Programme and as a consultant at the World Bank, the Inter-American Development Bank, and the Ministry of Economics of Argentina, among others. His fields of interest are international finance, development, macroeconomics, and resource-rich economies. During his doctoral studies at Princeton University he did research on debt-relief initiatives for highly indebted poor countries.

Marcelo Olarreaga is Professor of Economics at the University of Geneva and Research Fellow at the Centre for Economic Policy Research in London. Before joining the University of Geneva he worked as an economist in the Research Department of the World Bank, as well as in the Economics Research Division of the World Trade Organization. He has also been an invited professor at INSEAD (France), Institute CLAEH (Uruguay), SciencePo-Paris (France), Universidad de la República (Uruguay), and the University of Antwerp (Belgium). He holds an MA from the University of Sussex, and a PhD in Economics from the University of Geneva. He is currently doing research on the political economy of trade policy and trade agreements, barriers to developing countries' exports, and distributional and poverty impacts of trade reforms.

Preface

There has been a major shift in the focus of trade research and the development community in the last decade. Traditionally, much of the attention was on trade policy—tariffs, quotas—and the effects of such policies in creating an anti-export bias. High tariffs in developing countries act as a disincentive to export in a number of ways. At the same time, high tariffs in export destinations also reduce the ability of developing countries to contest markets. The analytical and policy focus of much of the literature was to identify the incentive effects of trade policies, with a particular emphasis by the development community on the importance of improving the effectiveness of preferential market access schemes. In many countries tariffs were lowered substantially in the 1990s and 2000s, and many OECD countries have improved the coverage and depth of their preferential market access programs for the poorest countries. Most observers would recognize that the "supply response" to these policy changes in the least developed countries was less than was hoped for. One result has been a shift in focus to analyze more broadly the determinants of competitiveness. Trade economists now emphasize the importance of real trade costs as a barrier to trade, ranging from factors such as bad infrastructure to delays and excessive paperwork in clearing customs and high costs of transport, especially for landlocked countries. The effect of such costs is to raise prices and make farmers and other producers in low-income economies less competitive. The indirect effect is to inhibit investment and job creation.

The focus of the present book is on a neglected source of such "real costs" for farmers in low-income countries: market power along the supply chain. An absence of competition among the providers of key inputs that are used in farming may result in transfers from farmers (and consumers) to the firms that provide intermediates such as seeds and fertilizer and transportation services and storage. Such firms can raise prices above what they would be if the market structure was competitive, to the detriment of farmers, and indeed the detriment of society as a whole. A lack of competition is likely to result in inefficiencies—and associated deadweight costs.

As is illustrated in this book, the exercise of market power along the supply chain will have a number of possible effects. Given that the impacts on prices will imply a redistribution of income across agents in the economy, there will also be implications for poverty and the attainment of poverty reduction objectives. In general, smallholders are likely to be poorer than the owners of the firms that supply them with services and tangible inputs. The analysis shows that the effects of market power on income distribution and the incomes of poor households can be significant. It also demonstrates that there is much heterogeneity, both across countries for a given crop, and within a country for different crops.

The bottom line is clear. Measures to increase competition—to make the market structure less concentrated—will have effects similar to those resulting from actions to reduce customs clearance times, facilitate the movement of goods across borders, and so forth. The latter are issues that are at the forefront of the policy agenda in many countries and the activities of development agencies. This is much less the case for the competition-related, market structure issues that are the center of attention in this volume. The analysis is therefore not just an interesting analytical exercise—it is of great policy significance as it suggests that more attention should be devoted to competition policy in low-income countries.

Bernard Hoekman   Stephen Yeo
Sector Director, Trade Department   Chief Executive Officer
Poverty Reduction and Economic Management   CEPR
The World Bank

Acknowledgments

We want to warmly thank Daniel Lederman, Aaditya Mattoo, and Bernard Hoekman for helping us put this project together and for all of their support during its implementation. We thank Jorge Balat, Huberto Ennis, Leonardo Gasparini, Sebastian Ludmer, Mariana Marchionni, and Alessando Nicita for their contributions to the book, and German Bet, Laura Jaitman, David Jaume, and Cecilia Peluffo for outstanding research assistance. Anil Shamdasani and the CEPR team did superb publishing work. We would also like to thank Philip Abbott, Gilles Alfandari, Francois Ruf, Daniel Sarpong, Daniel Sellen, Hardwick Tchale, and Marcella Vigneri for providing us with important information on the institutional arrangements for several countries. Silvia Chauvin helped with the value chains figures in Chapter 3. Michelle Chester patiently assisted us with the administration of the project.

We have received useful comments and suggestions from Dante Amengual, Irene Brambilla, Olivier Cadot, Daniel Lederman, Justin Lin, Will Martin, and Stephen Mink, and from numerous participants in seminar presentations. These comments helped us significantly improve the book. We remain, however, responsible for any omission and errors.

Financial support from the Bank Netherlands Partnership Program at the World Bank is gratefully acknowledged. All views expressed here are those of the authors and should not be regarded as those of the World Bank or its clients.

1

Introduction

1 OVERVIEW

The literature on trade and poverty is large and has grown extensively during the last decade or so (Winters et al. 2004; Goldberg and Pavcnik 2004, 2007; Porto 2007, 2010, 2011). Initially, this literature investigated whether trade reforms, meaning mostly border protection such as tariffs, quotas, or export taxes, affected poverty. The approach is based on the idea that trade reforms affect domestic prices, and domestic prices affect households via several channels. As consumers, households benefit from lower prices and are hurt by higher prices. As producers, households benefit from higher prices and are hurt by lower prices. As income earners, prices can affect wages and employment and thus trade can affect the labor income of the household. Other channels, such as changes in transfers or capital income, can also play a role. In the end, the impact of trade on poverty is ambiguous: it depends on the size of the price change (the pass-through), on whether the poor are net producers or net consumers of the goods affected by the trade reform, on the response and nature of the labor markets, and so on (see Deaton 1989, 1997; Hertel and Winters 2006; Hoekman and Olarreaga 2007; Nicita 2009; Porto 2005, 2006; Ravallion 1990).

In this book, we study how the internal structure of export markets and the level of competition affect poverty and welfare in remote rural areas in Africa. In sub-Saharan Africa, rural poverty is a widespread phenomenon. While most farmers produce for home consumption, some are engaged in high-value export agriculture. Here, we focus on export crops such as coffee, cotton, cocoa, and tobacco. For many African countries, these crops, which are typically produced by smallholders, are a major source of export revenue. In consequence, changes in export prices and in the conditions faced in export markets (both internally and externally) can play a big role in shaping poverty in the region. Traditionally, the literature has focused on how external conditions affect poverty, for example by addressing whether agricultural subsidies in the developed world affect world prices and how this in turn affects farm-gate prices. Our objective in this book is to explore domestic factors. In particular, we investigate the role played by the structure of competition in export agriculture supply chains.

In Africa, commercialization of export agriculture is produced along a supply chain where intermediaries, exporters, and downstream producers interact with farmers. Often, the sector is concentrated, with a few firms competing for the commodities produced by atomistic smallholders. This structure of the market conduces to oligopsony power: firms have market power over farmers and are able to extract some of the surplus that the export market generates. The extent of oligopsony power depends on the number of competitors and on the relative size of each competitor (the distribution of market shares). Changes in the configuration of the market will thus affect the way the firms interact with the farmers. In principle, tighter competition induced by entry or by policies that foster competition (e.g., merger or antitrust policies) can affect farm-gate prices and therefore household welfare and poverty. This is the topic of our investigation.

The relationship between firms and farmers in export markets in Africa is complex. On top of the standard game-theoretic interrelationship, where firms interact with each other and take into account the response of farmers when setting prices, many markets are characterized by the presence of outgrower contracts. When there are distortions in the economy, or missing markets (especially for credit and capital), it may be impossible for farmers to cover any start-up investments related to the production of the export crop. In those scenarios, farmers would not be able to purchase seeds, or the pesticides needed for cash crop production and the market for these crops can disappear. In Africa, one way to solve this issue is with outgrower contracts, whereby firms provide inputs on loan at the beginning of the season. These loans, and any interest bore, are then recovered at harvest time. While outgrower contracts can be a very useful instrument for making these markets work, they may fail, sometimes catastrophically, when there are enforceability problems. Clearly, an inadequate legal system may prevent enforceability. Equally importantly, the presence of too many players/firms interacting simultaneously can facilitate side-selling, a situation in which a farmer takes up a loan with one firm, sells to a different one at harvest, and thus defaults on the original loan. In these cases, it is possible for increased competition to make contract monitoring very costly. Interest payments may become too burdensome for the farmers. In extreme cases, this may lead to a vicious cycle in which the system fully collapses. Our analysis covers these scenarios.

Our analytical methodology has two main parts. The first is a game-theory model of supply chains in cash crop agriculture between many atomistic smallholders and a few exporters. The model provides the tools needed to simulate the changes in farm-gate prices of export crops given hypothetical changes in the structure of the supply chain. Farm-gate prices are set by firms. The firms buy raw inputs from the farmers (coffee beans, cotton seeds, etc.) and sell them in international markets at given prices. In contrast, the firms enjoy oligopsony power internally. The oligopsony game delivers the equilibrium farm-gate prices that the firms offer to the farmers. Given these prices, farmers allocate resources optimally and supply raw inputs to the firms and this supply affects the quantity that firms can supply in the export market. In equilibrium, firms take into account the supply response of the farmer when choosing optimal farm-gate prices.

Once the equilibrium of the model is found, and the solution is calibrated to match key features of the economy, we simulate various changes in competition. Our simulations cover a large number of general settings, from entry to exit. We study the impacts of the entrance of a small competitor, of a hypothetical merger between the two leading firms, and of the split of the leader into smaller competitors (the "small entrant," "leaders merge," and "leader split" simulations). We also explore scenarios with tightest, albeit still imperfect, competition (the "equal market shares" simulations) as well as a hypothetical "perfect competition" scenario. In all these cases, given the initial equilibrium, we find the new equilibrium of the model and study the changes in farm-gate prices. We also study simulations of changes in the level of competition with complementary policies that affect firms and farmers, and with changes in international prices. Finally, we combine all these simulations with a model that allows for outgrower contracts. In the end, we run seventy simulations with seventy corresponding changes in farm-gate prices.

The second component utilizes household surveys to assess the poverty impacts of those changes in the value chains. We follow a standard first-order effects approach, as in Deaton (1989, 1997). Using the microdata from the household surveys, we use income shares derived from the production of different crops to evaluate the income impacts of a given farm-gate price change. We investigate the average impact for all rural households, the distribution of these impacts across levels of living (e.g., for poor vis-à-vis nonpoor households) and the differences in impacts between male-headed and female-headed households.

We explore twelve case studies: the cotton sector in Zambia, Malawi, Burkina Faso, Côte d'Ivoire, and Benin; the coffee sector in Uganda, Rwanda, and Côte d'Ivoire, the tobacco sector in Malawi and Zambia, and the cocoa sector in Côte d'Ivoire and Ghana. We focus on those crops that are plausible vehicles for poverty eradication and on those countries where the household survey data needed for the poverty analysis is available.

2   MAIN RESULTS

In discussing the results from the simulations and the poverty impacts, we study the case of Zambian cotton in detail. We then briefly explore differences and similarities with the remaining eleven case studies. The Zambian cotton sector is our leading case because it has undergone several of the transformations our simulations aim to capture (i.e., privatization, entry, and exit) and because several outgrowers schemes have been implemented.

The main conclusion of our analysis for the case of cotton in Zambia is that competition among processors is good for farmers as it increases the farm-gate price of the crop and therefore it improves their livelihood. For instance, if the leading firm splits, the increase in income for the average cotton producer would be equivalent to 2.4 percent of his initial income. On the other hand, if the two largest firms in the Zambian cotton market merge, the income of the average producer would decline by 2.3 percent. The largest possible gain for the farmers occurs under perfect competition, where farmers would enjoy an income gain of 19.3 percent. The implementation of complementary policies or a positive international price shock intensify the positive effects of more competition and mitigate the negative effects of a reduction in the level of competition among ginneries. For example, the original increase of 2.4 percent in income for producers following the split of the leader becomes 2.8 percent under complementary policies for farmers, 3.1 percent when these policies affect only firms, and 3.5 percent when they affect both farmers and firms. With outgrower contracts, farms need to borrow to finance the production of export crops. In consequence, we find that, in all simulations, the gains from more competition and the losses from higher market concentration tend to be lower. While possible in theory (since we assume that the cost of enforcing these contracts increases with market competition and that those costs are transferred to producers through increasing borrowing costs), none of our simulations uncover a collapse of the market due to increased competition among ginneries.

The general conclusion that more competition among processing and exporting firms is beneficial for smallholders applies to the other case studies. Take, for instance, the case where the firm with the largest market shares splits. This would lead to an average income increase for producing households of 2.8 percent across all case studies. However, this average masks a lot of variability, with high gains for African cotton farmers and low gains instead for African coffee smallholders. For instance, in our baseline scenario, the leader split simulation would increase average households' income in cotton in Burkina Faso by 12.4 percent but only by 0.1 percent in coffee in Uganda. This does not come as a surprise, however, since the leading cotton firm in Burkina Faso controls 85 percent of the market, while the leading firm in Uganda controls only 14.3 percent of the coffee market. Another interesting simulation of increased competition is the case of equal market shares, which delivers the upper bound increase in income under imperfect competition. Here, the average effect is much larger than in the case of leader split. The average producer household would see its income grow by 9.1 percent across our case studies with cotton in Burkina Faso (20.9 percent) and Benin (20.1 percent) showing the largest gains. In contrast, the average household would receive less than 1 percent extra income in the equal market shares simulation in coffee in Uganda and Rwanda.

The finding that increases in competition among processors benefit farmers needs to be put into perspective. One important result from our simulations is that small changes in the level of competition are unlikely to have significant effects on farmers' livelihoods. This is captured by the small entrant simulation. Under this scenario, the income of households only increases by an average of a quarter of a percentage point for our case studies. The largest effects for this simulation are observed in cotton in Malawi (0.94 percent) and tobacco in Zambia (0.74 percent).

We are also interested in assessing the effects of reductions in competition among upstream firms. This is done by studying the effects of the merging of the largest two firms in the market and through the case of the "exit of the largest" (and most efficient) firm. In the first simulation, the average loss for farmers is 1.3 percent of their income. The largest loss is registered in the case of cotton in Côte d'Ivoire (3.8 percent) where the new merged firm would control three quarters of the market. In the exit of the largest firm simulation, the highest income loss for producer households takes place in the cotton sector of Burkina Faso, where the disappearance of SOFITEX (which controls 85 percent of the market) would lead to a decrease in farm income of 15.4 percent. In contrast, the smallest impacts of a reduction in competition are observed in the coffee sector in Uganda, where the loss would in fact be only around a tenth of a percentage point in both simulations.

To investigate the role of complementary policies, we compare our baseline scenario with cases where we introduce complementarities affecting farmers (for instance, extension services), affecting firms (infrastructure), or both. The main finding here is that these policies boost the income of households when there is an increase in competition and mitigate (or even revert) the income loss when there is a reduction in competition. In all cases, the largest effects are observed when the complementary factors affect both firms and farmers. Overall, the quantitative effects of these policies depend on the particular crop, country, and market structure, but they range from as low as a 0.36 percent (equal market shares simulation for coffee in Rwanda) to a 2.8 percent (perfect competition simulation for cotton in Côte d'Ivoire) income gains for the average producer household.

We also study the effects of a 10 percent exogenous increase in the international prices of the different export crops. Given the current market configuration for each crop and country in the study, the exogenous price increase leads to an average raise in producing households' income of 6.9 percent. The largest effect takes place in cotton in Burkina Faso (12.8 percent) and the smallest effect takes place in coffee in Rwanda (2 percent). We also allow for combinations of higher international prices and different changes in the level of competition among processors. Increasing competition boosts the positive effects of the price change, while a reduction in the competition damps its effects. For instance, in the case of perfect competition, the income gains for producing households would range from 68 percent (cotton in Burkina Faso) to 3.8 percent (coffee in Uganda), with an average effect across case studies of 29.6 percent. On the other hand, when the largest firm exits the market, the overall income effect of the increase international prices would range from −3.9 percent (cotton in Burkina Faso) and 11.3 percent (cocoa in Côte d'Ivoire) with an average income effect of 3.4 percent for all the case studies.

The survey data allows us to distinguish the effect of the different simulations on poor versus nonpoor households and across gender groups. In nine out of the twelve simulations, the benefits of more competition have a larger income effect in male-headed households than in the female counterpart. The three exceptions are the case of cotton in Benin and Côte d'Ivoire and coffee in Rwanda. The largest differences between genders are found in Burkina Faso–cotton, where the gains for male-headed households are 217 percent higher than the income gains of female-headed households, and in Benin–cotton, where instead the gains for female-headed households are 57 percent higher than the gains for male-headed households. It is noteworthy that in only four out of the twelve case studies, the increase in competition is pro-poor. This is because of the relatively low participation of poor households in the production of the export crop. The income gains are larger for the poor, on average, in the cases of coffee and cocoa in Côte d'Ivoire, coffee in Rwanda, and cotton in Zambia.

Turning to the models with outgrower contracts, we find that, in all case studies except for cotton in Burkina Faso, an increase in competition is beneficial for farmers and, in turn, a higher market concentration is prejudicial. As in the case of Zambia–cotton, the gains from increasing competition and the losses from more oligopsony power are lower (because of the borrowing costs). In general, the discrepancies with the results from models without outgrower contracts are rather small. Interestingly, the cotton sector in Burkina Faso is the only case where less competition is better for smallholders.

Three of the countries in our study have more than one case study. In Côte d'Ivoire we study cotton, coffee, and cocoa. In Malawi and Zambia we cover both cotton and tobacco. It is interesting, then, to describe how the same scenario and simulation has different effects upon crops in the same country. For instance, in Côte d'Ivoire, an increase in competition has a larger effect on producing households' income in cotton than in cocoa and coffee. If the leader firm in cotton, cocoa, and coffee were to split, the effect on income would be a 4.6 percent, 1.1 percent, and 0.6 percent increase, respectively. In the case of equal market shares, the increase in the income of households would be 14 percent, 10.5 percent, and 5.4 percent, respectively. The effect is also different for poor versus nonpoor households and across gender depending on the crop. Competition in coffee benefits more poor and male-headed households while, in cotton, female-headed and nonpoor households enjoy larger gains. In cocoa, competition benefits male-headed households slightly more while the effect is about the same among poor and nonpoor households. In Malawi we cannot directly compare the results between cotton and tobacco simulations, as the latter are slightly different from the standard simulation that we run for all the other case studies for reasons we will explain later. However, the overall effects seem to be of about the same magnitude, while, in both crops, male-headed and nonpoor households benefit the most from the increase in competition. Finally, in Zambia, the effect of competition has similar quantitative effects in cotton and tobacco. The leader split case would increase the income of households by 2.4 percent in cotton and by 3.2 percent in tobacco, while the equal market share case would generate a growth in income of 7.3 percent in cotton and of 7.2 percent in tobacco. In both crops male-headed households benefit the most, though only slightly in the case of cotton. Poor producing households gain more in cotton, while nonpoor benefit more in the case of increasing competition among tobacco exporters.

3 THE ORGANIZATION OF THE BOOK

In Chapter 2, we introduce the twelve case studies and we document how and why we chose them. We describe the availability of household surveys across countries and we explore crops that provide an important source of cash income for the economy. In Chapter 3, we describe the main institutional arrangements that characterize the supply chains in the each of the twelve case studies. This description includes the different vertical arrangements from different crops, whether the value chains are characterized by one or more layers, the structure of competition among firms and farmers in each layer, and whether there are market interlinkages. In Chapter 4, we develop the theoretical model of supply chains in export agriculture. The purpose of the model is to provide an analytical framework for studying how changes in the structure of the supply chain affect farm-gate prices. Finally, in Chapter 5, we combine the household survey with the farm-gate price changes to carry out the poverty analysis. We estimate the impact, at the farm level, of changes in the supply chain on household income.

2

Case Studies

In this chapter, we describe the twelve case studies that comprise our investigation on supply chains, agricultural exports, and poverty in sub-Saharan Africa. The case studies were selected following two criteria. First, the export crop had to have the potential to eradicate poverty, and, second, the microdata needed for the poverty analysis had to be available in the target country. We investigate twelve case studies covering four crops, namely cocoa, coffee, cotton, and tobacco, in eight countries, namely Benin, Burkina Faso, Côte d'Ivoire, Ghana, Malawi, Rwanda, Uganda, and Zambia.

The objective of this chapter is to document our selection of the case studies. To this end, we begin in Section 1 by looking at export data to assess how important different export crops are for different countries. Given the nature of our analysis, we only focus on crops that are a major source of cash income for the economy (thus leaving aside food crops). In Section 2, we explore the availability of household surveys in sub-Saharan countries and, for those countries where this data is available, we check whether the selected export crops are grown by a significantly large number of households and whether those crops generate a significant share of total household income. To document this, we describe summary statistics (sample size, gender structure, and demographic composition) from the household surveys used in the analysis. Finally, in Section 3, we use the microdata from these surveys to characterize those farmers that produce the export crops.

1 EXPORTS

To get a sense of the overall importance of the export crops for the local economy, we begin with a description of the export structure of each target country. Table A2.1 provides the summary statistics. In general, all the selected crops are very important for the economy of at least one of the countries. Cocoa is a crucial foreign exchange generator both in Côte d'Ivoire and Ghana, where it raises between 20 and 25 percent of all export revenue. Coffee exports account for more than 10 percent of the total exports in both Rwanda and Uganda. Cotton accounts for more than one-third of total exports in Benin and Burkina Faso. Finally, tobacco accounts for more than 70 percent of export earnings in Malawi.

1.1 Benin

Cotton is the main agricultural export of Benin, which, after Mali and Burkina Faso, is the largest cotton exporter in West Africa. Historically, cotton has represented around 70 percent of the value of agricultural exports and more than 30 percent of total export value (Table A2.1). However, the export value recently collapsed from $208 million in 2004 to $113 million in 2006. Part of this reduction was due to a decrease of 30 percent in the total volume exported. This crop generates revenues for some 325,000 small holders. Cotton lint constitutes 92 percent of the cotton export value, followed by cotton seed oil (6.8 percent) and seeds (1.1 percent). The main exports markets for Benin in 2007 were China (24.7 percent), India (8.2 percent), Niger (6.6 percent), Togo (5.4 percent), Nigeria (5.3 percent), and Belgium (4.6 percent). The total value of exports of goods and services only represents around 13 percent of Benin's GDP. This low number may indicate that there is room for further increases in the share of the external sector in Benin's economy.

1.2 Burkina Faso

Burkina Faso is one of the main producers and exporters of cotton in Africa. In 2006, cotton exports generated $235 million. This accounted for 81 percent of the agricultural exports and for 35 percent of all the revenue generated by exports (Table A2.1). Other important agricultural exports are cattle, sesame seed, and mangoes, but their export value is marginal in comparison with cotton. As in the case of Benin, cotton lint constitutes the bulk of cotton exports (96 percent of the export value), followed by cotton seed oil (2.7 percent) and seeds (1.1 percent). The main destination for Burkina Faso's exports in 2007 were China (29.6 percent), Singapore (15.7 percent), Thailand (7.2 percent), Ghana (6.4 percent), and Niger (4.8 percent). Exports of goods and services remain low, as they account for 11 percent of GDP on average.

1.3 Côte d'Ivoire

After oil, cocoa is the most important source of foreign revenue in Côte d'Ivoire, followed by rubber, coffee, bananas, cashew nuts, and cotton. Cocoa products account for more than 60 percent of total agricultural exports and for more than one-fifth of total export revenue (Table A2.1). This sector has generated around $2 billion per year of export income in recent years. Cocoa beans account for 73 percent of total cocoa exports, followed by cocoa paste (12 percent), cocoa butter (9 percent), husks and shell (3.5 percent), and powder and cake (2 percent). Côte d'Ivoire is the largest worldwide cocoa producer and exporter followed by Ghana and Indonesia.

Coffee is the second most important cash crop for the Ivorian economy. Coffee exports amounted to $166 million in 2006 (5.3 percent of total agriculture exports and 1.8 percent of total exports) up from $130 million in 2004. One-third of the coffee exports are coffee extracts, while the other two-thirds correspond to green coffee. Côte d'Ivoire is the third largest coffee exporter in Africa after Ethiopia and Uganda.

Cotton is also an important cash crop in the Ivorian Economy. The exports of the sector were $121 million in 2006 (1.3 percent of total export income). Most of the exports are cotton lint (93 percent), followed by cotton seed (5.1 percent) and cotton oil (1.3 percent). Côte d'Ivoire is the fourth largest cotton exporter in sub-Saharan Africa after Burkina Faso, Mali, and Benin.

The external sector is of vital importance for the Ivorian economy, with exports of goods and services accounting for more than 50 percent of the country's GDP in recent years. The main export partners are France (23.7 percent), the Netherlands (10.8 percent), the United States (10.2 percent), Nigeria (7.5 percent), and Italy (4.8 percent).

1.4 Ghana

Cocoa has traditionally been the main source of foreign income for the Ghanaian economy. This may change in the future as the country starts to export the recent oil discoveries. In 2006, cocoa generated $1.2 billion in exports revenue. This amounted to 79 percent of agricultural exports and one-fourth of all export revenue (Table A2.1). Ghana is the second largest producer and exporter of cocoa after Côte d'Ivoire. Cocoa beans are the main exporting product (86.6 percent) followed by cocoa butter and cocoa paste (both around 6 percent of cocoa exports).

The exporting sector accounts for more than one-third of total GDP, and this highlights the importance of the cocoa sector for the Ghanaian economy. The main markets for Ghanaian exports are the Netherlands (12.5 percent), the United Kingdom (8.3 percent), the United States (6.7 percent), Belgium (5.8 percent), France (5.6 percent), and Germany (4.4 percent).

1.5 Malawi

Tobacco is the most important export from Malawi, followed by maize, sugar, tea, and cotton. In 2006, it generated almost three-fourths of all export income ($432 million, up from $258 million in 2004, see Table A2.1 for details). Malawi is the third largest exporter of tobacco after Brazil and the United States. However, the main difference between these two countries is that almost all Malawian exports are unmanufactured tobacco.

Cotton is another important cash crop for the Malawian economy, generating $32.6 million in 2006 (around 5 percent of all export income). Cotton lint accounts for 94 percent of all cotton exports, with the remaining 6 percent coming from cotton seeds.

Exports are roughly one-fifth of total GDP and the main exports markets for Malawi are South Africa (12.6 percent), Germany (9.7 percent), Egypt (9.6 percent), the United States (9.5 percent), Zimbabwe (8.5 percent), Russia (5.4 percent), and the Netherlands (4.4 percent).

1.6   Rwanda

Coffee is the main agriculture export in Rwanda, accounting for 60 percent of all agricultural exports in 2006 and 17.5 percent of total export revenues. The sector generated exports for $48 million in 2006 (Table A2.1). In 2007, the total export value decreased to $32 million, remaining ahead of tea, the second largest agricultural export with $30 million. Almost all exports of Rwandan coffee are green coffee.

Major export markets for Rwanda in 2007 were the United Kingdom (18.7 percent), Kenya (18.6 percent), Belgium (14 percent), China (12.5 percent), and Switzerland (4.7 percent).

1.7   Uganda

As in Rwanda, coffee is the most important cash crop in Uganda. Other important crops are tobacco and tea. Total coffee exports (99 percent of them green coffee) amounted to almost $190 million in 2006. This amount corresponded to 42 percent of all agricultural exports and 12.5 percent of all exports (Table A2.1). Uganda is the second largest coffee exporter in sub-Saharan Africa.

In 2008, the three largest markets for exports were Sudan (14.3 percent), Kenya (9.5 percent), and Switzerland (9.0 percent).

1.8   Zambia

Cotton and Tobacco are the two most important cash crops in Zambia. Together they generated almost half of the agricultural exports (Table A2.1). However, they only account for less than 2 percent each of total export revenues as copper is by far the most important foreign revenue generator in Zambia. Almost all tobacco exports ($75 million in 2006) are unmanufactured. Cotton lint exports are the largest exporting cotton item (91.5 percent) followed by cotton seed (7 percent) and carded and combed cotton (1 percent).

The three main destinations for Zambian exports are Switzerland, South Africa, and Egypt.

1.9   Final Remarks

From this analysis, it follows that most of the agricultural exports in the countries that we study involve little local processing. This is more clearly seen in Table A2.2, which shows the composition of exports of cotton, tobacco, coffee, and cocoa for each country for 2006.

In the top panel, we observe that more than 90 percent of the cotton exported by our target countries is cotton lint. Unfortunately, we do not have detailed and reliable information on cotton yarn exports. However, these countries have a low spinning installed capacity given their cotton potential production. Burkina Faso, Benin, and Côte d'Ivoire are among the top twenty world exporters of cotton lint but none of them are among the top twenty exporting countries of cotton yarn or apparel.

Almost all of the tobacco exported by the two tobacco-producing countries in our study is unmanufactured (second panel). This is quite common among developing countries. In Brazil, the largest exporter, 98 percent of their tobacco exports are unmanufactured.

The composition of coffee exports is presented in the third panel of Table A2.2. Green coffee accounts for most coffee exports. This is not unusual, however, since other large coffee exporters (Brazil, Vietnam, and Colombia) also sell mostly green coffee. Roasted and instant coffee is produced in the consuming countries.

Finally, the bottom panel of Table A2.2 shows the composition of cocoa exports in Côte d'Ivoire and Ghana. Most of their exports are in the rudimentary form of beans: 85 percent in Ghana and 75 percent in Côte d'Ivoire in comparison with 69 percent in Indonesia and 1 percent in Brazil (the other two big international producers of cocoa). Brazil exports 65 percent of its cocoa production as cocoa butter. None of the top five exporters of cocoa are among the top twenty exporters of chocolate.

2   THE HOUSEHOLD SURVEYS

In order to perform the poverty analysis, we need household survey data with detailed information on crop production and income. The available household surveys for the eight target countries in sub-Saharan Africa are listed in Table A2.3.

In the case of Benin, we use the "Questionnaires des indicateurs de base du bien-être" conducted in 2003. The survey covered 5,350 households out of a population of 1.4 million households. Rural households accounted for 61.5 percent of total respondents. In Burkina Faso, we use the "Enquête Burkinabe sur les conditions de vie des ménages," also from 2003, which surveyed 8,500 households (0.48 percent of the total population) of which 69.4 percent were located in rural areas. In Côte d'Ivoire, we utilize the "Enquête niveau de vie ménages" studying 10,801 of the existing 3.2 million households in the country. Households classified as rural were 47.9 percent of the total. In Ghana, we use the "Ghana living standards survey" of 1998. This survey reviewed the standard of living of 5,998 Ghanaian households, 63.3 percent of them residing in rural areas. Information about Malawian households is taken from the "Integrated household survey" of 2004. This survey covers 11,280 households (coverage rate of 0.42 percent), 87.2 percent of which were in rural areas. In Rwanda, the most recent available survey is the "Enquête intégrale sur les conditions de vie des ménages" from 1998. This survey covers 6,420 households amounting to 0.4 percent of the household population. Households in rural areas are 82.1 percent of the total households interviewed. The

"Uganda national household survey" of 2005 interviewed 7,425 households from a population of 5.2 million households. The share of rural households is 77.12 percent. Finally, in the case of Zambia, we use the "Living conditions monitoring survey III" from 2003. This survey covers 4,837 households (a coverage rate of 0.23 percent) of which 47.9 percent were located in rural areas.

Table A2.4 presents a brief demographic characterization of the target countries. All of these countries are relatively small in terms of population. Benin is the smallest country with 6.7 million inhabitants and, with a population of 28.9 million, Uganda is the largest. In all countries the average age of the population is very low, ranging from 19.5 years in Uganda to 24.4 years in Burkina Faso. Except for the case of Burkina Faso, where they are about the same, in all the other countries the rural population largely surpasses the urban population. The rural population is on average younger than the urban population, except in Côte d'Ivoire, Malawi, Rwanda, and Zambia. The national male share oscillates between 0.464 in Rwanda and 0.498 in Côte d'Ivoire. There is no discernable pattern for male shares across urban and rural areas. The male share is larger than the female shares only in urban areas of Burundi and Malawi.

Average household size and its age composition are presented in Table A2.5 at the national, urban, and rural level. Ghana has the smallest average household size, with 4.4 members; Burkina Faso has the largest, with 5.6 members. Rural households are, on average, larger than urban households, except in Rwanda and Zambia. Rural household size ranges from 4.7 to 5.9 members (with an average of 5.2) while urban household size ranges from 4.0 to 5.5 members (with an average of 4.8). For the countries in the study, the 0–15 age group comprises 49.1 percent of all household members in rural areas and 42.5 percent in urban areas. The 16–29 age group represents 22.5 percent and 29.8 percent of the rural and urban households, respectively. Those between thirty and forty-nine years of age represent, on average, 17.7 percent and 19.8 percent of the household members in rural and urban areas. The last age group, those fifty years old or older, represents only 9.6 percent and 7.3 percent of the members of rural and urban households, respectively. The demographic age structure of rural and urban households is similar across all target countries with the exception of Burkina Faso where the 16–29 age group has a larger share than the 0–15 group in the members of urban households.

3   THE DISTRIBUTION OF INCOME AND EXPORT CROP INCOME

In what follows, we use the household survey data to characterize the distribution of income in the target countries. Since we are interested in the impact on poverty of changes in the supply chain in export agriculture, we begin here by plotting densities of per capita expenditures. These densities are estimated nonparametrically with kernel methods (Deaton 1997; Pagan and Ullah 1999).

The results are reports in Figures A2.1–A2.8, with one figure for each country in the study. Each figure has three panels. Panel (a) reports the density for per capita expenditures for the total population at the national, rural, and urban level. Since we are also interested in gender-specific impacts, we estimate those densities for male-headed and female-headed households in panels (b) and (c), respectively.

There are three key conclusions that emerge from the examination of the per capita expenditure densities. First, there are significant differences between urban and rural households. The urban densities are always shifted to the right of the rural densities, both in male-headed and female-headed households. This is particularly evident in the case of Burkina Faso, Ghana, Malawi, and Rwanda. Second, the rural density is similar to the national density in most cases (with the exception of Côte d'Ivoire), again regardless of the gender of the household head. This is consistent with the data in Table A2.4, which shows that the rural population is much larger than the urban population for most of the countries in our study. Third, male-headed households typically enjoy higher levels of per capita expenditure level, both for urban and rural households, than female-headed households.

We now turn to the analysis of households' income shares. Results are reported in Tables A2.6–A2.13. We present the descriptive statistics for the total population of households (panel (a)) and separately for male-headed (panel (b)) and female-headed households (panel (c)). The bottom panels present the summary statistics for the subsample that includes only those households that produce at least one of the crops under study. The first column in each table reports statistics from the national sample, the second column reports statistics from the urban sample, and the third column reports statistics from the rural sample. Since our focus is mainly on rural households, we also report statistics across quintiles of per capita expenditure for rural households. In each table, the first row reports the average per capita expenditures and the following rows report the average income shares (in percentage). We identify the share of income derived from agriculture and, within this category, we also report the share derived from the export crop under study. For completeness, we report the share of income derived from home-production activities as well as from other sources (wages, nonfarm businesses, and transfers).

Data for Benin is in Table A2.6. The share of agricultural income in total income for rural households is 34 percent for the whole sample and 56.3 percent for those households that produce cotton, the main export crop of the country. Cotton generates 6.6 percent of total income for the average rural household, and 33.8 percent for the average rural cotton producer. This crop is particularly important for the poorest farmers since it generates 10.4 percent and 7.1 percent of total income for households in the first and second quintiles of the income distribution, respectively. Among producers, cotton generates about one-third of the total income in each of the quintiles.

Panels (b) and (c) highlight some of the differences in income shares between male-headed and female-headed households. Cotton is mostly an important source of income for female-headed households, accounting for 7.6 percent of their total income—in contrast to 1.1 percent in male-headed households—for the total rural population. Conditional of being a cotton producer, cotton income accounts for 33.3 percent and 21.8 percent of total income in female-headed and male-headed households, respectively.

Table A2.7 presents income shares for the case of Burkina Faso. In our data, agricultural sales play a minor role, relative, for example, to income from home production. However, if we consider only the subsample of producers, agricultural income amounts to 70.5 percent of the total rural household income. The most important crop is cotton, which generates 1.31 percent of the income of the average rural household and 56.4 percent of the income of the average cotton producer. Among producers, cotton is a more important source of income for male-headed households (56.4 percent) than for female-headed households (17.7 percent). For male-headed households, cotton generates a similar share of income across quintiles. Instead, female-headed households in the second quintile earn a significantly higher share of income from cotton than the rest of the quintiles (31 percent of their total income).

The case of Côte d'Ivoire is presented in Table A2.8. Around 52 percent of the total income of rural households comes from agriculture; for export crop producers (any of the three major crops in Côte d'Ivoire), agriculture accounts for 77 percent of total income. The relevant export crops are cocoa (with an income share of 17.1 percent), coffee (6.8 percent), and cotton (4.2 percent). Conditional on being an export crop producer, the income shares are 38.5 percent, 15.3 percent, 9.5 percent, for cocoa, coffee, and cotton, respectively. The share of cocoa is similar across the first four quintiles, but declines for the richest rural households. Coffee is particularly important for households in the first and second quintiles. In contrast, the importance of cotton as an income generator increases with household income: while households in the first quintile only derive 0.8 percent of their income from cotton, the cotton share for households in the last quintile is 8.6 percent. On average, rural male-headed households depend more heavily on agricultural income (64.6 percent). Rural female-headed households only get 36.8 percent of their income from agriculture, cocoa being the only significant contributor (with 4.1 percent of the household income). Conditional on being a producer, agricultural income is important for both genders (78.1 percent for male-headed and 63.2 percent for female-headed households).

Rural households in Ghana (Table A2.9) receive 29 percent of their income from agricultural activities (45.9 percent if they are cocoa producer). Agricultural income is particularly important for the first two quintiles, where households get one-third of their income from agriculture; these shares decline sharply for households in the last quintile, who get only 23 percent of their income from this activity. Conditional on being a cocoa producer, the average rural household gets a similar share of income from agriculture regardless of the quintile. For the average rural household, cocoa contributes 4.8 percent of the total income in male-headed households and 2.8 percent of the income in female-headed households (24.1 percent and 22.2 percent respectively for the subsample of producers). For both genders, households in the third quintile are the ones that more heavily depend on cocoa with 6.3 percent (male-headed) and 4.2 percent (female-headed).

Malawi (Table A2.10) is one of the countries in our study with the lowest income share coming from agricultural sales, with only 11.6 percent for the average rural household (34.3 percent for producers). This share is even smaller for female-headed households at 7 percent (29.4 percent for producers). Most of the income of rural households comes from home-production activities. This source of income declines with the level of consumption of the household and the share of agricultural income increases up to 15.4 percent for the average rural household in the last quintile (42.3 percent for producers). Tobacco (with a share of 3.8 percent) and cotton (with a share of 0.5 percent), are the most important crops (the figures are 21.8 percent and 2.7 percent respectively for producers).

On average, Rwandan rural households get 18.8 percent of their income from the commercialization of agriculture products (Table A2.11). This share increases to 28.3 for the households producing the export crops in our study. The share for male-headed households is slightly higher, at 20.1 percent. As in the case of Malawi, the share of agriculture income increases with the level of household consumption. Those in the last quintile get 25.8 percent of their income from agriculture. Among producers, the agriculture share does not drastically change across quintiles. Coffee is the main cash crop, contributing slightly less than 1 percent of total household income. Among producers, instead, coffee—with an average share of 8 percent—is an important source of household income, in particular for households in the first quintile (with a share of 11.57 percent).

The case of Uganda (Table A2.12) is very similar to the case of Rwanda. On average, a rural household generates 15.1 percent of its income from agricultural products but this average is very different across quintiles. The share of agricultural income for rural households in the first quintile is only 5 percent, while, for those in the fifth quintile, the share is 25.7 percent. Among producers we observe a similar pattern, but the shares are higher. Male-headed households rely more on agricultural income than female-headed households. Coffee is also the main cash crop here, contributing 2.4 percent of the rural household income (8.2 percent if they are producers).

The last country in our analysis is Zambia (Table A2.13). Around one-fifth of rural household income comes from the commercialization of agricultural products (36.4 percent among producers). This percentage is similar across quintiles, with slightly higher shares for the poorest households in the total sample, and slightly higher (21.8 percent and 2.7 percent respectively for producers) shares for the richest households among producers. Cotton and tobacco are the main sources of agricultural income. Cotton contributes, on average, 3.2 percent (23.3 percent among producers) of the total income in male-headed rural households and 2.1 percent (23 percent for producers) in the case of female-headed households. The contribution of tobacco is 0.8 percent and 0.4 percent for male-headed and female-headed rural households (5.9 percent and 4.6 percent, respectively, for the subsample of producers).

To show the importance of the relevant crops for the rural households in the eight target countries across the entire income distribution more effectively, Figures 2.9 to 2.16 display nonparametric regressions of the income shares derived from different export crops on the log of per capita household expenditures. These regressions are estimated using local polynomials (see Pagan and Ullah 1999). For each crop–country pair, we estimate this regression for the total rural sample, and for the subsamples of male-headed and female-headed households.

In Benin (Figure A2.9), the share of income coming from cotton declines with the level of per capita expenditure of the household. The decline is more pronounced in the case of female-headed households. On the other hand, in the case of Burkina Faso (Figure A2.10), the importance of the income share derived from cotton grows with the level of per capita expenditure (particularly for male-headed households). The share of coffee and cocoa decline with per capita expenditure in Côte d'Ivoire (Figure A2.11); cotton shares, in contrast, monotonically increase. In Ghana, the share of cocoa income first increases with income, but then declines at the right tail of the income distribution (Figure A2.12). Figure A2.13 shows that the share of income generated by tobacco increases with the level of per capita expenditure of the typical Malawian rural household, whereas the share of income coming from cotton has an inverted U-shape. In Rwanda (Figure A2.14), on average, the share of income from coffee increases with the level of expenditure of the rural household. We observe a similar pattern for coffee in Uganda (Figure A2.15) but with a decline in the share of coffee for the richest rural households. In Zambia (Figure A2.16) both the share of income from tobacco and cotton increase with the level of per capita consumption of the rural household.

APPENDIX: TABLES AND FIGURES

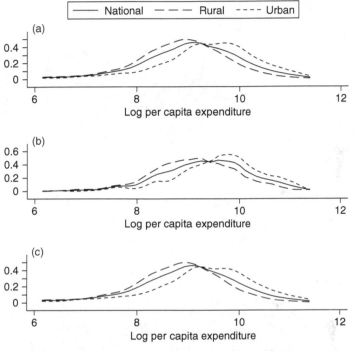

Figure A2.1: *Per capita expenditure density for Benin.*

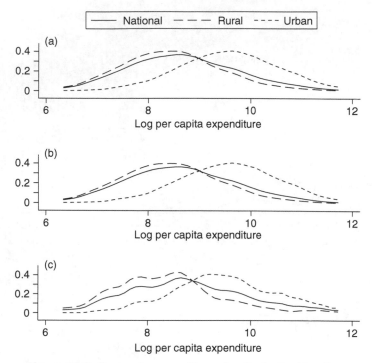

Figure A2.2: *Per capita expenditure density for Burkina Faso.*

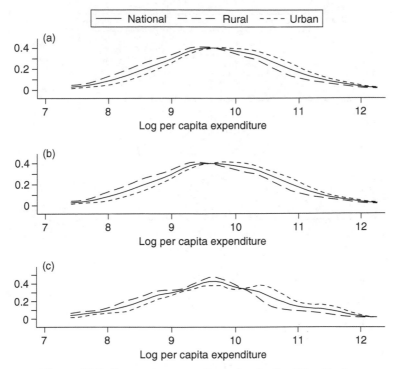

Figure A2.3: *Per capita expenditure density for Côte d'Ivoire.*

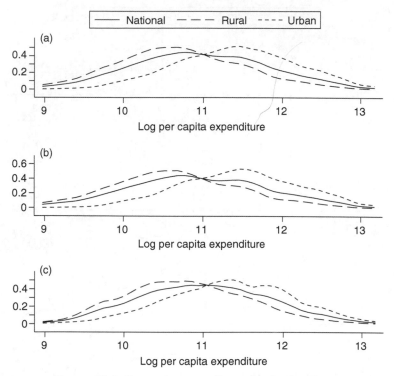

Figure A2.4: *Per capita expenditure density for Ghana.*

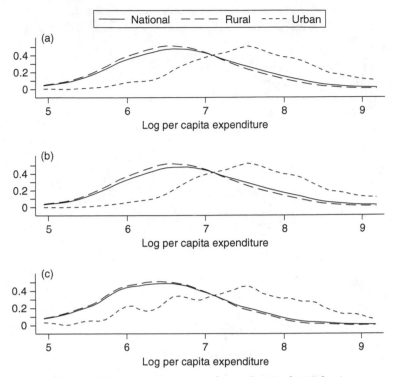

Figure A2.5: *Per capita expenditure density for Malawi.*

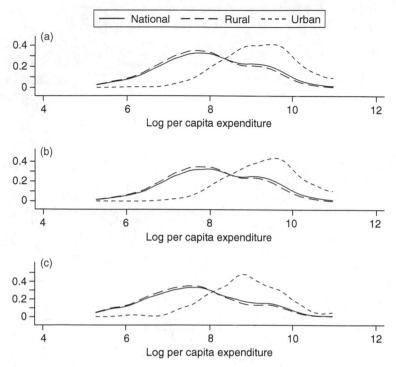

Figure A2.6: *Per capita expenditure density for Rwanda.*

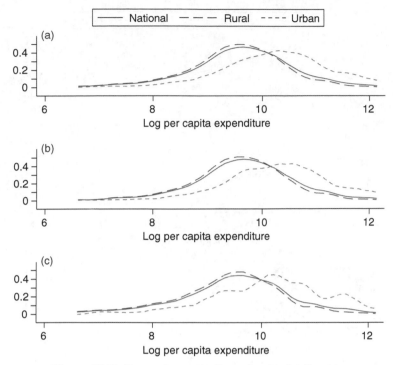

Figure A2.7: *Per capita expenditure density for Uganda.*

Supply Chains in Sub-Saharan Africa

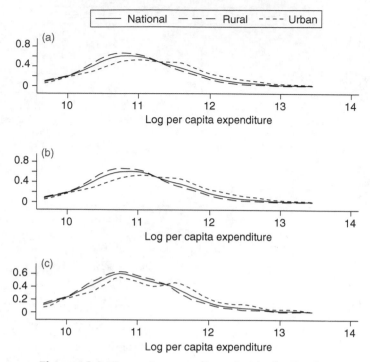

Figure A2.8: *Per capita expenditure density for Zambia.*

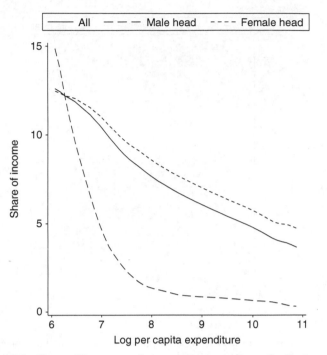

Figure A2.9: *Share of income and per capita expenditure for Benin: cotton.*

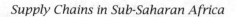

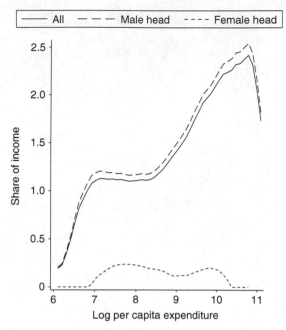

Figure A2.10: *Share of income and per capita expenditure for Burkina Faso: cotton.*

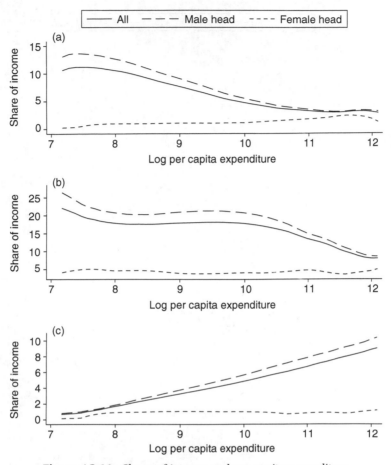

Figure A2.11: *Share of income and per capita expenditure for Côte d'Ivoire: (a) coffee; (b) cocoa; (c) cotton.*

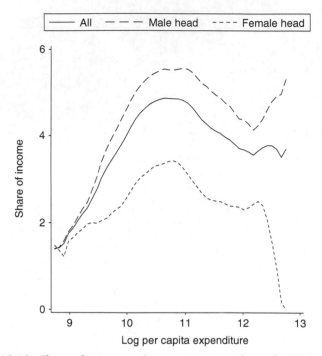

Figure A2.12: *Share of income and per capita expenditure for Ghana: cocoa.*

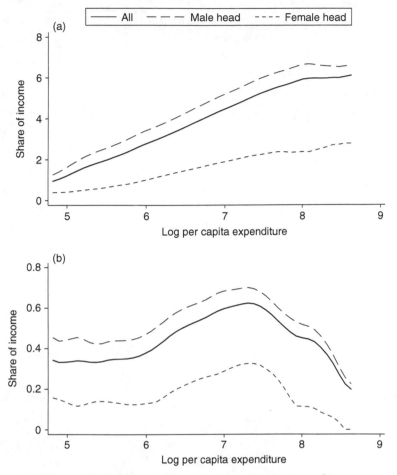

Figure A2.13: *Share of income and per capita expenditure for Malawi: (a) tobacco; (b) cotton.*

Supply Chains in Sub-Saharan Africa

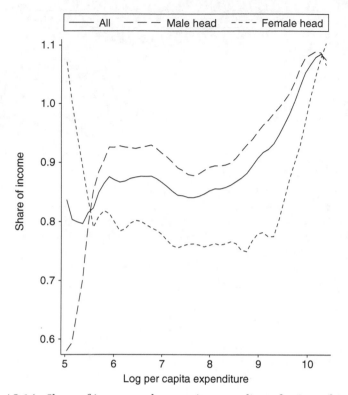

Figure A2.14: *Share of income and per capita expenditure for Rwanda: coffee.*

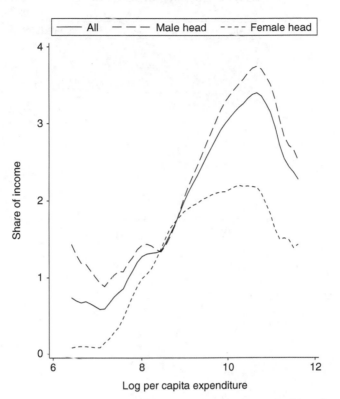

Figure A2.15: *Share of income and per capita expenditure for Uganda: coffee.*

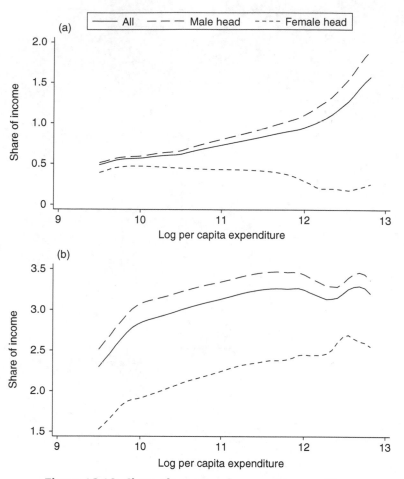

Figure A2.16: *Share of income and per capita expenditure for Zambia: (a) tobacco; (b) cotton.*

Table A2.1: *Agricultural exports in sub-Saharan Africa.*

Country – crop	2004	2005	2006
(1) Benin – cotton			
Cotton exports (thousands of $)	208,128	181,448	113,306
– Percentage of agricultural exports	75	69	33
– Percentage of total exports	39	31	N/A
Exports of goods and services as percentage of GDP	13	13	N/A
(2) Burkina Faso – cotton			
Cotton exports (thousands of $)	270,329	213,614	235,290
– Percentage of agricultural exports	81	78	81
– Percentage of total exports	49	39	35
Exports of goods and services as percentage of GDP	11	10	12
(3) Côte d'Ivoire – cocoa, coffee, cotton			
Cocoa exports (thousands of $)	2,124,649	1,988,939	1,946,273
– Percentage of agricultural exports	68	66	62
– Percentage of total exports	28	24	21
Coffee exports (thousands of $)	130,255	113,436	166,007
– Percentage of agricultural exports	4	4	5
– Percentage of total exports	2	1	2
Cotton exports (thousands of $)	163,256	148,336	121,026
– Percentage of agricultural exports	5	5	4
– Percentage of total exports	2	2	1
Exports of goods and services as percentage of GDP	49	51	53
(4) Ghana – cocoa			
Cocoa exports (thousands of $)	984,034	914,605	1,224,309
– Percentage of agricultural exports	77	79	79
– Percentage of total exports	28	26	27
Exports of goods and services as percentage of GDP	39	32	36

Table A2.1: *Continued.*

Country - crop	2004	2005	2006
(5) Malawi – tobacco, cotton			
Cotton exports (thousands of $)	16,443	12,302	32,648
– Percentage of agricultural exports	4	3	6
– Percentage of total exports	3	2	5
Tobacco exports (thousands of $)	257,974	320,715	431,787
– Percentage of agricultural exports	64	71	73
– Percentage of total exports	39	57	73
Exports of goods and services as percentage of GDP	25	20	19
(6) Rwanda – coffee			
Coffee exports (thousands of $)	28,458	36,966	48,008
– Percentage of agricultural exports	88	57	60
– Percentage of total exports	14	15	17
Exports of goods and services as percentage of GDP	10	10	10
(7) Uganda – coffee			
Coffee exports (thousands of $)	124,236	172,942	189,841
– Percentage of agricultural exports	35	42	42
– Percentage of total exports	12	13	12
Exports of goods and services as percentage of GDP	14	14	15
(8) Zambia – cotton, tobacco			
Cotton exports (thousands of $)	126,075	62,542	66,992
– Percentage of agricultural exports	35	19	21
– Percentage of total exports	6	3	2
Tobacco exports (thousands of $)	60,383	63,473	75,205
– Percentage of agricultural exports	17	20	23
– Percentage of total exports	3	3	2
Exports of goods and services as percentage of GDP	38	34	38

Source: FAO and WDI.

Table A2.2: *The composition of agricultural exports*
(2006; all values are percentages).

Crops	Benin	Burkina Faso	Côte d'Ivoire	Ghana	Malawi	Rwanda	Uganda	Zambia
(1) Cotton								
Carded, combed	0	0	0	—	0	—	—	1
Lint	92	96	93	—	94	—	—	92
Linter	0	0	0	—	0	—	—	0
Waste	0	0	0	—	0	—	—	0
Seed	1	1	5	—	6	—	—	7
Seed oil	7	3	1	—	0	—	—	0
(2) Tobacco								
Unmanufac.	—	—	—	—	100	—	—	100
Manufac.	—	—	—	—	0	—	—	0
(3) Coffee								
Extracts	—	—	33	—	—	0	0	—
Husks, skins	—	—	0	—	—	0	0	—
Roasted	—	—	0	—	—	0	0	—
Substitutes	—	—	0	—	—	0	0	—
Green	—	—	66	—	—	100	99	—
(4) Cocoa								
Beans	—	—	73	87	—	—	—	—
Butter	—	—	9	6	—	—	—	—
Paste	—	—	12	6	—	—	—	—
Husks, shell	—	—	4	0	—	—	—	—
Powder, cake	—	—	2	1	—	—	—	—

Source: FAO.

Table A2.3: *List of sub-Saharan Africa household surveys.*

Country	Year	Survey	Households	Rural share (%)	Sample share (%)	Households (millions)
Benin	2003	Questionnaire des indicateurs de base du bien-être	5.350	61.53	0.39	1.4
Burkina Faso	2003	Enquête Burkinabe sur les conditions de vie des ménages	8.500	69.41	0.48	1.8
Côte d'Ivoire	2002	Enquête niveau de vie ménages	10.801	47.87	0.34	3.2
Ghana	1998	Ghana living standards survey	5.998	63.34	0.14	4.4
Malawi	2004	Integrated household survey	11.280	87.23	0.42	2.7
Rwanda	1998	Enquête intégrale sur les conditions de vie des ménages	6.420	82.10	0.40	1.6
Uganda	2005	Uganda national household survey	7.425	77.12	0.14	5.2
Zambia	2003	Living conditions monitoring survey III	4.837	47.88	0.23	2.1

Table A2.4: *Population, age and gender composition.*

Country	National			Urban			Rural		
	Population	Age	Male	Population	Age	Male	Population	Age	Male
Benin	6.7	21.7	48.7	2.4	22.7	48.7	4.3	21.1	48.7
Burkina Faso	9.9	24.4	48.5	1.9	25.2	49.6	8.0	24.2	48.3
Côte d'Ivoire	17.1	22.2	49.8	8.6	21.7	49.8	8.3	22.7	49.8
Ghana	19.5	23.4	47.8	6.8	24.1	46.8	12.8	23.0	48.3
Malawi	12.5	21.3	49.2	1.4	20.6	51.1	11.1	21.4	49
Rwanda	8.0	21.0	46.4	0.8	19.9	46.9	7.1	21.2	46.3
Uganda	28.9	19.5	48.8	4.6	19.8	47.8	24.3	19.4	49.0
Zambia	11.2	20.9	49.0	4.7	20.7	49.2	6.6	21.0	48.9

Source: based on the household surveys (Table A2.3).

Table A2.5: *Demographic decomposition (household size by age group).*

Country	National					Urban					Rural				
	All	0–15	16–29	30–49	50+	All	0–15	16–29	30–49	50+	All	0–15	16–29	30–49	50+
Benin	4.9	2.4	1.1	1.0	0.5	4.5	2.0	1.1	0.9	0.4	5.3	2.7	1.0	1.0	0.5
Burkina Faso	5.6	2.3	1.5	1.1	0.6	5.0	1.6	1.7	1.1	0.5	5.7	2.5	1.4	1.1	0.7
Côte d'Ivoire	5.4	2.4	1.5	1.1	0.5	4.9	2.0	1.5	1.0	0.3	5.9	2.7	1.4	1.1	0.6
Ghana	4.4	2.0	1.0	0.9	0.5	4.0	1.7	1.0	0.8	0.4	4.7	2.3	0.9	0.9	0.6
Malawi	4.6	2.2	1.2	0.7	0.5	4.4	1.9	1.5	0.8	0.2	4.7	2.3	1.1	0.7	0.5
Rwanda	5.0	2.4	1.3	0.9	0.4	5.2	2.3	1.7	0.9	0.3	4.9	2.4	1.2	0.8	0.4
Uganda	5.5	2.9	1.3	0.9	0.4	5.0	2.3	1.6	0.8	0.3	5.6	3.0	1.3	0.9	0.4
Zambia	5.3	2.5	1.4	0.9	0.4	5.5	2.5	1.7	1.0	0.3	5.2	2.5	1.3	0.8	0.5

Source: based on the household survey data (Table A2.3).

Table A2.6: *Per capita expenditure and income sources in Benin.*

Sample	National total	Urban total	Rural total	q_1	q_2	q_3	q_4	q_5
(a) National								
Per capita expenditure	14,557	21,080	10,193	2,054	4,719	7,325	11,117	26,082
Share agriculture	25.84	13.32	34.04	38.92	37.70	35.53	32.91	24.78
– Cotton	5.35	3.47	6.59	10.39	7.05	6.71	4.58	3.98
Share home-production	26.79	22.64	29.50	44.32	31.60	27.08	22.58	21.13
Share other	47.37	64.04	36.46	16.76	30.7	37.39	44.51	54.09
(b) Male-headed								
Per capita expenditure	16,850	21,837	12,664	2,278	4,746	7,322	11,161	26,217
Share agriculture	11.50	4.42	17.36	27.18	21.87	18.46	18.34	9.21
– Cotton	0.90	0.61	1.14	4.07	1.27	0.38	1.32	0.26
Share home-production	18.99	14.37	22.81	37.81	28.39	26.14	15.45	16.73
Share other	69.51	81.21	59.83	35.01	49.74	55.4	66.21	74.06
(c) Female-headed								
Per capita expenditure	14,099	20,903	9,753	2,033	4,715	7,325	11,108	26,043
Share agriculture	28.71	15.41	37.01	40.00	40.24	38.40	35.85	29.32
– Cotton	6.24	4.14	7.56	10.97	7.97	7.77	5.24	5.06
Share home-production	28.35	24.59	30.70	44.92	32.11	27.24	24.02	22.41
Share other	42.94	60	32.29	15.08	27.65	34.36	40.13	48.27

Table A2.6: *Continued.*

Sample	National total	Urban total	Rural total	q_1	q_2	q_3	q_4	q_5
(d) Producers								
Per capita expenditure	8,139	10,251	7,325	1,890	4,699	7,298	11,106	23,407
Share agriculture	56.3	55.55	56.53	51.79	54.74	57.4	64.28	64.85
– Cotton	33.76	36.56	32.89	30.86	32.16	33.94	34.63	36.99
(e) Producers (males)								
Per capita expenditure	7,925	11,048	6,138	1,913	4,887	7,294	10,330	20,960
Share agriculture	54.17	44.12	57.24	58.42	58.73	60.51	55.36	34.47
– Cotton	24.08	31.63	21.77	20.82	17.18	11.54	37.2	33.61
(f) Producers (females)								
Per capita expenditure	8,150	10,198	7,377	1,889	4,690	7,298	11,151	23,473
Share agriculture	56.39	56.02	56.5	51.44	54.55	57.32	64.71	65.36
– Cotton	34.15	36.76	33.35	31.38	32.89	34.49	34.51	37.04

Source: based on household surveys (see Table A2.3).

Table A2.7: *Per capita expenditure and income sources in Burkina Faso.*

Sample	National total	Urban total	Rural total	q_1	q_2	q_3	q_4	q_5
(a) National								
Per capita expenditure	12,163	26,187	8,480	1,243	2,641	4,399	7,429	25,756
Share agriculture	4.15	1.48	4.73	2.85	2.98	3.86	5.88	7.91
– Cotton	1.10	0.13	1.31	1.08	0.93	1.04	1.29	2.21
Share home-production	48.59	16.21	55.60	66.67	59.57	55.97	50.36	46.08
Share other	47.26	82.31	39.67	30.48	37.45	40.17	43.76	46.01
(b) Male-headed								
Per capita expenditure	11,769	25,593	8,470	1,250	2,647	4,394	7,441	25,359
Share agriculture	4.40	1.63	4.93	3.00	3.11	4.00	6.13	8.17
– Cotton	1.19	0.15	1.39	1.17	0.97	1.1	1.37	2.32
Share home-production	50.17	17.78	56.42	67.54	60.46	57.04	51.00	47.06
Share other	45.43	80.59	38.65	29.46	36.43	38.96	42.87	44.77
(c) Female-headed								
Per capita expenditure	16,612	29,579	8,629	1,157	2,557	4,468	7,223	33,017
Share agriculture	1.34	0.72	1.69	0.95	1.19	1.90	1.83	2.95
– Cotton	0.1	0	0.15	0	0.41	0.13	0	0.22
Share home-production	30.68	8.21	43.31	55.79	47.38	40.85	39.88	27.64
Share other	67.98	91.07	55.00	43.26	51.43	57.25	58.29	69.41

Table A2.7: *Continued.*

Sample	National total	Urban total	Rural total	q_1	q_2	q_3	q_4	q_5
(d) Producers								
Per capita expenditure	26,034	31,136	18,245	1,451	2,693	4,511	7,624	38,753
Share agriculture	70.79	91.09	70.52	71.52	64.24	68.86	71.64	73.11
– Cotton	55.92	87.41	55.51	58.79	52.68	49.77	56.25	7.93
(e) Producers (males)								
Per capita expenditure	25,608	30,860	17,840	1,460	2,655	4,532	7,611	37,698
Share agriculture	71.72	91.09	71.46	71.52	65.26	70.65	71.64	74.46
– Cotton	56.78	87.41	56.37	58.79	53.84	51.61	56.25	8.96
(f) Producers (females)								
Per capita expenditure	31,483	34,140	25,245	1,307	2,987	3,885	8,098	56,690
Share agriculture	29.75	—	29.75	—	45.17	29.46	—	14.26
– Cotton	17.74	—	17.74	—	31.03	9.15	—	13.07

Source: based on household surveys (see Table A2.3).

Table A2.8: *Per capita expenditure and income sources in Côte d'Ivoire.*

Sample	National total	Urban total	Rural total	q_1	q_2	q_3	q_4	q_5
(a) National								
Per capita expenditure	29,931	35,756	23,386	3,625	8,109	13,583	23,098	70,970
Share agriculture	41.36	29.47	51.99	59.53	57.59	50.11	48.70	41.50
– Cotton	2.89	1.36	4.24	0.81	2.36	4.91	5.58	8.61
– Coffee	5.39	3.75	6.81	11.91	9.00	4.95	4.16	2.81
– Cocoa	14.60	11.69	17.12	17.53	17.67	18.87	18.41	12.48
Share home-production	4.64	2.75	6.34	8.74	8.38	5.87	3.92	4.00
Share other	54	67.78	41.67	31.73	34.03	44.02	47.38	54.5
(b) Male-headed								
Per capita expenditure	30,381	35,967	24,112	3,641	8,151	13,536	23,131	71,727
Share agriculture	45.30	33.13	56.11	64.63	61.35	55.29	52.74	44.29
– Cotton	3.38	1.64	4.93	0.93	2.33	6.04	6.59	9.76
– Coffee	6.33	4.40	7.98	14.41	10.55	5.94	4.79	2.89
– Cocoa	17.02	13.79	19.82	20.38	20.41	22.54	21.74	13.54
Share home-production	4.90	2.93	6.66	9.10	8.83	6.23	4.20	4.21
Share other	49.8	63.94	37.23	26.27	29.82	38.48	43.06	51.5
(c) Female-headed								
Per capita expenditure	27,606	34,611	19,798	3,551	7,895	13,788	22,955	65,675
Share agriculture	22.43	11.74	32.11	36.75	38.61	28.08	31.04	22.45
– Cotton	0.50	0.03	0.92	0.25	2.51	0.09	1.17	0.71
– Coffee	0.87	0.59	1.14	0.72	1.16	0.73	1.39	2.23
– Cocoa	2.95	1.56	4.12	4.81	3.82	3.28	3.85	5.27
Share home-production	3.40	1.88	4.79	7.16	6.10	4.36	2.68	2.53
Share other	74.17	86.38	63.1	56.09	55.29	67.56	66.28	75.02

Table A2.8: *Continued.*

Sample	National total	Urban total	Rural total	q_1	q_2	q_3	q_4	q_5
(d) Producers								
Per capita expenditure	29,892	35,354	24,330	3,561	8,154	13,546	23,001	73,379
Share agriculture	77.97	79.37	77.36	75.47	78.65	79.55	76.67	76.31
– Cotton	8.23	5.61	9.54	1.74	5.16	11.25	12.27	21.24
– Coffee	15.37	15.43	15.3	25.65	19.66	11.34	9.13	6.93
– Cocoa	41.63	48.14	38.48	37.78	38.59	43.26	40.46	30.8
(e) Producers (males)								
Per capita expenditure	29,215	34,254	24,154	3,544	8,164	13,518	22,947	73,323
Share agriculture	78.57	79.74	78.07	76.04	79.36	80.52	77.08	77.24
– Cotton	8.33	5.74	9.65	1.72	4.48	11.73	12.4	22.27
– Coffee	15.59	15.45	15.6	26.49	20.25	11.53	9	6.61
– Cocoa	41.93	48.4	38.74	37.47	39.16	43.75	40.87	30.89
(f) Producers (females)								
Per capita expenditure	37,138	45,930	26,468	3,821	8,023	13,920	23,522	74,011
Share agriculture	64.21	66.79	63.17	62.46	65.05	58.4	68.58	60.92
– Cotton	5.95	0.86	7.42	2.37	18.17	0.88	9.84	3.97
– Coffee	10.29	14.66	9.22	6.66	8.39	7.26	11.71	12.38
– Cocoa	34.92	39.11	33.28	44.73	27.65	32.61	32.5	29.25

Source: based on household surveys (see Table A2.3).

Table A2.9: *Per capita expenditure and income sources in Ghana.*

Sample	National total	Urban total	Rural total	q_1	q_2	q_3	q_4	q_5
(a) National								
Per capita expenditure	93,515	136,077	66,940	14,753	27,426	41,344	63,763	170,249
Share agriculture	22.47	11.63	28.96	33.47	32.49	30.21	26.21	23.18
– Cocoa	2.91	0.84	4.15	2.39	4.42	5.69	4.26	3.82
Share home-production	24.62	8.73	34.15	47.10	40.13	35.21	29.31	21.03
Share other	52.91	79.64	36.89	19.43	27.38	34.58	44.48	55.79
(b) Male-headed								
Per capita expenditure	93,405	141,895	65,394	14,487	27,220	41,161	63,436	170,681
Share agriculture	24.11	10.66	31.53	36.00	36.24	32.92	27.74	24.92
– Cocoa	3.44	1.04	4.76	2.39	5.24	6.30	4.98	4.76
Share home-production	25.36	8.48	34.67	47.94	38.03	36.05	29.05	22.85
Share other	50.53	80.86	33.8	16.06	25.73	31.03	43.21	52.23
(c) Female-headed								
Per capita expenditure	93,740	125,774	70,396	15,480	27,895	41,798	64,376	169,375
Share agriculture	19.09	13.35	23.14	26.59	23.94	23.53	23.28	19.57
– Cocoa	1.82	0.49	2.76	2.40	2.56	4.18	2.89	1.88
Share home-production	23.12	9.18	32.96	44.82	44.89	33.11	29.82	17.26
Share other	57.79	77.47	43.9	28.59	31.17	43.36	46.9	63.17

Table A2.9: *Continued.*

Sample	National total	Urban total	Rural total	q_1	q_2	q_3	q_4	q_5
(d) Producers								
Per capita expenditure	83,122	124,121	71,297	15,829	27,437	40,859	63,374	192,875
Share agriculture	46.22	49.34	45.89	42.55	48.14	44.81	44.21	49.27
– Cocoa	23.99	27.13	23.65	18.62	22.03	25.49	22.89	27.98
(e) Producers (males)								
Per capita expenditure	83,538	125,681	72,380	15,730	27,122	40,769	62,985	211,379
Share agriculture	47.51	48.4	47.42	42.25	50.46	45.94	46.25	50.94
– Cocoa	24.38	27.31	24.07	17.04	21.95	25.05	25.27	29.96
(f) Producers (females)								
Per capita expenditure	81,897	120,512	67,855	16,212	28,880	41,222	64,160	143,971
Share agriculture	41.56	52.78	40.39	43.74	37.05	40.22	39.54	43.24
– Cocoa	22.56	26.45	22.15	24.82	22.44	27.3	17.45	20.78

Source: based on household surveys (see Table A2.3).

Table A2.10: *Per capita expenditure and income sources in Malawi.*

Sample	National total	Urban total	Rural total	q_1	q_2	q_3	q_4	q_5
(a) National								
Per capita expenditure	1,385	3,643	1,078	274	498	742	1,129	2,709
Share agriculture	10.52	2.88	11.55	6.82	9.63	11.89	13.90	15.40
– Tobacco	3.47	0.86	3.82	1.41	2.68	4.06	4.80	6.10
– Cotton	0.41	0.00	0.47	0.33	0.37	0.49	0.72	0.44
Share home-production	40.82	10.04	44.97	56.76	49.76	47.08	41.56	30.01
Share other	48.66	87.08	43.48	36.42	40.61	41.03	44.54	54.59
(b) Male-headed								
Per capita expenditure	1,488	3,768	1,142	279	499	742	1,128	2,742
Share agriculture	11.64	2.86	12.97	8.11	10.99	13.22	14.98	16.39
– Tobacco	4.09	0.81	4.59	1.92	3.30	4.81	5.38	6.86
– Cotton	0.48	0.00	0.56	0.44	0.45	0.57	0.80	0.50
Share home-production	39.25	9.08	43.79	57.09	49.29	46.25	40.86	29.10
Share other	49.11	88.06	43.24	34.3	39.72	40.53	44.16	54.51
(c) Female-headed								
Per capita expenditure	1,037	2,935	875	265	498	744	1,131	2,539
Share agriculture	6.72	2.99	7.04	4.22	5.76	7.51	9.92	10.32
– Tobacco	1.37	1.14	1.39	0.38	0.93	1.59	2.67	2.18
– Cotton	0.18	0.00	0.20	0.11	0.14	0.21	0.44	0.13
Share home-production	46.11	15.39	48.71	56.08	51.09	49.80	44.12	34.65
Share other	47.17	81.62	44.25	39.7	43.15	42.69	45.96	55.03

Table A2.10: *Continued.*

Sample	National total	Urban total	Rural total	q_1	q_2	q_3	q_4	q_5
(d) Producers								
Per capita expenditure	1,255	2,866	1,205	292	496	755	1,132	2,598
Share agriculture	34.39	36.42	34.34	23.47	28.35	33.8	36.2	42.35
- Tobacco	21.97	27.97	21.82	13.64	17.29	21.63	22.36	28.52
- Cotton	2.63	0	2.69	3.2	2.39	2.59	3.37	2.06
(e) Producers (males)								
Per capita expenditure	1,294	3,207	1,238	294	498	756	1,135	2,610
Share agriculture	34.91	34.79	34.91	24.97	29.01	34.66	36.11	42.07
- Tobacco	22.3	26.32	22.21	14.61	7.92	22.13	22	28.47
- Cotton	2.64	0	2.7	3.37	2.47	2.63	3.27	2.08
(f) Producers (females)								
Per capita expenditure	920	845	923	277	481	745	1,107	2,398
Share agriculture	29.96	45.64	29.41	15.21	23.64	26.96	36.96	46.98
- Tobacco	19.12	37.28	18.49	7.92	12.79	17.7	25.44	29.48
- Cotton	2.52	0	2.61	2.29	1.86	2.31	4.22	1.73

Source: based on household surveys (see Table A2.3).

Table A2.11: *Per capita expenditure and income sources in Rwanda.*

Sample	National total	Urban total	Rural total	q_1	q_2	q_3	q_4	q_5
(a) National								
Per capita expenditure	6,487	18,074	5,215	602	1,451	2,599	5,100	16,228
Share agriculture	17.25	2.26	18.84	11.15	14.91	19.24	23.61	25.41
– Coffee	0.80	0.02	0.88	0.87	0.79	0.96	0.70	1.09
Share home-production	42.89	6.35	46.76	56.50	50.30	47.10	41.66	38.04
Share other	39.86	91.39	34.4	32.35	34.79	33.66	34.73	36.55
(b) Male-headed								
Per capita expenditure	7,060	19,660	5,585	635	1,463	2,606	5,105	15,555
Share agriculture	18.18	1.91	20.06	11.14	16.16	20.44	23.72	25.77
– Coffee	0.82	0.02	0.91	1.03	0.78	0.97	0.75	1.06
Share home-production	39.60	4.28	43.69	53.08	46.61	45.27	41.00	35.75
Share other	42.22	93.81	36.25	35.78	37.23	34.29	35.28	38.48
(c) Female-headed								
Per capita expenditure	5,271	13,993	4,447	562	1,428	2,584	5,085	18,419
Share agriculture	15.28	3.25	16.30	11.16	12.63	16.67	23.29	24.23
– Coffee	0.75	0.02	0.81	0.68	0.81	0.96	0.56	1.16
Share home-production	49.93	12.21	53.16	60.51	57.01	51.00	43.62	45.52
Share other	34.79	84.54	30.54	28.33	30.36	32.33	33.09	30.25

Table A2.11: *Continued.*

Sample	National total	Urban total	Rural total	q_1	q_2	q_3	q_4	q_5
(d) Producers								
Per capita expenditure	6,159	9,020	6,030	623	1,438	2,628	5,115	15,225
Share agriculture	28.28	26.15	28.3	29.79	28.22	30.01	24.67	29.04
– Coffee	7.96	2.17	8.02	11.52	8.76	8.06	5.99	7.34
(e) Producers (males)								
Per capita expenditure	6,210	13,034	6,074	642	1,489	2,657	5,168	13,799
Share agriculture	28.44	27.98	28.44	28.26	29.8	30.8	21.79	30.93
– Coffee	7.43	2.41	7.48	10.34	8	7.68	6.28	6.67
(f) Producers (females)								
Per capita expenditure	6,026	7,042	5,909	582	1,339	2,555	4,947	21,798
Share agriculture	27.8	21.8	27.87	33.62	24.57	28.03	33.92	20.09
– Coffee	9.57	1.62	9.67	14.5	10.51	8.99	5.04	10.56

Source: based on household surveys (see Table A2.3).

Table A2.12: *Per capita expenditure and income sources in Uganda.*

Sample	National total	Urban total	Rural total	q_1	q_2	q_3	q_4	q_5
(a) National								
Per capita expenditure	26,514	53,670	20,780	3,675	9,085	13,964	21,219	54,102
Share agriculture	13.19	3.88	15.14	5.00	10.44	14.16	20.09	25.69
– Coffee	2.05	0.40	2.40	1.22	2.30	2.57	3.19	2.67
Share home-production	49.08	47.35	49.45	41.49	54.19	54.74	51.83	45.16
Share other	37.73	48.77	35.41	53.51	35.37	31.1	28.08	29.15
(b) Male-headed								
Per capita expenditure	26,795	55,137	21,042	3,850	9,112	13,970	21,264	51,916
Share agriculture	14.91	4.59	16.99	5.75	11.27	15.31	21.46	28.41
– Coffee	2.29	0.49	2.65	1.20	2.40	2.83	3.44	3.11
Share home-production	49.23	46.76	49.73	41.96	55.35	55.30	51.49	44.13
Share other	35.86	48.65	33.28	52.29	33.38	29.39	27.05	27.46
(c) Female-headed								
Per capita expenditure	25,749	50,118	20,049	3,344	9,008	13,943	21,071	61,558
Share agriculture	8.53	2.20	10.01	3.57	8.33	10.79	15.23	15.99
– Coffee	1.41	0.19	1.69	1.28	2.05	1.82	2.33	1.14
Share home-production	48.67	48.74	48.66	40.59	51.28	53.13	53.05	48.80
Share other	42.8	49.06	41.33	55.84	40.39	36.08	31.72	35.21

Table A2.12: *Continued.*

Sample	National total	Urban total	Rural total	q_1	q_2	q_3	q_4	q_5
(d) Producers								
Per capita expenditure	24,012	47,873	22,882	4,260	9,402	14,066	21,367	46,836
Share agriculture	24.69	24.88	24.68	17.35	19	23.33	26.18	30.44
- Coffee	8.18	6.91	8.23	8.63	7.59	7.96	8.33	8.66
(e) Producers (males)								
Per capita expenditure	25,293	55,403	23,888	4,113	9,454	14,074	21,469	48,177
Share agriculture	26.94	30.06	26.81	18.49	20.35	25.38	29.1	32.02
- Coffee	8.64	8.11	8.66	8.7	7.54	8.43	9.09	9.07
(f) Producers (females)								
Per capita expenditure	19,657	23,807	19,450	4,721	9,278	14,036	21,042	40,593
Share agriculture	17.09	10.59	17.4	13.79	15.77	15.85	16.92	23.08
- Coffee	6.64	3.61	6.78	8.44	7.7	6.25	5.94	6.77

Source: based on household surveys (see Table A2.3).

Table A2.13: *Per capita expenditure and income sources in Zambia.*

Sample	National total	Urban total	Rural total	q_1	q_2	q_3	q_4	q_5
(a) National								
Per capita expenditure	80,764	107,191	66,597	25,641	43,127	60,424	86,042	169,201
Share agriculture	13.54	2.54	19.61	20.34	21.38	19.45	17.27	18.41
– Tobacco	0.47	0	0.73	0.43	0.7	0.72	0.7	1.35
– Cotton	1.92	0.02	2.97	1.97	3.25	3.99	2.55	3.27
Share home-production	25.86	2.18	38.91	42.17	39.83	39.24	37.62	32.71
Share other	60.6	95.28	41.48	37.49	38.79	41.31	45.11	48.88
(b) Male-headed								
Per capita expenditure	81,515	108,948	66,475	25,714	43,122	60,430	85,817	166,574
Share agriculture	13.94	2.69	20.23	21.47	21.59	20.09	17.43	19.47
– Tobacco	0.52	0	0.81	0.54	0.59	0.8	0.86	1.61
– Cotton	2.05	0.01	3.18	2.13	3.54	4.26	2.61	3.42
Share home-production	25.08	1.74	38.12	42.07	39.46	38.22	36.29	31.23
Share other	60.98	95.57	41.65	36.46	38.95	41.69	46.28	49.3
(c) Female-headed								
Per capita expenditure	77,739	99,565	67,066	25,389	43,146	60,400	86,863	179,898
Share agriculture	11.86	1.88	17.06	16.34	20.46	16.42	16.62	13.77
– Tobacco	0.26	0.02	0.39	0	1.18	0.36	0.07	0.22
– Cotton	1.4	0.03	2.11	1.41	2.01	2.71	2.31	2.62
Share home-production	29.12	4.13	42.15	42.53	41.4	44.07	42.8	39.14
Share other	59.02	93.99	40.79	41.13	38.14	39.51	40.58	47.09

Table A2.13: *Continued.*

Sample	National total	Urban total	Rural total	q_1	q_2	q_3	q_4	q_5
(d) Producers								
Per capita expenditure	68,064	81,291	65,810	24,695	43,305	60,417	87,480	153,442
Share agriculture	36.29	20.79	36.38	34.98	37.35	36.19	33.26	39.75
– Tobacco	5.68	3.71	5.69	5.06	5.4	4.61	5.5	8.48
– Cotton	23.17	11.64	23.23	23.49	24.87	25.47	20.13	20.48
(e) Producers (males)								
Per capita expenditure	68,131	87,224	64,885	24,654	43,421	60,769	87,568	150,609
Share agriculture	36.57	12.63	36.71	35.43	35.96	36.41	34.55	41.51
– Tobacco	5.89	0.6	5.92	5.81	4.06	4.78	7.09	9.62
– Cotton	23.19	9.62	23.26	22.75	24.25	25.5	21.56	20.38
(f) Producers (females)								
Per capita expenditure	67,807	58,848	69,346	24,847	42,683	58,987	87,257	164,377
Share agriculture	34.6	64.84	34.4	31.93	50.33	34.57	29.15	29.43
– Tobacco	4.36	20.54	4.26	0	17.89	3.4	0.45	1.79
– Cotton	23.05	22.53	23.05	28.47	30.59	25.33	15.58	21.11

Source: based on household surveys (see Table A2.3).

3

Institutional Arrangements

This chapter describes the main institutional arrangements in each of the value chains to be considered in the analysis. This description includes the different vertical arrangements from different crops, whether the value chains are characterized by one or more layers, the structure of competition among firms and farmers in each layer, and whether there are market interlinkages. For each crop we describe the main characteristics of its world market and the specific institutional arrangement in the countries being studied. More importantly for our simulations, for each case study we present a list of the main processing/exporting firms and their respective market share.

1 COTTON

The cotton plant is native to tropical countries but cotton production is not limited to the tropics, as the emergence of new varieties and advances in cultivation techniques have led to the expansion of its culture. Whereas the plant is a perennial tree by nature, under extensive cultivation it is mostly grown as an annual shrub. The collected seed cotton goes through the ginning process that separates the fiber from the cotton seeds. The major end uses for cotton fiber (85 percent of the commercial value of the seed cotton) include wearing apparel, home furnishings, and other industrial uses. Through the spinning process the cotton fiber is made into yarns and threads for use in the textile and apparel sectors (wearing apparel accounts for approximately 60 percent of cotton consumption). The cotton seeds provide edible oil and seeds that are used for livestock food (UNCTAD: see http://unctad.org/infocomm/anglais/cotton/chain.htm). Figure 3.1 depicts a stylized value chain for the cotton sector.

The production of cotton is crucially important to several developing countries. In 2006–7, the four main producing countries were China, India, the United States, and Pakistan and accounted for approximately three quarters of world output. Although Africa is not the largest cotton exporter (it accounts for 10–15 percent of world exports), cotton is of critical importance to many African countries. Cotton is the largest source of export receipts in several West and Central African countries. The cotton sector is also key to rural poverty reduction, with cotton-related activities accounting for a large share

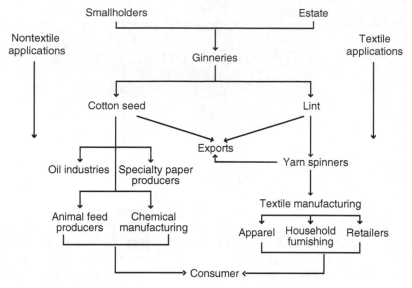

Figure 3.1: *Cotton stylized value chain.*

of rural employment. Almost all exports from West African countries are raw cotton, which means that processing opportunities at the domestic level are not fully exploited. The four main exporters of cotton lint are the United States, India, Uzbekistan, and Brazil while, the four largest importers of cotton lint are China, Turkey, Bangladesh, and Indonesia.

Global cotton consumption has increased by 2 percent per year since the 1940s. This is this despite the fact that cotton share in textile fibers has been declining because of the increase in chemical textiles. Regardless of increasing local processing (especially in developing countries), cotton is still the main traded agricultural raw material, with more than 30 percent of cotton production (approximately 6.3 million tonnes of fiber) traded per annum since the beginning of the 1980s. Cotton consumption has shifted to developing countries, mainly as a reflection of rising wage levels in developed countries. In the textile sector, labor accounts for about one-sixth of production costs. This means that raising labor costs eroded the competitive edge of developed countries, and contributed to the shifting of cotton processing to low-cost economies (UNCTAD).

1.1   Cotton in Benin[1]

Cotton is the main cash crop and the largest source of export receipts for Benin. The average annual production of cotton grain is 350,000 tonnes. The

---

[1] This section is largely based on Gergely (2009), Saizonou (2008), and World Bank (2005).

sector generates 45 percent of fiscal revenue (excluding custom duties) and, on average, contributes 13 percent of the national GDP. This crop is of particular importance for rural welfare since cotton-related activities generate monetary revenue for approximately two million people in 350,000 cotton farms.[2] Cotton accounts approximately for 20 percent of the total cultivated area in the country. Two-thirds of the cotton production takes place in the north of the country (départements of Borgou and Alibori). At the industrial level, cotton represents around 60 percent of the industrial tissue through twenty ginning companies, five textile plants, three crushing mills, and one company producing cotton wool. Gearing activities during a campaign (around six months) create more than 3,500 jobs at the national level. The cotton value chain generates important spillover effects in other sectors such as transportation, retail, and construction.

The origin of cotton production in Benin is similar to other French West African countries. Cotton emerged as a cash crop in the 1950s, under the direction of the French parastatal Compagnie Française pour le Développement des Fibres Textiles (CFDT). After independence, cotton production was shifted to national monopolies, with CFDT retaining a minority share. In Benin, as was generally the case elsewhere, a monopoly marketing board, the SONAPRA, controlled all stages of the production process: distribution of seeds and inputs, provision of credit and other services to producers, ginning, and the final exports. Once a year and before the growing season, the SONAPRA established a single price for seed cotton and inputs, with some adjustments possible based on its financial outcome. The cost of the inputs provided by the organization was reimbursed directly via a deduction from the purchase price of cotton (World Bank 2005).

The process of liberalization of the Beninese cotton commodity chain started during the 1992–93 campaign. It implied a progressive disengagement of the state from the provisioning and distribution of inputs. Import and distribution operations were taken over gradually by private national operators, whose numbers have increased over time. At the same time, producer organizations were given responsibilities so that they could participate fully in the process of the transfer of competencies in the domains of input supplies, support to the supervision of farmers, and the commercialization of cotton grain. In the industrial sector, liberalization started in 1994, with the accreditation granted by the state to private promoters of factories for the production of cotton grain.

There are three major functions in the Beninese cotton chain: the production of cotton grain, the provision of inputs, and the production of cotton fiber (shelling). The actors involved in these three functions are structured

---

[2]This number comes from the 2002 agricultural census. However, due to the decline observed in the last few years, some estimate that the number of farms growing cotton has declined to 120,000 (Gergely 2009).

in organizations or "families": the family of the producers represented by FUPRO–Benin (Fédération des Unions de Producteurs du Bénin), the family of the importers and input distributors represented by the Professional Group of Agricultural Input Distributors, and the family of cotton grain producers represented by the Professional Association of Cotton Grain Shelling factories of Benin (APEB). The Cotton Inter-professional Association (AIC) coordinates the three families of organizations (Saizonou 2008).

Until 1999, producers' prices were fixed by the government. From that year onward, the responsibility was supposedly transferred to the AIC. The new price mechanism established that seed cotton price was to be determined through negotiations between cotton producers and ginners, with the AIC acting as a facilitator. Usually, for the upcoming marketing year, a base price is set in March–May. The final producer price is then fixed in October, when the harvest is about to begin using the cotton world market price as a reference and deducting the customary processing and marketing cost. According to the institutional design, CSPR–GIE is the technical unit of the AIC in charge of the management of physical and financial flows. It receives support from the producer organizations in order to animate primary collection markets for cotton grain. The cotton grain shelling factories ensure transportation of the products but are only responsible for the quantities that they have been allocated. Since the 2006–7 season, the CSPR–GIE has had total control over the physical flows, which permits it to ensure 100 percent payment of the actors (Saizonou 2008). Despite the liberalization process and the price mechanism described below, in practice, the government remained a key player in determining the price, since the price-setting mechanism is somewhat vague and the stakeholders rarely reach a price agreement. Furthermore, the behavior of producer prices of the last few years seems to show that the price-setting mechanism has not changed to a large extent, as local prices have remained sticky despite considerable world price fluctuations.

Benin prohibits exports of cotton seeds. The seeds are ground locally and exported as cotton lint or oil. Each cotton company is allocated a quota proportional to its installed capacity, which contributes toward segmenting the market and restricting entry and competition. Ginneries are required to pay to the CSRP an advance of 40 percent prior to delivery of the seed cotton as a security (Gergely 2009). The country has an installed ginning capacity of twenty units with a total shelling capacity of up to 587,000 tonnes per year, which significantly exceeds the average annual production of 350,000 tonnes. Ten plants belong to SONAPRA, while private actors, either foreign companies (LBC/Aiglon, Louis Dreyfus, Kamsal, IBECO, MCI, and Sodicot) or the local private sector (Talon and cooperatives) have invested in the private plants (SONAPRA retained a 35 percent share in each of them). The effective allocation of grains often differs from the quota based on the installed capacity. In our simulations we will use the allocation of the 2007–8 campaign, where SONAPRA accounted for 55 percent of the market, followed by LCB

Table 3.1: *Market shares in export supply chains: cotton.*

	Benin		Burkina Faso		Côte d'Ivoire	
Ranking	Firm	Share	Firm	Share	Firm	Share
1	SONAPRA	55.1	SOFITEX	5.0	Ivoire Coton	45.0
2	SOCOBE	6.8	SOCOMA	10.0	CIDT	29.0
3	Ibeco	6.2	Faso Coton	5.0	LCCI	16.0
4	LCB	10.0			DOPA	6.0
5	MCI	3.4			SICOSA	4.0
6	ICB	8.4				
7	CCB	8.5				
8	SODICOT	1.6				

	Malawi		Zambia	
Ranking	Firm	Share	Firm	Share
1	Great Lakes	50.0	Dunavant	44.0
2	Clark Cotton	50.0	Cargill	32.0
3			Amaka	13.0
4			Mulungushi	6.0
5			Continental	5.0
6			Mukuba	1.0

with 10 percent, CCB with 8.5 percent, and ICB with 8.4 percent of the market (see Table 3.1 for details).

In theory the cotton industry covers the whole value chain (spinning, weaving, printing, and garment making) but the activity in the textile sector has been shrinking in the last decade and now processes less than 2 percent of the lint production. The sector that produces for the domestic market and the Nigerian market is represented by SOBETEX (a French private group), COTEB (a partnership between the government and European investors), and SITEX (a joint venture between the government and Chinese investors). The sector is facing increased competition from imports and second-hand garments, in particular because of the high cost of energy and the low productivity of labor (Gergely 2009). All companies are facing considerable financial difficulties and the government is in the process of privatizing them. Despite the interest of the government in the sector, Benin has so far failed to demonstrate a comparative advantage in textiles.

Recently, a new strategic plan for the revival of the agricultural sector (and the cotton subsector in particular) has been adopted. The plan will promote the development of the agricultural commodity chains within the framework of public/private partnerships. The plan retains the structure of the commodity chains that has been in development since 2000 in the interprofession associations. As part of this plan, SONAPRA has been partially privatized in September 2008. The Société Commune de Participation (SCP) was provisionally declared the successful bidder. As a result, a public–private joint venture called the Société Pour le Développement du Coton (SODECO) will be created which will retain 33.5 percent ownership. The remaining shares will be held by the government of Benin (33.5 percent) and the private sector (33 percent).

1.2   Cotton in Burkina Faso[3]

Cotton is the main cash crop in Burkina Faso, generating income for approximately two million people in the country. It is also the main source of foreign revenue, accounting for 40 percent of total exports. The production is concentrated in the western part of the country (Comoé, Kossi, Mouhoum, and Kénédougou). While a minority of producers cultivate relatively large areas (up to twenty-five hectares), most of the cotton farms are family owned and small scale (typically from three to five hectares).

Cotton production in Burkina Faso is semi-privatized, and is often cited as a model of reform away from the old vertically integrated state-owned cotton companies (Hanson 2008). The process of privatization of the sector began in 1998 when the government sold some of its shares to the producers' organization (UNPCB). The subsequent partial privatization of the cotton sector in Burkina Faso created three regional cotton companies. SOFITEX, the core of the former parastatal operates in the western part of the country, owns thirteen gins, making up approximately 85 percent of the ginning capacity (Table 3.1). Faso Coton was formed in 2004, operates in the central region with a single gin located in Ouagadougou, and controls 5 percent of the market. SOCOMA, which operates three gins in the eastern region, is the second private company created in 2004 and has a market share of 10 percent. After three consecutive years of significant losses from 2005 to 2007, the three cotton companies initiated a recapitalization process. DAGRIS—a French parastatal and former shareholder in many African cotton and oilseed companies that was privatized in January of 2008 (becoming Geo Coton)—did not participate in the recapitalization of its shares in SOFITEX. The government of Burkina Faso assumed those shares and subsequently created a financial institution called "Fonds Burkinabe de Développement Economique" to broker the sale of the shares to the private sector.[4]

A distinguishing feature of the cotton sector is the degree of organization of the producers at the local and regional level. Since 1996, producers have

---

[3] This section is largely based on Hanson (2008), WTO (2004a), and Yartey (2008).

[4] The capital structure of the three companies in 2008 was as followed. SOFITEX was owned by the state (65 percent), UNPCB (30 percent), and private banking (1 percent). SOCOMA's larger shareholders were Geo Coton (34 percent) and UNPCB (20 percent). FASO Coton was owned by Reinhart AG (31 percent), IPS (29 percent), others (20 percent), and UNPCB (10 percent).

joined together in cotton producers' groups (GPCs), which took over from village groups. The GPCs have a cooperative structure that facilitates the supply of inputs and agricultural machinery, and seeks to ensure proper management of loans and an increase in crop yields. Recent estimates show around 250,000 cotton producers, organized in 8,000 producers' cooperatives that form 170 departmental cooperative groups and seventeen regional unions. At the national level, the producers are represented by the National Union of Burkina Cotton Producers (UNPCB). The state handed over part of the capital of the SOFITEX in 1998 to the UNPCB to allow producers to take a leading role in managing the subsector (WTO 2004a).

The ginning companies are in charge of the transportation from the primary markets to the ginning plants. The producers' associations are paid net of inputs purchased and the proceeds are then distributed among the members of the association. Most of the seed cotton is ginned and 98 percent of the lint is then exported mainly to Southeast Asia (66 percent) and Europe (20 percent). Burkina Faso also produces and exports seed oil, mainly through SN-Citec.

Until recently, there was a guaranteed producers' base price that was set before the crop year. The system included the possibility of bonus payments (in case of profit, the producers received a higher price the following season[5]) similar to the system applied in Côte d'Ivoire and Benin. Since the 2007–8 campaign the system has been changed in favor of a market-based producer price-setting mechanism. The new mechanism aligns domestic producer prices with world market prices and thus makes producers share part of the risk. However, to limit excessive price fluctuations for producers, who have little access to credit, the producer floor price is smoothed by basing it on a five-year centered average of world market prices. A discount is then applied to the average to protect the smoothing fund, set up to finance major deviations of actual prices from the producer floor price. When world prices are low, the fund makes payments to ginning companies. When world prices rise, the fund is replenished (Yartey 2008). The system is administrated by the Inter-Professional Cotton Association and the fund is financed by assistance from the EU, the French Development Agency, and is sustained by payments made by the cotton companies.

1.3 Cotton in Côte d'Ivoire[6]

Cotton is the third most important crop for the Ivorian economy but ranks far behind cocoa and coffee in terms of export revenues generated. Despite this, cotton contributes significantly to livelihood in rural areas. Most of the

---

[5] The return premium was divided: 50 percent to growers, 25 percent to the state, and 25 percent to the ginning companies.

[6] This section is largely based on the UNCTAD online report (see references for details).

production takes place in the north of the country and is done by small-scale farmers, who, on average, own four hectares and receive a low share of world prices, averaging around 54 percent and reaching 63 percent in recent years. The area planted to cotton has grown steadily since 1960, with a leveling off around 1989, a jump in area planted at the time of the 1994 devaluation, and subsequent decline in recent years due to the civil conflict. Seed cotton yields also grew over the 1960s and 1970s, but stagnated and varied erratically until the devaluation. As a result, production grew until 1987, and again after the devaluation, with increased variability. Seed cotton is ginned in the country and the cotton lint production has mirrored seed cotton production. Most lint is exported and some cotton seed has also been exported since 2000.

Until the late 1990s, a single vertically integrated state enterprise ("Compagnie Ivoirienne de Développement des Textiles," or CIDT) was responsible for organizing virtually all services needed for cotton production and marketing, utilizing the institutional frameworks derived from French colonial heritage (UNCTAD). The privatization of this parastatal company was an objective of international donors, but was resisted by the government. Due to agronomic[7] and institutional differences, the cotton sector in Côte d'Ivoire was managed somewhat differently from cocoa or coffee and the institutional arrangement and its evolution are somewhat different.

The privatization of CIDT began in 1998, when it was broken into regional companies, but each of those held a monopoly over their region, and the state did not divest a majority interest in those companies until 2002. This did not lead to competition, as the price of seed cotton remained the same for the three zones; in addition, each company retained exclusive purchasing rights within its zone. Three new companies were set up. "CIDT nouvelle" is active in the south of the country. The government has expressed its readiness to relinquish its share (a proposed deal was to sell 80 percent of the state's shares to producers) but the negotiations on the purchase of CIDT nouvelle have been stalled due to the civil conflict affecting the country. The second company is "Cotton-Ivoire," an equity joint venture active in the northwest of the country. The Aga-Khan group and the Swiss-based cotton-trading firm "Paul Reinhart" have joined venture interests in the company. The state retains a 30 percent share in the venture. The third company is LCCI, a subsidiary of the Switzerland-based Aiglon group. LCCI is primarily active in the northeast. Each company is responsible for the purchasing of cotton throughout its allotted area. This is often implemented by signing contracts, with growers stipulating the area to be planted and the quantity of seed cotton to be delivered.

The market remained geographically segmented until the introduction of two new companies, DOPA and SICOSA. The original three companies felt

---

[7]Cotton is more input demanding, requiring fertilizer, pesticides, and variety changes over time.

penalized because they had invested in inputs and extension services for producers. To resolve this situation, a new system was developed to guarantee seed cotton supply to the cotton companies and to secure reimbursement of their investment in seed cotton inputs. Under this system, the companies sign a contract with the producers through their cooperatives for the provision of inputs and extension services. The extension services could be provided by any private company chosen by the cooperative. In return, via their cooperatives, the producers are engaged to deliver their seed cotton to the cotton company. As of March 2006, the market shares for the ginning companies were: Ivoire Coton 45 percent, CIDT 29 percent, LCCI 16 percent, DOPA 6 percent, and SICOSA 4 percent (Table 3.1).

1.4   Cotton in Malawi[8]

In recent years, cotton has become an important crop for a Malawian economy looking to broaden an agricultural export base that is heavily reliant on tobacco. The cotton sector has about 120,000 smallholder farmers, three ginning companies, and three main input providers. Cotton production has increased since the 2003–4 campaign after a long period of decline that started in the late 1980s. This negative trend was the result of several factors, including the structure of the industry, the dominance of the public sector in the purchasing of cotton, decreased productivity, and declining world prices. On top of that, the integrated cotton, textile, and garment value chain with intra-sector linkages collapsed with the financial problems of the only remaining textile company (David Whitehead and Sons) in the 1990s.

The sector has recovered since the 2003–4 campaign, partly due to the establishment of the Cotton Development Association (CDA). The CDA provides treated seed and pesticides to cotton farmers under contract farming arrangements. A further important change was the improved ginning outturn from 33 percent to 38 percent, which improves the overall crop value. The improvements in the cotton price on the international market have also contributed to the recent favorable performance of the sector. Up until 2003–4, cotton yields averaged about 600 kg/ha, but since then, through a number of emerging cotton development initiatives and the slight increase in the ginners, average yield has improved to about 900 kg/ha and production has considerably increased to about 50,000 tonnes during the 2007–8 campaign from only 14,700 tonnes five years before (Tchale and Keyser 2009).

The estimated production cost for un-ginned seed cotton for Malawi is lower than other countries, except for Mozambique and Nigeria. This implies that Malawi has some competitive edge against its neighbors in the production of cotton, and consequently the exportation of lint. Arguably, part of this

---

[8]This section is largely based on RATES (2003) and Tchale and Keyser (2009).

competitive advantage is lost due to the government cotton price policy.[9] Every year, the government of Malawi sets a minimum seed cotton price with 2–3 percent deduction from gross sales for outgrower costs. This price is probably higher than the one that would exist in a collusion of the two ginning companies. This higher price is compensated for by reducing the ginner's investment in outgrower extension and other services, thereby threatening the sustainability of high quality and productivity in the cotton subsector. The price-setting policy has recently generated conflict between the government and the ginneries as the minimum set price established by the government in 2009 was much higher than the price ginneries were willing to pay after the international price collapsed following the 2008 crisis.

The two main components of the cotton value chain in Malawi are the cotton producers, typically small holders, and the three existing ginning companies. The major cotton growing areas are the Lower Shire Valley (50 percent of total production), the Southern region upland areas around Balaka (30 percent), and the Lakeshore area around Salima (20 percent). Until recently, virtually all the cotton was sold within Malawi to the two ginning companies, Great Lakes Cotton Company and Clark Cotton Malawi (both subsidiaries of international companies) that each have half the market (Table 3.1). The market structure is currently changing, as a new company has been established. The Malawian government, in association with China, has created the Malawi Cotton Company. The company is comprised of a cotton ginnery, a textile manufacturing plant and cooking oil extraction. The company will also process cotton seed cake.

Seed cotton is sold to the ginneries in three different ways: through traders, by producer organizations, and directly to ginners. Traders operate in remote areas, providing transportation to central markets. They often pay cash, and they often pay it in advance of the announcement of the price for the current campaign by the ginneries. In general they offer poor conditions for the farmers and the CDA has tried to discourage the sale to middlemen by opening several buying points. Sales made through the farmers' association have been increasing over time. The purchases made by these associations are often limited by the amount of available cash. In general, they offer better prices and deliver other services such as training, organizing inputs, and transportation. Farmers located close to the four ginneries and to the ginners' own buying points can sell directly to the ginning companies, receiving a better price but having to organize and afford the cost of transportation.

Each of the original two ginning companies owns two plants. After the seed cotton is ginned, the ginneries are left with cotton lint and cotton seed. A

---

[9]The other reason for the very narrow competitive edge in the lint export market is due to the low ginning output in Malawi compared with other countries. This is an area that provides the greatest scope in terms of improving the ginner's profit, which could then be cascaded to the net farmer profit through investment in required services for the producer (Tchale and Keyser 2009).

proportion of the cotton seed (often around 10 percent) is set aside for the ginners to provide the farmers with seeds for the following year. Most of the rest is exported to South Africa, undersupplying the two or three active seed crushing companies that exist in Malawi. Historically a higher proportion of cotton lint has been sold to the local textile company (David Whitehead and Sons) but financial problems led to a drop in its output and local ginneries started to export most of the cotton lint to South Africa and South Asian countries. The garment industry in the country is small and does not use local textile as all the fabric for the cut, make, and trim garment firms is imported.

1.5   Cotton in Zambia[10]

Cotton is one of the main cash crops and it is produced almost entirely by small-scale farmers in Zambia. In 2003, around 11 percent of the farmers grew cotton. The largest 20 percent of farmers accounted for half of the production and sale of this crop. Cotton production is heavily concentrated in the Eastern province, with over one-third of all households in that province producing the crop and accounting for about a two-thirds share of national production during the 2003 harvest season. Central and Southern provinces follow, with 16 percent of farmers growing the crop in the Central province and accounting for 19 percent of national production, and 12 percent growing in the Southern Province and accounting for 13 percent of national production (Tschirley and Kabwe 2007).

Until 1994, the sector was dominated by a state monopoly (LINTCO) that was responsible for every activity in the industry. The reform period began in 1994 when LINTCO was broken up and its ginneries sold to Lonrho (later succeeded by Dunavant) and Clark Cotton (Koyi 2005). Since then, the production has gone through four phases: a rapid expansion through 1998, with production increasing from less than 20,000 tonnes in 1995 to over 100,000 tonnes in 1998; a rapid decline in 1999 and 2000, spurred in large measure by a serious credit default crisis; production in 2000 falling to less than 50,000 tonnes; a sustained and rapid recovery from 2000 to 2006, and a sharp decline in 2007, driven by the kwacha appreciation crisis of the previous year (Tschirley and Kabwe 2007).

In the first eight years following the privatization of LINTCO, Zambia's cotton sector operated as a concentrated, market-based system with almost no government involvement, even on a regulatory basis. Extra-market coordination, whether across ginning firms or between ginners, organized farmers, and other stakeholders, was minimal. Since 2002 the Zambian government has developed a more noticeable presence in the sector, and efforts at sector-wide coordination have increased production markedly (Tschirley and Kabwe 2007). Starting in 2005, two developments increased the level of effort put into

---

[10]This section is largely based on Koyi (2005) and Tschirley and Kabwe (2007, 2009).

sector-wide coordination. First, the Zambia National Farmers' Union (ZNFU) finalized the creation of the Cotton Association of Zambia (CAZ) to represent farmer interests in the sector, providing the Ginners' Association with an organized private sector body with whom to communicate on key issues. Second, efforts at revision of the Cotton Act became a focus of intense collaboration across stakeholders.[11] The government has also launched an initiative to complement existing private outgrower schemes: the Cotton Outgrower Credit Fund (COCF).

There has been no government mandated price, nor any pricing guidance of any kind from government, since liberalization in 1994. Dunavant has typically acted as a price leader, announcing a minimum preplanting price to farmers, which may be adjusted upwards at the start of the buying season. Cargill typically follows Dunavant's pricing, while smaller ginners frequently pay higher prices than Dunavant. New entrants in the market have led to increased competition among private firms and prices have become a key tool for attracting buyers. However, there remains a great deal of variability in the level of input credit support offered to smallholders by the various ginners. These differences may allow the companies offering less or no support to use price to attract sellers who may have received input support from another company. The appreciation of the Kwacha in 2006 led to a conflict over the domestic price of cotton. The government openly tried to influence prices and the farmers attempted for the first time in an organized way (through CAZ) to negotiate the prices paid by the ginners. The analysis of Tschirley and Kabwe (2007) shows that while Zambian companies have paid nominal prices comparable to those in Tanzania, where more companies compete for the cotton crop, a detailed cross-country analysis demonstrates that Zambia pays a substantially lower share of its realized ex-ginnery price to farmers than in Tanzania. The key issue is that Zambia enjoys a very high price premium on world cotton markets and therefore ginning companies could arguably pay a higher price than they have been paying.

The value chain in cotton includes the production of cotton seeds at the farm level, the production of cotton lint, the production of cotton yarn, and, eventually, the production of textiles. In Zambia, most of the production of

---

[11] In March 2006 a sub-committee was formed consisting of six members to consult stakeholders: Cotton Ginners Association, Cotton Development Trust, Food Security Research Project, Cotton Association of Zambia, Ministry of Agriculture, and co-operatives. Some stakeholders felt that the act was not strong enough to regulate the industry and control the production and marketing of seed cotton. The main concern for processors is the increase in "side buying" due to the proliferation of companies buying seed cotton and with over 200,000 farmers producing cotton, prosecution of defaulters would be extremely expensive. They asked for an increase in the penalty for purchasing seed cotton without proper licensing and for the implementation of a register of producers that have requested financing. The report of this committee was presented to the parliament in February 2009 and a new Cotton Act is under consideration.

cotton seeds is devoted to the exports of cotton lint and, to a much lesser extent, of cotton yarn. In the case of exports of cotton lint, the farmers produce cotton, which is purchased by the ginneries to produce cotton lint.[12] Cotton lint is then exported to world markets. World markets for cotton lint are best described as competitive. Farmers are atomized and cannot exert monopoly power when selling the cotton seeds. Instead, it is assumed that the ginneries can act monopsonistically over farmers. The number of ginneries has increased in recent years with Dunavant remaining as the dominant company with 44 percent of the installed ginning capacity. Cargill is the second largest firm, controlling 32 percent of the market, followed by Amaka (13 percent), Mulungushi (6 percent), Continental (5 percent), and Mukuba with only 1 percent of the total installed capacity (Table 3.1).

Another destination of farm cotton is to produce cotton yarn. In this case, the production of the farmers is processed by the ginneries into cotton lint and then sold as cotton yarn. This may involve another layer down the value chain. However, Zambia's spinning industry appears to absorb a small and declining share of the country's lint production. The last available data indicates that, in 2002, the country's four operating spinning mills processed less than 10,000 tonnes of lint, or less than one quarter of lint production in the country. Swarp (a spinner) estimated in 2002 that 90 percent of Swarp's lint needs are met by purchases from Dunavant and Clark (now Cargill); the balance appears to come from smaller ginners. Mukuba Textiles and Mulungushi Textiles both have gins within their premises and purchase seed cotton for processing. Starflex, Excel, Mulungushi, and Kafue all experienced serious financial problems in the early 2000s, which led to temporary and sometimes prolonged shutdowns (RATES 2003). The other smaller spinners indicate that they periodically import to meet their lint needs when they are unable to reach agreement on price with local ginners. Despite the problems that these value-added sectors have faced, their combined size is not trivial when compared with cotton lint: total exports of yarn, woven fabric, and apparel totaled US$23.5m in 2002 (over US$21m from yarn), compared to US$30m in lint exports (Tschirley and Kabwe 2009).

2   COCOA

Cocoa is grown on trees and the cocoa fruits grow directly on the stems and branches. In West Africa, where most of the cocoa is produced on small family

---

[12]Historically, independent cotton traders—individuals trading cotton who do not own and are not employed by a ginning company—played a major role as the middlemen between farmers and ginneries. However, due to market conditions, they largely disappeared after 2000.

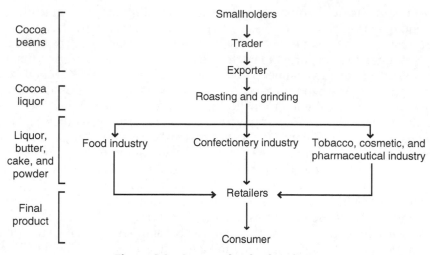

Figure 3.2: *Cocoa stylized value chain.*

farms,[13] they are collected most intensively in the harvest seasons of December and June. The cocoa fruits are cut down by hand. Machines cannot be used because it is not possible to harvest all beans at the same time. The seeds are fermented on the ground for around seven days and dried for approximately three weeks, before being packed in bags and exported. Figure 3.2 shows a simple representation of the cocoa value chain from the small holder to the consumer.

West Africa is the primary producer of cocoa today. Côte d'Ivoire, Ghana, Nigeria, and Cameroon produce two-thirds and export three-quarters of total world cocoa production. Côte d'Ivoire and Ghana are the largest producers. The third largest producer is Indonesia and other big producers are Brazil, Malaysia, and Ecuador. Most exports are directed to Europe and the United States, which are the two largest processors and consumers of cocoa.

Over the last ten years the global cocoa production has increased at an average annual growth rate of 2.7 percent, producing 3.7 million tonnes during 2007–8. Consumption has shown similar patterns. However, during the second half of the 1980s, excessive cocoa production led to a divergence between supply and demand, caused by excess production of cocoa. Over the last thirty years there has been a relative decline in the price of cocoa because of an increased in the supply of cocoa into world markets. This is due to entry of new producer countries and to more efficient processing methods. The price decline was partially reversed in 2001 due to changing stock-holding behavior of the industries, social unrest in Côte d'Ivoire, and lower yields of cocoa.

---

[13] This is in contrast to cases like Brazil and Malaysia, where large commercial plantations dominate.

2.1   Cocoa in Côte d'Ivoire[14]

Côte d'Ivoire is the largest cocoa producer, accounting for around 40 percent of total cocoa supply. The sector is the most important for the Ivorian economy, contributing with 15 percent of GDP, 35 percent of the total exports, and 20 percent of the government revenue in 2007. It employs 700,000 households (35 percent of the total). Despite its importance and resilience, the sector has been greatly affected in recent years by the civil conflict in the country, low yields, volatile international prices, and excessive taxation.[15]

The institutional development behind agricultural policy, and indeed all policy evolution, was conditioned by Côte d'Ivoire's experience as a French colony (Abbott 2007). Following independence the "Caisse de stabilisation des prix des produits agricoles" (Caistab) was established to regulate farm-gate and export prices (both for cocoa and coffee), provide extension service and inputs, and to collect substantial taxes. The Caisse was not directly involved with the transportation of cocoa from the farm gate (controlled by private traders called traitants) and permitted "private" exporters to operate within a system of quotas (Losch 2002). The Caisse was relatively successful in insulating farmers from the ample variation of international prices observed between the 1970s and the 1990s.

The reform process started in 1987 and, in the middle of the 1990s, the state's control was diminished in order to reduce marketing costs, raise producer prices, and encourage the creation of producers' organizations. The reforms increased production, but did not lead to sufficient changes for farmers, which brought about further liberalization reforms in 1999 when the Caistab was disbanded and the producer price was fully liberalized.

The Caistab was replaced by four agencies to manage and monitor the sector. The Autorité de Régulation du Café/Cacao (ARCC) is the regulatory authority in charge of defining and enforcing a regulatory framework ensuring competition at all levels of the value chain. The Fonds de Régulation et de Controle (FRC) is a financial regulation fund managing the price stabilization system through taxes of cocoa exports and forward selling. The Bourse du Café/Cacao (BCC) is a marketing bourse managed by farmers and exporters, responsible for managing export operations. The Fonds de Développement et de Promotion des Producteurs de Café et Cacao (FDPCC) is a development fund established by producers, funded by voluntary levy, to finance demand-driven development programs. Through these agencies the government has

---

[14]This section is largely based on Abbott (2007), Losch (2002), and Wilcox and Abbott (2004).

[15]Ivorian cocoa farmers received the lowest farm-gate prices among a sample of cocoa-producing countries: 40 percent less than farmers in Ghana, 50 percent less than farmers in Cameroon or Nigeria, and 60 percent less than a producer in Brazil or Indonesia. The major factor behind the low farm-gate prices is taxation. Trading margins, in-country transportation, exporter costs, local processing, and maritime freight are other contributing factors.

tried to strengthen the position of farmers by providing information about prices and encouraging farmers to form cooperatives to gain more bargaining power.

These four structures have been in charge of the regulation of the cocoa (and coffee) sector since 2001. However, the system has suffered a number of drawbacks due to external (decline in world market prices) and internal factors (civil conflict, an excessive tax burden on cocoa farmers who provide $5 billion in fiscal levies and $1.4 billion on para-fiscal levies, and apparent corruption cases leading to the arrest of some of the officials in charge of these agencies). Currently, the system configuration is in the process of being revised. Two committees, formed in September 2008, are reviewing past reforms and audits of the sector and revisiting the role of the sector's four agencies, with a view to formulating a new institutional and regulatory framework for the sector.

The elimination of the Caisse de Stabilisation had an impact on the cocoa market configuration allowing some backward integration by the market's new entrants: the multinational firms. The state of the sector and the civil conflict does not allow us to gather recent statistics. However, according to the Bureau d'Etudes Techniques et de Développement (BNETD), the market share enjoyed by cooperatives has decreased from 32 percent during the 1998–99 season to 18 percent in the post-liberalization season of 2000–2001, leaving almost 80 percent to be funneled through middlemen. Once the cocoa arrives at the port of Abidjan or San Pedro, it is conditioned for export (usinage) and shipped to processors mainly by multinational exporters who, in the cases of Archers Daniels Midland (ADM), Cargill, and Barry Callebaut, are themselves processors. Therefore the farm-gate price is now the residual of the "c.i.f." price less transportation, conditioning, taxes, and other associated marketing costs, which may include rents to exporters (Wilcox and Abbott 2004). Fourteen firms controlled three-quarters of the cocoa that was declared for export in 1999–2000, the year the Caisse was dissolved. Three years later, these fourteen firms controlled more than 85 percent of the export market, with the top five firms among the sixty-one exporters controlling almost half of the total exports.[16] Table 3.2 provides detailed market shares for these fourteen companies. The three largest are Cargill West Africa with 16.4 percent of the export market, ADM Cocoa Sifca with 11.9 percent, and Tropival with 8.3 percent.

---

[16]Wilcox and Abbott (2004) note that these reports only allow us to figure out the nominal ownership of cocoa exporters as some anecdotal information leads us to believe that several smaller companies are acting on behalf of the larger exporters or that there is overlapping ownership.

Table 3.2: *Market shares in export supply chains: cocoa.*

Ranking	Côte d'Ivoire		Ghana	
	Firm	Share	Firm	Share
1	ADM Cocoa Sifca	11.9	PBC	32.83
2	Armajaro	3.3	Akuapo	11.97
3	Barry Callebaut	3.1	Olam	10.71
4	Cargill West Africa	16.4	Adwumapa	8.62
5	Cemoi	3.8	Fed	7.04
6	Cipexi	6.0	Kuapa	5.91
7	Cocaf	4.4	Transroyal	5.72
8	Dafci and IFCO	4.5	Armajaro	5.7
9	Delbau	4.7	Cocoa Gh	3.17
10	Outspan Ivoire	5.2	Diaby	2.7
11	Proci	6.0	Others	5.63
12	Sifca-Coop	4.9		
13	Tropival	8.3		
14	Zamacom	3.4		
15	Others	14.1		

2.2 Cocoa in Ghana[17]

Ghana provides one-fifth of the total world supply of cocoa beans. The country was the world's leading producer of cocoa by 1911, a position it retained until the mid 1970s when it was overtaken by Côte d'Ivoire. The sector has been of vital importance for the Ghanaian economy, not only for the 1.6 million smallholder farmers growing cocoa (production has always been small-farm based, mostly on plots of three hectares or less, with plantations never having been of much importance) but also for the government and other economic sectors associated with the activity. With the recent discovery of oil fields, it is expected that the sector will become less determinant for the government in terms of revenue source.

Until World War II, internal and external marketing were handled by private firms, but during the war the colonial government took over the purchase of cocoa. In 1947 the Cocoa Marketing Board (CMB) was established (after 1979 it was renamed The Ghana Cocoa Board or COCOBOD). It was omnipresent in the cocoa industry and covered extension services, input marketing, and the maintenance and rehabilitation of roads in cocoa-producing villages (Brooks et al. 2007). The CMB was the only authorized buyer and exporter of cocoa. The CMB carried out its activities through its subsidiaries the Produce Buying Company (PBC) and the Cocoa Marketing Company (CMC). The Quality Control Division (QCD) is responsible for ensuring that the overall quality of the beans is kept to the high standard for which Ghanaian cocoa is known worldwide.

---

[17] This section is largely based on Brooks et al. (2007), Laven (2007), Lundstedt and Pärssinen (2009), and Vigneri and Santos (2007).

While initially set up to protect farmers from price volatility, the CMB gradually turned into an instrument of public taxation. Rents were extracted by keeping producer prices well below the world price, and by using an overvalued exchange rate to make payments to farmers. Between 1967 and 1977, the system for purchasing and marketing cocoa gradually broke down as the economic situation deteriorated. An extensive economic recovery programme was implemented in the mid 1980s. Efforts to improve the efficiency of COCOBOD led to wide-ranging changes to its structure and activities. Transport of cocoa shifted to the private sector after 1984. From the 1988–89 campaign, COCOBOD began phasing out input subsidies, and this led to a substantial increase in input prices. Staff levels were reduced from over 100,000 in the early 1980s to just over 5,100 staff by 2003 (Brooks et al. 2007). The internal marketing system was liberalized in 1993 allowing Licensed Buying Companies (LBCs) to compete with the PBC. In addition, the PBC was partly privatized in 2000 and introduced on the Ghanaian stock exchange. COCOBOD owns 40 percent of the stocks directly and another 30 percent indirectly through its ownership of a major stakeholder (Lundstedt and Pärssinen 2009).

Despite the reforms, the Ghanaian government still plays an important role in the cocoa sector. Through COCOBOD, the government controls cocoa quality, hands out licenses, finances, and controls activities of private companies. As we will describe below, it also sets producer prices and margins and sells and exports to manufacturing and processing companies.

The farm-gate price for cocoa in Ghana is determined in a very unique way because of the country's unique marketing arrangements. The ceiling price is determined by the international price of cocoa to which the government then nets out a variety of margins to pay for the many layers of its intervention in the sector. The Producer Price Review Committee (PPRC) is very much in charge of how the floor price paid to the farmer is ultimately determined, and this committee is made up of a variety of stockholders ranging from the Ministry of Finance, industry representatives, the COCOBOD, LBCs, farmers representatives, and the University of Ghana. The producer price is a price floor, i.e., the LBCs are not allowed to purchase cocoa for less than the producer price, but, in practice, the price paid to the farmers is not raised above this minimum level. This producer price is set at the beginning of each crop year and is constant throughout the seasons. In addition to setting the producer price, the PPRC sets a yearly fixed purchase price, i.e., the price that the LBCs receive from selling the cocoa to COCOBOD. This price corresponds to the buyer's margin and is set taking into account average transport costs, commissions paid to purchasing clerks, and other costs faced by the LBC. Each LBC receives the same buyer's margin.

The system contemplates the existence of a price stabilization mechanism. When there is a discrepancy between the actual and the predicted price because of fluctuations in the world price of cocoa, this implies a surplus or deficit with respect to the target level set at the beginning of the campaign.

The surplus is divided between the government and the farmers (in the form of yearly bonuses after payment), while the deficit is covered by the government alone (Lundstedt and Pärssinen 2009).

Despite the fact that the number of registered LBCs has increased gradually since the liberalization reform,[18] the number of companies that are active players in the local market remains much smaller as fewer than ten of them purchase up to 90 percent of the total harvest. Table 3.2 portrays the ranking of LBCs by market shares calculated as the five-year average between 2004–5 and 2008–9. PBC has the largest market share with a market share of around 32.8 percent. The second largest LBC is the domestically owned company Akaufo Adamfo, which has an average market share of 12 percent. Olam, with its approximate market share of 11 percent, is the third largest LBC.

LBCs can be divided into four categories depending on the ownership structure of the company. The first category comprises the former subsidiary of COCOBOD, the PBC. The second category of LBCs consists of domestically owned LBCs. The third type of companies is the farmer-based fair trade cooperative Kuapa Kokoo that was established in 1993 by a group of farmers with support from a British NGO. The last category of LBCs comprises the two international companies, Singaporean-owned Olam and British-owned Armajaro.[19] The international companies have access to foreign capital, an advantage that makes them less dependent on the seed fund. When dividing the market shares into its categories, Lundstedt and Pärssinen (2009) show that domestically owned LBCs have increased their shares over the five-year period, while the shares of both Kuapa Kokoo and of Olam and Armajaro have decreased. The PBC strongly decreased its market shares in 2005–6 and 2006–7.

The liberalization process has also meant that the number of LBCs per village increased by around 30 percent between 2002 and 2004, which implies that the potential trading partners of cocoa farmers have increased significantly over the years (Lundstedt and Pärssinen 2009). This deregulation in the domestic segment of the supply chain was expected to bring competition among different private buyers and to generate a number of production incentives to the farmers. Most notably, one would have expected competition to emerge by means of price bonuses and/or premiums over the guaranteed price to characterize the new marketing arrangement. One would also have expected this, in turn, to both stimulate farmers' supply and to increase traders' own share of the domestic market. However, what makes cocoa Ghana's cocoa marketing system unique is the virtual absence of any

---

[18]Initially, six companies were granted licenses to operate on the internal market while today there are twenty-six active LBCs, including the PBC.

[19]Both Olam and Armajaro are leading suppliers of cocoa and other commodities (such as coffee and sugar) on the world market and operate in all main cocoa-producing countries. In Ghana they operate as buying companies, but their expertise includes origination, exporting, and processing of cocoa (Lundstedt and Pärssinen 2009).

price-based competition mechanism. LBC competition for cocoa supplies—which is fierce, if anecdotal evidence is to be believed—is based on the provision of different services (Vigneri and Santos 2007). Examples of this lack of price competition include allowing community representatives to select the purchase clerks or choosing one that is capable, trustworthy, and motivated to serve farmers' needs. Incentive packages offered by LBCs may comprise cash payments, bonuses, gifts, rewards, subsidized inputs, credit and training, and other investments looking to maintain durable social relations with their suppliers. According to a survey of farmers, the main reasons by farmers for choosing a particular buyer are cash payments, social relations with the purchasing clerk, provision of credit, and, in the case of the PBC, accountability (Laven 2007). For our purposes, it does not matter whether competition brings about an increase in prices or a decrease in costs.

The liberalization of the internal market has not led to liberalization of the external front. The PBC is the only company that is allowed to export. Originally, the government imposed some minimum volume of purchase requirements over three consecutive years for the LBCs to be able to export 30 percent of their purchases. During the first years of the reform, the LBCs did not have enough profit margins and volumes of cocoa to cross the export bar. However, now that some of them seem ready to start exporting, the government has decided not to grant them the required license to export. The reason advanced by the government for maintaining the monopsony structure of the sector is to guarantee high quality and contract fulfilment, for which Ghanaian cocoa receives a price premium on the world market. In contrast, most LBCs report that they want to enter and would be capable of entering the export sector and that COCOBOD deliberately hold them back from engaging in external marketing. International processing and manufacturing companies do not oppose the system in Ghana, most likely because Ghana is the only country in the world offering a consistent supply and relatively low price of high quality cocoa (Lundstedt and Pärssinen 2009).

3   COFFEE

Coffee is grown in tropical and subtropical regions around the equator. The two types of coffee plants widely cultivated are Robusta and Arabica. Ripe coffee cherries are harvested manually and undergo primary processing in the producing country before they are exported. The primary processing is carried out to separate the coffee bean from the skin and pulp of the cherry. There are two alternative methods for doing this: wet and dry. The end products of both methods are coffee beans, referred to in the trade as "green" coffee. Wet processing produces "mild" coffee, usually of the Arabica type, and the dry method produces "hard" coffee, either Hard Arabica or Hard Robusta. The distinction is important as Mild Arabica, Hard Arabica, and

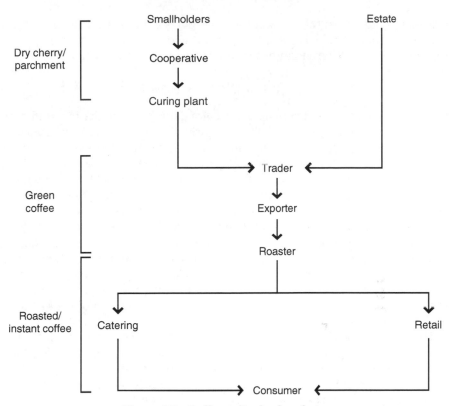

Figure 3.3: *Coffee stylized value chain.*

Hard Robusta coffees are traded separately (Tropical Commodity Coalition (www.teacoffeecocoa.org)). Figure 3.3 shows the value chain for coffee.

Brazil, Vietnam, Colombia, Indonesia, and Ethiopia are the main producers and exporters of green coffee, with Brazil's share close to one-third of the total market. Uganda, Côte d'Ivoire, and Kenya are also among the top twenty exporting nations. Most of the coffee produced is consumed in high-income countries. The United States, Germany, Italy, Japan, and France are the top five importers. More than 80 percent of the production is traded internationally as green coffee, generally packed in 60 kg bags. Green coffee is available to buyers either directly or via the spot markets in the United States and Europe. International buyers are generally concerned with the uniformity and consistency of green coffee and they require information on the type of coffee, the type of primary processing, the country of origin, and the official grade standard.

Globally, coffee for home consumption is mostly purchased in supermarkets. The food retail sector is highly concentrated in the United States, the

United Kingdom, and Northern Europe and plays a dominant role in the food marketing chain. There is also an important and growing market for specialties and product differentiation that is been exploited by smaller producers.

3.1   Coffee in Côte d'Ivoire[20]

Coffee plantations were first established alongside smallholder farms in Côte d'Ivoire at the beginning of the 1920s. Historically, coffee was a very important source of income for small holders in Côte d'Ivoire and the second source of foreign exchange after cocoa for the government. During the 1960s and 1970s the country was Africa's largest coffee exporter. Some 300,000 coffee planters managed 1,200,000 hectares of plantations. However, mismanagement of the sector and the economy and low relative international prices for coffee have led to a decline of the sector. In the mid 2000s the sector was characterized by a coffee grove getting old (65 percent of the plantations were more than twenty-five years old[21]) and low output figures (around 150,000 tonnes per year) and yields (250 and 350 kg/ha). The civil conflict has affected the production of coffee and cocoa less as they are mainly produced in the south of the country. However, the conflict has led to the resumption of export taxes and increased trader margins.

The evolution of the institutional setting for the coffee sector has been similar to that of cocoa. In 1964 the Caisse de Stabilisation des Prix des Produits Agricoles (CAISTAB) was created as a price stabilization and support fund for the cocoa and coffee sector. The CAISTAB was in charge of the primary collecting and the transportation and export of the crops. It also provided extension and inputs but the state intervened little in the production process itself. It paid the farmers, through private agents, a preannounced price for their crops and sold the output on international markets. The difference between these two prices, net of marketing cost, was a surplus that constituted an important part of the government's revenue. However, from the late 1980s onward, international prices dropped below the producer prices and the surpluses became deficits (Benjamin and Deaton 1993).

The CAISTAB shielded coffee farmers from much of the international price variations, with remarkably stable nominal, domestic coffee prices over a period of enormous change in international prices (Abbott 2007). However, by the beginning of the 1990s the stabilization lacked reserves, had accumulated important debts, and could not continue to guarantee producers'

---

[20] This section is largely based on Abbott (2007) and Benjamin and Deaton (1993).

[21] In recent years, the situation has slightly improved, with a program for the regeneration of the groves that has been set up for 170,000 ha. The diagnostic is that the intensification of the output through the improvement of the coffee-tree plantations, the rejuvenation of the plantations, the maintenance of the groves, and the use of input location is necessary to regain the interest of the coffee culture in Côte d'Ivoire.

prices.[22] This crisis marked the beginning of a gradual liberalization process. International donors pushed for the privatization of the parastatal but the process was slow because it was resisted by the government. The CAISTAB and the cocoa and coffee sectors were finally privatized in 2000. The BCC (Coffee and Cocoa Marketing Exchange) and ARCC (Coffee and Cocoa Regulatory Authority) took over CAISTAB functions. The reform process continued through the 2000s aiming at improving producer prices and productivity, marketing arrangements, and the monitoring of the sector by government and public and private agencies. However, the results of these reforms have been disappointing as the producers' price and the competitiveness of the sector as a whole has not improved. As was mentioned in the section regarding cocoa in Côte d'Ivoire, the sector has been undergoing a new set of reforms since late 2008. Partially because of this flowing state of the system and also because of the civil conflict, it was not possible to find reliable information on coffee exporters' market shares. For that reason, in our simulations we decided to use the same market shares that we have for the case of cocoa in Côte d'Ivoire.

3.2 Coffee in Rwanda[23]

The production of coffee is well spread in Rwanda. Around 400,000 smallholders[24] produce coffee on approximately 52,000 hectares of land. There are no large estates producing coffee and only Arabica varieties are grown (WTO 2004b). The country's altitude and rainfall generate excellent agro-ecological conditions to cultivate this crop.

Historically, coffee has been one of the main sources of foreign earnings for the Rwandan economy and several of the state's public finance crises have been associated with strong fluctuation in the international price of coffee. The civil conflict at the beginning of the 1990s greatly affected the production of coffee, and this has only started to recover in the last few years. Since 2000, the volume of production has increased but always below the stipulated targets. An important development has been the improvement in the quality of the exported coffee. This has allowed Rwanda to take advantage of market niches favoring the trading of premium blends. The reported quantity and quality of Rwanda's coffee is affected by unofficial exports and imports of cherries to and from the surrounding region. The restrictions on ordinary coffee sales during the first period of the coffee season mean that some producers prefer to sell illegally for higher prices in neighboring countries.

Coffee was introduced at the beginning of the twentieth century and was the main economic commodity during the colonial period. After independence,

---

[22]In the 1989–90 crop year, producer prices for cocoa paid by the CAISTAB were reduced by 50 percent, and by 40–50 percent for coffee (Trivedi and Akimaya 1992).

[23]This section is largely based on Habyalimana (2007), Loveridge et al. (2003), and WTO (2004b).

[24]Each of them has on average 165 coffee trees.

Table 3.3: *Market shares in export supply chains: coffee.*

	Rwanda		Uganda	
Ranking	Firm	Share	Firm	Share
1	Rwacof	30.4	Ugacof Ltd.	16.2
2	Rwandex	29.2	Kyagalanyi Coffee Ltd.	14.0
3	CBC	22.8	Kawacom (U) Ltd.	13.3
4	Agrocoffee	13.7	Ibero (U) Ltd.	9.3
5	SICAF	3.9	Job Coffee	8.3
6			Great Lakes	7.2
7			Lakeland Holdings Ltd.	7.2
8			Kampala Domestic Store	5.6
9			Savannah Commodities	4.9
10			Pan African Impex	4.7
11			Others	9.4

the Rwanda Coffee Authority, OCIR-Café, was created with the mission of supervising coffee-related activities in the country, from production to commercialization (OCIR: see www.rwandacafe.com). However, the coffee industry was liberalized in the mid 1990s and, consequently, since then the coffee board has not been engaged in coffee processing, marketing, or exports. However, OCIR-Café still distributes seedlings and insecticides and provides certification on quality standards. It is remunerated by growers at 3 percent of their export sales price. The organization also issues licenses to private coffee traders (WTO 2004b). The liberalization of coffee policies seems to have increased yields by taking the poorest fields out of production. The 1990s saw a large reduction in the proportion of farmers cultivating coffee fields—nationally 55 percent of smallholders grew coffee in 1991 versus only 30 percent in 2002 (Loveridge et al. 2003).

In the marketing link of the value chain, middlemen collect coffee beans from door to door, bulk them, and deliver them to large buyers, who transport them to Kigali for hulling and export. Almost every village counts a middleman, but some middlemen extend their services over more than one village. Large buyers are generally located in Kigali (Habyalimana 2007). At present, secondary processing of coffee is handled mainly by five factory exporters.[25] Their market shares in 2005 were: Rwacof 30.4 percent, Rwandex 29.2 percent, CBC 22.8 percent, Agrocoffee 13.7 percent, and SICAF 3.9 percent (Table 3.3). Until recently, the government owned 51 percent of Rwandex. After several privatization attempts, the company was divided in two and sold in June 2009 to foreign investors. Due to significant private sector investments in coffee washing stations the amount of fully washed coffee has increased from 1 percent to 20 percent of production from 2002 to 2007. However, many washing

---

[25]Primary processing is done by the producers themselves using traditional or semi-modern methods. Only a small quantity is processed at modern washing stations.

stations are not profitable because of high operating costs, weak manage-ment, and financial issues. Stakeholders across the industry point out the lack of suitable infrastructure investment as the main constraint for the develop-ment of the coffee sector.

The fix-price policy for producers was abandoned in 1997 and replaced by an indicative weekly price. This "floating" price is announced before the end of each week as a baseline for negotiations between coffee producers and buyers. The calculation of this price is based on a "moving scale" which takes into account the various elements related to coffee picking, processing, transportation, and export (WTO 2004b).

3.3   Coffee in Uganda[26]

Uganda produces two types of coffee: Arabica coffee, which comprises about 70 percent of the world's coffee production but only 10 percent of Uganda's coffee production; and Robusta coffee, which comprises about 30 percent of the world's production and 90 percent of Uganda's production. Robusta is grown in the central part of Uganda in the Lake Victoria crescent, and across the west, southwest, and east of the country. Arabica beans are grown at higher altitude, in the areas of Mount Elgon along Uganda's western bor-der with Kenya and in southwestern Uganda along the Rwenzori mountain range. This widespread cultivation places Uganda among the top ten coffee-producing countries in the world. Approximately 500,000 smallholder fam-ilies are engaged directly in its production, with over seven million people depending on the crop for their livelihood (Masiga et al. 2007). The crop once generated more than 95 percent of the export income but its importance has declined over time as nontraditional exports have picked up and coffee now represents only around 20 percent of total export earnings. Despite this, the sector potentially has an important poverty reduction role since it occupies a much larger part of the population than other activities.

Until 1991, the roles of stakeholders in the coffee supply chain were clearly segregated. The smallholders produced, harvested, and dried their coffee. The dried cherry was then sold to either primary cooperative societies or private stores. Primary societies sold their coffee to cooperative unions, while the private stores sold the beans either to huller operators who, after hulling, sold the coffee to the Coffee Marketing Board (CMB). The CMB in turn reprocessed the crop and exported it as green coffee. The prices paid at each level were predetermined by the authorities and did not change with movements in the international coffee market (Masiga et al. 2007).

The Coffee Marketing Board monopoly was abolished in 1991 and the entity was split into two entities: the Coffee Marketing Board Limited (CMBL), which

---

[26]This section is largely based on Cheyns et al. (2006), Masiga et al. (2007), and Vargas Hill (2010).

is responsible for export, but on a par with private exporters, and the Uganda Coffee Development Authority (UCDA). The end of the monopoly opened up the possibility of cooperatives and private operators exporting coffee directly and nearly all exporters became vertically integrated. The supply chain for exported coffee was dominated by coffee processing and trading companies. Private traders and the old cooperative trading system gradually lost ground to private exporters. In recent years, multinational coffee companies have became also important in Uganda, generating an alternative channel for exporting coffee (Cheyns et al. 2006).

Since the liberalization of the internal coffee market in 1992, farmers have been free to decide how and to whom to sell their coffee. For the majority of farmers the price is negotiated at the time of sale and payment is not made until then. Transactions at the farm level are quite small and farmers usually sell as individuals, only in a few cases selling as a group. Most coffee sales are made at the farm gate to small traders.[27] These small-scale traders act as aggregators either for bigger independent traders, who often own a store or mill, or for exporters and their agents (Vargas Hill 2010).

After the coffee has been milled, it is transported to Kampala and sold to exporters. Coffee exporters in Uganda have to be registered with the Ugandan Coffee Development Authority (UCDA). The number of registered coffee subsector players at post-harvest levels was 324 in 2007–8 comprising 30 exporters, 19 export graders, 271 primary processors, and 4 roasters. At the export level, over 90 percent of the volume was handled by ten companies, with the largest being Ugacof Ltd. (16.2 percent), Kyagalanyi Coffee Ltd. (14 percent), Kawacom (U) Ltd. (13.3 percent), Ibero (U) Ltd. (9.3 percent), and Job Coffee (8.3 percent; see Table 3.3 for more details). Almost 75 percent of Ugandan coffee is exported to the European Union. More than 50 percent of Uganda coffee was bought by five companies, namely Sucafina (14.3 percent), Decotrade (11.3 percent), Drucafe (9.6 percent), Bernard Rothfos (8.5 percent), and Olam International Ltd. (7.7 percent). This level of concentration in Ugandan coffee exports is a reflection of the concentration in the coffee world markets for both traders and roasters.

4   TOBACCO

Tobacco is usually cultivated annually. Harvesting is the first step in the tobacco value chain. This activity is generally labor intensive and involves removing the leaves from the plant stalks. Once harvested, the leaves are cured to remove all of the natural sap. Tobacco is stored, aged, blended, conditioned, cased, cut, dried, and flavored. After the curing and storage period,

---

[27]The majority of Ugandan producers sell their coffee in the form of dry cherries locally known as kiboko, which are then milled (the cherry is separated from the husk) by the traders who buy the coffee.

the tobacco is graded according to color, texture, aroma, and size and sold in auctions or directly through a contract system. The next two steps in the value chain (often done in importing countries) are cigarette manufacturing and packaging. The cigarettes are manufactured by machine and put through quality control checks, wrapping, and printing. They are then inserted into packs and wrapped to preserve the quality. The last steps are the marketing and distribution. Figure 3.4 represents the value chain of tobacco.

The annual production of tobacco leaf is around seven million tonnes, of which almost 40 percent is produced in China, followed by Brazil and India both producing around 10 percent of the global production. A significant amount of tobacco is consumed domestically and the rest exported. Brazil, the United States, and Malawi are the top three exporting nations, while Zimbabwe, Mozambique, and Zambia are among the top twenty. Developed countries are still the main importers of tobacco leaf as they are the ones producing and exporting cigarettes and other tobacco products.

4.1   Tobacco in Malawi[28]

Tobacco is the single most important export crop for Malawi, contributing over 65 percent of foreign earnings. While the exact percentage may change from year to year, tobacco typically accounts for 43 percent of the agricultural GDP, 13 percent of overall GDP, and 23 percent of the country's total tax revenue. Out of a total workforce of about five million people, FAO (2003) estimates that around one million people (20 percent of the total labor force) are involved in the tobacco industry to some degree, either as producers, as laborers on estates or in processing factories, or as buyers or transporters.[29] The number of hectares dedicated to the crop generally varies between 120,000 and 145,000. During the 2009 marketing campaign, 82 percent of the tobacco sold was burley, while flue-cured tobacco accounted for 15 percent of the total proceedings. Malawi is the first tobacco exporter and the second largest tobacco producer in sub-Saharan Africa after Zimbabwe. These two countries account for 75 percent of the total production in sub-Saharan Africa. The outstanding position in tobacco export of Malawi is only partially explained by agro-ecological conditions as they are not outstanding and are not very different from other countries in sub-Saharan Africa. Instead, the two most important factors to explain this phenomenon are the fact that the varieties of burley tobacco grown in Malawi are relatively low in nicotine and path dependency as it was the crop of choice by both of the early European settlers and the new political elites after independence in 1964 (Poulton et al. 2007).

---

[28]This section is largely based on FAO (2003), Jaffe (2003), Poulton et al. (2007), Tchale and Keyser (2010), van Donge (2002), and World Bank (2008).

[29]Although some of this engagement is part-time and/or casual, the integrated household survey (IHS) of Malawi records income from tobacco sales as the main source of household (cash) income in the major growing districts in the country (Poulton et al. 2007).

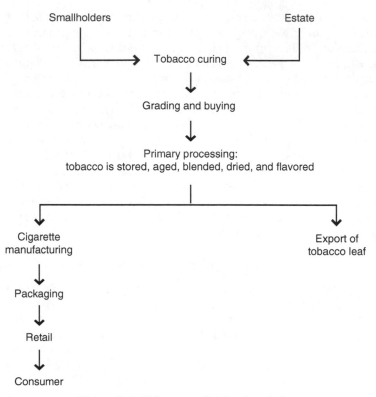

Figure 3.4: *Tobacco stylized value chain.*

Before 1989, the Tobacco Control Commission closely controlled production activity. All tobacco producers had to obtain a license from the government regulatory body. The system was biased against smallholders as only estates and landowners were eligible to apply for a production license. Moreover, to be allowed to sell tobacco directly on the auction floor, a grower had to reach a certain production scale. This was the case until early 1995 when Malawi embarked on a structural adjustment program that, among other things, allowed smallholder farmers to produce cash crops. These measures contributed significantly to the rapid expansion in tobacco production. The minimum quantity requirement to sell output in the auction market was overcome with the introduction of "intermediate buyers" for tobacco allowing small farmers to produce tobacco (FAO 2003).

The value chain of tobacco in Malawi is relatively simple as most of the exported tobacco is unmanufactured. The intermediate buyers functioned as the middlemen between small-scale tobacco growers and the auction market, buying tobacco leaf from many small-scale growers at a negotiated price and them selling them on the auction floor at the market price (FAO 2003). Tobacco

Table 3.4: *Market shares in export supply chains: tobacco.*

Ranking	Malawi Firm	Share	Zambia Firm	Share
1	AOI	34.0	Zambia Tobacco Leaf	47.61
2	Universal (LIMBE)	29.0	Alliance One Tobacco	16.34
3	Africa Leaf	16.0	Tombwe Tobacco	25.21
4	Premium	13.0	Associated Tobacco	10.84
5	Malawi Leaf	5.0		
6	ATC	2.0		
7	Wallace	1.0		

leaf is generally sold in auction markets[30] owned by Auction Holding Limited (four floors: Limbe, Lilongwe, Chinkhoma, and Mzuzu), in which the government, through the Agricultural Development and Marketing Corporation (ADMARC), has majority of the shares. Currently, there is a demand among private sectors players that are interested in providing alternative tobacco auction services. The government has agreed to open the auction system but it has yet to prepare the draft bills for legislation.

The tobacco buyers in Malawi have been described as an "oligopsony" where each of the few buyers exerts a disproportionate influence on the market. Increasing competition is one of the key elements in the agenda for the Malawian tobacco sector (van Donge 2002; World Bank 2008). The tobacco buyers are represented by the Tobacco Exporters Association of Malawi (TEAM).[31] In 2008 there were only six companies registered to buy tobacco: Limbe Leaf Tobacco Company Limited, Alliance One Tobacco (AOI), Africa Leaf, Premium Tama, Malawi Leaf, ATC, and RWJC Wallace. Their market shares for burley tobacco, reported in Table 3.4, were: AOI 34 percent, Universal (Limbe) 29 percent, Africa Leaf 16 percent, Premium 13 percent, Malawi Leaf 5 percent, ATC 2 percent, Wallace 1 percent. The market shares for flue-cured tobacco were: AOI 33 percent, Universal (Limbe) 45 percent, Africa Leaf 14 percent, Premium 3 percent, Malawi Leaf 2 percent, ATC 3 percent.

Despite the good conditions for growing burley tobacco in Malawi, the competitive edge is quite narrow. This is mainly due to high costs along the value chain. The key burley tobacco production costs at the farm-level include fertilizer, seed, chemicals, and labor. At the assembly level, the major costs that

[30]There are suggestions to introduce more rural satellite auction markets which will invariably reduce the congestion at the main auction markets and reduce the participation of intermediate traders.

[31]This association was formally established in 1930 and it is involved in negotiations and dialogue with all stakeholders in the tobacco industry on behalf of the buyers. Originally, membership in TEAM was restricted to tobacco buyers and exporters but has since been extended to processing organizations and manufacturers (World Bank 2008).

reduce producers' net profit include the high cost of transport and intermediation, including the auction floors. In addition to these costs, there are other hidden costs such as storage charges at the rural depots and the costs related to the long waiting time to offload the tobacco at the floors. The costs related to levies and taxes were already substantially reduced following the tobacco sector reforms undertaken in 2005 (Jaffe 2003; World Bank 2008). The only cost element in which significant cost reduction may be possible is in the tobacco transport system. According to sector experts, the tobacco transport system is the most costly mainly due to inefficiencies in the tobacco marketing system. As was previously mentioned, the government is studying to open satellite auction floors and the deregulation of the auctioning system to diminish these transportation costs. The authorities also have allowed tobacco contract farming and marketing arrangements that, in principle, bypassed the auctioning system, but this policy was later suspended (Tchale and Keyser 2010).

4.2   Tobacco in Zambia[32]

Tobacco is, with cotton, the main agriculture exports of Zambia and one the main sources of income diversification away from copper. Historically, tobacco production was carried out in large-scale commercial farms in the hands of expatriates. After gaining independence in 1964, the participation of smallholders increased. Around 40 percent of the tobacco production auctioned is contributed by small-scale farmers. In the 2003–4 season it is estimated that about 2,000 small-scale farmers participated in the growing of tobacco on a contract basis, averaging about 0.5–1 ha per farmer (Likulunga 2005). The main areas of tobacco production are Mukonchi, in the Kabwe district of the Central Province; Kalomo, in the Southern Province; Kaoma, in the Western Province; and several areas in the Eastern Province.

There is not an auction system like in Malawi. Tobacco is bought at buying stations established by merchants at strategic points in the growing districts. Most of this tobacco is then exported to Malawi, where it is processed and sold to cigarette manufactures that sell in world markets (Balat and Porto 2008). A few companies dominate the market. In 2006 the Lusaka floor market shares, reported in Table 3.4, were: Zambia Leaf Tobacco 47.61 percent, Alliance One Tobacco 16.34 percent, Tombwe Tobacco 25.21 percent, and Associated Tobacco, 10.84 percent. Given the liberalized nature of the sector, these companies are also able to contract small-scale farmers directly, offering them inputs on credit as well as extension services. The contracts are signed directly between the small-scale farmers and the tobacco company.

---

[32]This section is largely based on Balat and Porto (2007) and Likulunga (2005).

The other key institutional players of the Zambian tobacco sector are the Tobacco Board of Zambia and the Tobacco Association of Zambia. The Board was created by the Tobacco Act of 1967 with the objective of promoting, controlling, and regulating the production, marketing, and export of tobacco. The Tobacco Association of Zambia is the growers' association, which owns and manages the auction floors.

4

Exporters and Farmers: A Model of Supply Chains in Agriculture

In this chapter, we study a theoretical model of supply chains in export agriculture. The purpose of the model is to provide an analytical framework for studying how changes in the structure of the supply chain affect farm-gate prices. These farm-gate price changes will feed into the poverty analysis of Chapter 5.

We present a game-theory model of supply chains in export agriculture.[1] There are two main actors in the model: firms and farmers. There is a large number of farmers who must choose to produce home-consumption goods or exportable goods. They are atomistic and face exogenous farm-gate prices offered by the firms. These prices and the characteristics of the farmer (land endowment, productivity) determine the allocation of resources of each farmer to the "export market" or to home-production activities.

Farm-gate prices are set by firms. The firms buy raw inputs from the farmers (coffee beans, cotton seeds) and sell them in international markets. We assume that these firms are small in international markets and thus take international commodity prices (for coffee or cotton), as given. In contrast, the firms enjoy monopsony power internally. There are only a few firms in each market, and they compete in an oligopsony to secure the raw input provided by the farmers. The oligopsony game delivers the equilibrium farm-gate prices that the firms offer to the farmers. Given these prices, farmers allocate resources optimally and supply raw inputs to the firms and this supply affects the quantity that firms can supply in the export market. In equilibrium, firms take into account the supply response of the farmer when choosing optimal farm-gate prices.

The solution to the game depends on various parameters. On the firm side, the equilibrium depends on both the number of firms and on their share of the market. In other words, it matters whether the market is characterized

---

[1] Our model builds on the ideas and the analytical framework developed by, among many others, Salop (1979), Barnum and Squire (1979), Singh et al. (1986), De Janvry et al. (1991), Benjamin (2001), Horn and Levinsohn (2001), McMillan et al. (2003), Taylor and Adelman (2003), Syverson (2004), Sheldon (2006), Sexton et al. (2007), Kranton and Swamy (2008), Ennis (2009), Cadot et al. (2010), and Ludmer (2010).

by symmetrical firms or, instead, by a large dominant firm and many small competitors. Firm characteristics, such as production costs, also matter. On the farmer side, the equilibrium depends on factor endowments, preferences, and farm productivity (costs) in export agriculture. These factors determine the export supply response of the farmers and how this is affected by the structure of the market. Our model incorporates all of these features.

Once the equilibrium of the model is found, and the solution is calibrated to match key features of the economy, we study comparative static results. The main purpose of these exercises is to compute the changes in farm-gate prices that we need for the poverty analysis. We explore a variety of comparative static results. Given the initial structure of the market (that is, the number of firms and their market shares), we simulate various changes in competition. Our simulations cover a large number of general settings, from entry to exit. We study the impacts of the entrance of a small competitor, of a hypothetical merge of the two leading firms, and of the split of the leader into smaller competitors. In all these cases, given the initial equilibrium, we find the new equilibrium of the model and study the changes in farm-gate prices, profits, and farmer utility (for different farmers). In the simulations, we take into account both firm and farm responses. This means that our comparative static results allow firms to adjust prices and quantities separately (implying that market shares may change in equilibrium). Farmers also adjust crop supply, and this is, in turn, taken into account by the firms when choosing the new equilibrium prices. In this sense, while the model is a partial equilibrium model of the agricultural export markets, it incorporates responses from all agents and their feedback in determining the equilibrium.

We also study a number of additional simulations. Concretely, we focus on the impact of complementary policies that affect firms, complementary policies that affect farmers, and changes in international prices. These simulations work in the same fashion. For instance, we shock the production costs faced by firms, the production costs of the farmers, and the international commodity prices, and solve the model for the new equilibrium, allowing for all market interactions.

An important feature of our simulations is that we can study complementarities between domestic policies, international prices, and competition policies. To do this, we explore comparative static results where we change various parameters both separately and simultaneously and we compare the different equilibria. These exercises allow us to learn, for instance, whether a given change in competition policies (such as entry) can be amplified by complementary factors such as infrastructure.

Finally, we study outgrower contracts. Many markets in Africa are characterized by distortions and missing markets and this impedes the optimal allocation of resources. This is critical in export agriculture. If credit is needed upfront to undertake the necessary investments in export cropping (purchase of seeds, fertilizers, pesticides), then a malfunctioning credit market may push farmers out of the export market, even in the case of relatively high farm-gate prices.

To study these issues, we extend our model by including outgrower arrangements. In these arrangements, firms cover upfront a fraction of the farmer's crop production costs. Farmers repay these costs at the harvest time after paying an interest rate on the loan. The key feature of the extended model is that the interest rate charged by the firms may depend on the structure of the market, that is, on the number of firms and also on their market shares. This is because the legal system is imperfect and thus we assume that firms cannot perfectly monitor farmers. In consequence, farmers may default on the loan, and even side-sell to other exporters.

Increases in competition thus have two opposing effects, one effect via higher farm-gate prices, which encourages export participation and reduces poverty, and another via a potentially higher interest rate, which hinders export participation and increases poverty. This analysis introduces new interesting dimensions to the discussion of competition policies and poverty in sub-Saharan Africa.

The chapter is organized as follows. In Section 1, we introduce the basic structure of the standard model without outgrower contracts. In Section 2, we explain how we set up the simulations and in Section 3, we discuss the main results. In Sections 4 and 5, we extend the standard model to include outgrower contracts and we present the simulation results.

1   THE ECONOMY

We study an economy where individuals are endowed with (small) pieces of productive land. These agents must choose between being "peasants," who live in autarky and consume all their home production, or "farmers" who grow and sell exportable goods and buy consumption goods from the market. The main assumption driving our results is simply that market-acquired consumption goods are a superior good. In other words, a diversified consumption portfolio becomes desirable as the person's wealth increases.

In terms of behavior, this means that poorer individuals will home-consume 100 percent of their endowment, while richer families (in terms of initial endowment) will trade a fraction of their endowment in the market, in exchange for other goods. That is to say, the superior-goods assumption generates a wealth effect driving the peasant/farmer occupation decision in this economy.

The structure of the market for the tradeable good will naturally have a strong impact on the equilibrium prices of the endowments. In particular, perfect competition among buyers of the farmers' produce will deliver higher equilibrium prices than monopsony or oligopsony situations. In turn, higher prices for the farmers' produce means higher wealth for individuals. And through the wealth effect, this means that the more competitive the market structure is, the more individuals will leave autarky and become farmers. In consequence, as competition increases, the richest peasants will become farmers. Autarky behavior will move down along the distribution of income.

1.1   The Model

More formally, this is a one-period endowment economy populated by a measure I of farmers and a finite number n of exporters. Farmers are identical in preferences but are heterogeneous in the size/productivity of their farms. Specifically, each farmer i is endowed with a farm that can produce e_i units of crop. e_i takes values on an interval $[\underline{e}, \bar{e}]$ and its distribution over values is represented by the continuously differentiable probability function $F(e)$, density $f(e)$.

1.2   Farmers

Individual farmers are identical in their preferences, but are heterogeneous in the size/productivity of their farms. Their Cobb–Douglas utility function defined on home consumption h and market goods m is given by

$$u(h, m) = h^\alpha (m + c)^{1-\alpha}.$$

The constant c is a preference parameter and implies that $m = 0$ can be a rational choice—marginal utility of m will be finite even for $m = 0$. The level c will effectively play the role of imposing a "subsistence" level $\hat{e}$ of the endowment that must be consumed by farmers. Poor farmers whose initial endowment is lower than the subsistence level will live in autarky. Rich farmers, instead, whose endowment e_i is larger than the "subsistence" level $\hat{e}$ will sell part of the "surplus" $e_i - \hat{e}$ to the market (and self-consume the rest). We will also show that the cutoff "subsistence" level is decreasing in p. The intuition is a wealth effect (or equivalently, in this simple one-period endowment economy, income effect). When p is higher, farmers are richer, and therefore can afford to diversify their consumption goods.

Each farmer $i \in I$ is endowed with a farm with productivity e_i. The farmer operates the farm and its output can be either consumed by the farmer or sold to exporters in the market. The optimization problem is

$$V(e_i; p, r) = \max_{h,m} h^\alpha (m + c)^{1-\alpha}$$

$$\text{subject to } m + ph \leqslant (p - \lambda r)e_i, \quad h \geqslant 0, \quad m \geqslant 0,$$

where e_i is individual i's initial endowment, p is the price for farmers of the crop, $r > 0$ is the interest rate. Preferences are parameterized by $0 < \alpha < 1$. We now discuss the different pieces of the optimization problem.

We begin with the budget constraint. The farmer produces e_i units of crop, of which he will apply h units to his own consumption. The remaining units will be sold to the exporters at a market price of p. In addition, we allow for the possibility of a liquidity constraint affecting the home-market decision. The liquidity constraint is parameterized by λ. When $\lambda = 0$, there is no liquidity constraint. When $\lambda > 0$, the interpretation is that a farmer planning to produce output of $(e_i - h)$ for the market will need to borrow an amount $\lambda \cdot (e_i - h)$ beforehand. The farmer will then need to pay an interest rate r on the borrowed amount. This possibility of liquidity constraints is introduced to study outgrower contracts later on (Sections 4 and 5). For the remainder of the section, however, we will leave outgrower contracts aside, thereby assuming that $\lambda = 0$.

1.3 Exporters

There are n exporters who sell the crop at an international price of P. They buy from farmers at the internal market price of p. These are Cournot oligopsonists. They choose how much quantity to demand from the market at the prevailing price p, and they understand and correctly anticipate that their own demand behavior affects p.

The problem faced by an exporter is then to maximize revenues:

$$\Pi(P, p, c_j^p) = \max_{q_j}(P - p - c_j^p) \cdot q_j,$$

where q_j and c_j^p are, respectively, the demanded quantity and the unit cost of production of exporter j. In principle, exporters may face different marginal costs and this determines the equilibrium market shares.

1.4 Markets and Equilibrium

Individuals sell their output to exporters. Each exporter chooses its individual demand from the farmers. The price P at which exporters sell their output in the international markets is exogenously given in this model. The domestic price p earned by farmers is determined in equilibrium, given farmers' aggregate supply and exporters' aggregate demand. We next define an equilibrium for this economy.

Definition 4.1. An equilibrium in this economy is a collection of individual decisions and prices

$$\{(h_i)_{i \in I}, (m_i)_{i \in I}, \{q_j\}_{j=1}^n, p, r\}$$

such that:

1. for each farmer i, (h_i, m_i) maximizes utility given price p and interest rate r,
2. for each firm j, (q_j) is a best-response to the other firms' decisions $(q_k)_{k \neq j}$, to farmers' aggregate behavior and

3. the goods market clears:

$$\int_{i \in I} (e_i - h_i)\, di = \sum_{j=1}^{n} q_j.$$

Condition 1 is the standard requirement that a farmer's behavior be utility maximizing given the structure of the problem. Farmers take prices as given and act accordingly.

The optimality condition for exporters introduces oligopolistic competition. Firms chose demanded quantities in anticipation of their own effect on farmers' aggregate behavior, in a context of strategic interaction with other firms. Equilibrium in the economy requires that firms' decisions be a Cournot–Nash equilibrium of the game between firms, given the farmers' aggregate supply function.

Condition 3 is a standard market clearing condition requiring that output sold by farmers to the market coincides with the aggregate demand from exporters.

1.5 Farmer Solution

We begin with the solution to the problem of the farmers. With $\lambda = 0$, the Lagrangian and first-order conditions are

$$\mathcal{L} = h^\alpha (m + c)^{1-\alpha} + u_1(pe_i - ph - m) + u_2 h + u_3 m,$$

$$\frac{\partial \mathcal{L}}{\partial h} : \quad \alpha \frac{h^\alpha (m + c)^{1-\alpha}}{h} - u_1 p + u_2 = 0,$$

$$\frac{\partial \mathcal{L}}{\partial m} : \quad (1 - \alpha)\frac{h^\alpha (m + c)^{1-\alpha}}{m + c} - u_1 + u_3 = 0.$$

The complementary slackness conditions are

$$u_1(pe_i - ph - m) = 0, \qquad u_2 h = 0, \qquad u_3 m = 0,$$

$$u_1 \geqslant 0, \qquad u_2 \geqslant 0, \qquad u_3 \geqslant 0.$$

It is simple to show that any solution must have $h > 0$, since marginal utility of h converges to ∞ when $h \to 0$. Therefore, $u_2 = 0$ will always hold. Moreover, we look for a solution with $m > 0$. This implies $\mu_3 = 0$, and the first-order conditions become

$$\frac{\partial \mathcal{L}}{\partial h} : \quad \alpha \frac{h^\alpha (m + c)^{1-\alpha}}{h} - u_1 p = 0,$$

$$\frac{\partial \mathcal{L}}{\partial m} : \quad (1 - \alpha)\frac{h^\alpha (m + c)^{1-\alpha}}{m + c} - u_1 = 0.$$

From this we can solve

$$\alpha \frac{h^\alpha (m + c)^{1-\alpha}}{h} = p(1 - \alpha)\frac{h^\alpha (m + c)^{1-\alpha}}{m + c} \quad \Rightarrow \quad m = \frac{1 - \alpha}{\alpha}ph - c.$$

Using the budget constraint, we get

$$pe_i = ph + m \quad \Rightarrow \quad pe_i = ph + \frac{1-\alpha}{\alpha}ph - c$$

$$\Rightarrow \quad h = \frac{\alpha}{p}(pe + c)$$

$$\Rightarrow \quad m = (1-\alpha)pe_i - c\alpha$$

We get the standard response functions with Cobb–Douglas utility, for which it is optimal to assign constant shares of the budget to each consumption good.

Note that this can only be a solution provided $m \geqslant 0$. Therefore, we can solve for the cutoff level of parameters:

$$m = (1-\alpha)pe_i - c\alpha \geqslant 0 \quad \Leftrightarrow \quad e_i \geqslant \frac{\alpha}{1-\alpha}\frac{c}{p}.$$

Define the cutoff level

$$\hat{e}(p) \equiv \frac{\alpha}{1-\alpha}\frac{c}{p}.$$

For any $e_i \leqslant \hat{e}(p)$, the optimal responses are

$$m = 0, \qquad h = e_i.$$

For any $e_i \geqslant \hat{e}(p)$, the optimal responses are the usual Cobb–Douglas budget allocation rules:

$$ph = \alpha(pe_i + c), \qquad m + c = (1-\alpha)(pe_i + c).$$

In this sense, we interpret $\hat{e}(p)$ as a "subsistence" endowment level. Poor farmers whose e_i is lower than this "subsistence" level live in autarky and self-consume 100 percent of their endowment. Note that the cutoff "subsistence" level is decreasing in p. The intuition is an income effect. At higher p, farmers are richer, and therefore can afford to diversify their consumption goods.

The individual farmer's market supply function is

$$s(p;e) = \max\{e - h, 0\} = \max\left\{e - \alpha\left(e + \frac{c}{p}\right), 0\right\}.$$

With some algebra, this can be rewritten as

$$s(p;e) = (1-\alpha)\max\{e - \hat{e}(p), 0\}.$$

The interpretation of this equation is that each farmer supplies a percentage $1 - \alpha$ of the "subsistence surplus" $e - \hat{e}(p)$.

The indirect utility function is

$$e \leqslant \hat{e}(p) \quad \Rightarrow \quad V(e;p) = e^\alpha c^{1-\alpha},$$

$$e \geqslant \hat{e}(p) \quad \Rightarrow \quad V(e;p) = \frac{\alpha^\alpha(1-\alpha)^{1-\alpha}}{p^\alpha}(pe + c).$$

This function is strictly increasing. To the left of $\hat{e}(p)$, it is strictly concave. It has a convex kink at $e = \hat{e}(p)$, and is linear to the right of $\hat{e}(p)$. To see this, consider the derivative:

$$e < \hat{e}(p)$$

$$\Rightarrow \quad \frac{\partial V(e;p)}{\partial e} = \alpha \frac{c^{1-\alpha}}{e^{1-\alpha}} > 0 \quad \text{and} \quad \frac{\partial^2 V(e;p)}{\partial e^2} = -\alpha(1-\alpha)\frac{c^{1-\alpha}}{e^{2-\alpha}} < 0,$$

$$e > \hat{e}(p)$$

$$\Rightarrow \quad \frac{\partial V(e;p)}{\partial e} = \alpha^\alpha(1-\alpha)^{1-\alpha}p^{1-\alpha} > 0 \quad \text{and} \quad \frac{\partial^2 V(e;p)}{\partial e^2} = 0.$$

It takes simple algebra to see that the kink at $\hat{e}(p)$ is convex. The left-hand first derivative for $\hat{e}(p)$ is smaller than the right-hand first derivative:

$$e > \hat{e}(p) \equiv \frac{\alpha}{1-\alpha}\frac{c}{p} \quad \Rightarrow \quad (1-\alpha)p > \alpha\frac{c}{e}$$

$$\Rightarrow \quad \alpha^\alpha(1-\alpha)^{1-\alpha}p^{1-\alpha} > \alpha^\alpha\alpha^{1-\alpha}\frac{c^{1-\alpha}}{e^{1-\alpha}} = \alpha\frac{c^{1-\alpha}}{e^{1-\alpha}}.$$

The shape of the supply function will be relevant for the exporters' decision. Note that, over the range where $s(p;e) > 0$, the individual supply function is strictly increasing and strictly concave:

$$\frac{\partial s(p;e)}{\partial p} = \frac{c}{p^2}\alpha > 0,$$

$$\frac{\partial^2 s(p;e)}{\partial p^2} = -2\frac{c}{p^3}\alpha < 0.$$

However, the function has a kink at the level which implies $e = \hat{e}(p)$. It is globally weakly increasing but not concave.

We can now easily derive the aggregate supply of export crops that firms will face. Integrating across individuals, we get

$$S(p) \equiv \int_{\underline{e}}^{\bar{e}} s(p;e)f(e)\,de$$

$$= (1-\alpha)\int_{\underline{e}}^{\bar{e}} \max\{e - \hat{e}(p), 0\}f(e)\,de$$

$$= (1-\alpha)\int_{\hat{e}}^{\bar{e}} (e_i - \hat{e}(p))f(e)\,de.$$

Thus, the aggregate supply function is

$$\frac{S(p)}{1-\alpha} = \int_{\hat{e}}^{\bar{e}} e_if(e)\,de - \hat{e}(p)(1 - F(\hat{e}(p))).$$

What is the shape of the aggregate supply function? To avoid carrying around the term $(1 - \alpha)$, which is strictly positive, we look at the shape of

$$\tilde{S}(p) \equiv \frac{S(p)}{1-\alpha}.$$

First, to see that the aggregate supply function is nondecreasing in p, note that:

$$\frac{d\tilde{S}(p)}{dp} = \frac{\partial \tilde{S}(p)}{\partial \hat{e}(p)} \frac{\partial \hat{e}(p)}{\partial p}.$$

The second term is decreasing in p as mentioned before:

$$\frac{\partial \hat{e}(p)}{\partial p} = -\frac{\alpha}{1-\alpha} \frac{c}{p^2} = -\frac{\hat{e}(p)}{p} < 0.$$

The first term is

$$\frac{\partial \tilde{S}(p)}{\partial \hat{e}(p)} = -\hat{e}(p) f(\hat{e}(p)) - (1 - F(\hat{e}(p))) + \hat{e}(p) f(\hat{e}(p))$$

$$= -(1 - F(\hat{e}(p))) \leqslant 0.$$

This establishes that the aggregate supply function is nondecreasing:

$$\frac{S'(p)}{1-\alpha} = \tilde{S}'(p)$$

$$= \frac{\partial \tilde{S}(p)}{\partial \hat{e}(p)} \frac{\partial \hat{e}(p)}{\partial p}$$

$$= -(1 - F(\hat{e}(p))) \left(-\frac{\hat{e}(p)}{p} \right)$$

$$= (1 - F(\hat{e}(p))) \left(\frac{\hat{e}(p)}{p} \right)$$

$$\geqslant 0.$$

What about the second derivative?

$$\frac{d\tilde{S}'(p)}{dp} = \frac{c}{p^2} \frac{\alpha}{1-\alpha} \partial \frac{\partial(1 - F(\hat{e}(p)))}{\partial \hat{e}(p)} \frac{\partial \hat{e}(p)}{\partial p} + (1 - F(\hat{e}(p))) \frac{\partial(\hat{e}(p)/p)}{\partial p}$$

$$= f(\hat{e}(p)) \left(\frac{c}{p^2} \frac{\alpha}{1-\alpha} \right)^2 - (1 - F(\hat{e}(p))) 2 \frac{c}{p^3} \frac{\alpha}{1-\alpha}.$$

This reduces to

$$\frac{d\tilde{S}'(p)}{dp} = f(\hat{e}(p)) \left(\frac{\hat{e}(p)}{p} \right)^2 - (1 - F(\hat{e}(p))) 2 \frac{\hat{e}(p)}{p^2}.$$

The sign of this derivative is not unambiguous. We can look for conditions under which it will be negative:

$$\tilde{S}''(p) < 0 \quad \Leftrightarrow \quad f(\hat{e}(p)) \left(\frac{\hat{e}(p)}{p} \right)^2 - (1 - F(\hat{e}(p))) 2 \frac{\hat{e}(p)}{p^2} < 0$$

$$\Leftrightarrow \quad \frac{f(\hat{e}(p)) \hat{e}(p)}{1 - F(\hat{e}(p))} < 2.$$

Note that there is not a straightforward intuition for this term. This condition reads as follows: take any p. Then the aggregate supply function will be locally concave at p if, evaluated at the "subsistence level" $\hat{e}(p)$ corresponding to such p, the distribution function $F(\cdot)$ satisfies

$$\frac{f(\hat{e}(p))}{1 - F(\hat{e}(p))} < \frac{2}{\hat{e}(p)}.$$

This condition basically puts a bound on "mass points." In other words, for $S(p)$ to be locally concave at a given p, the distribution function must satisfy the condition that probability does not "grow too fast" (i.e., too high an $f(\hat{e}(p))$ relative to the "remaining" probability $1 - F(\hat{e}(p))$).

While this condition will hold in the simulations that we run below, it is useful to discuss the shape of the supply function. This is because this discussion illustrates some of the major issues that drive the economic decision of the farmers and their participation in export markets. To this end, let's do a thought experiment in which we start off with a very low price (say, $p = 0$) for the traded good, and we increase it gradually to see how the economy responds.

When the market price for the exportable good is very low, all farmers are poor and they all self-consume their endowment. As the price of the tradeable good increases, all farmers experience a positive wealth effect. This effect entices them to diversify their consumption portfolio by selling part of their endowment to the market to buy other goods. Mathematically, as the price increases, the "subsistence level" of endowment starts decreasing. However, for sufficiently low prices this "subsistence level" is still higher than each and every farmer's endowment (including the rich).

The wealth effect is larger for "richer" farmers, which means that as the endowment value increases, these people are the first to experience the cutoff moment in which the market value of their endowment surpasses their "subsistence level." Therefore, there is a first, low price p that acts as a trigger for rich farmers to start selling part of their endowment to the market in exchange for market consumption goods. After rich farmers have entered the market, there is a region of prices where rich farmers are selling their goods, but poor farmers are still below their "subsistence levels," and therefore are operating in autarky and self-consumption. In such regions where only the rich are trading, the slope of the aggregate supply curve is just the slope of the rich farmers' individual supply curves—the individual supply curves of poor farmers still has zero slope. Hence, in this region the aggregate supply curve will be locally concave. Eventually the price raises enough to bring poor farmers to the market as well. This happens when the value of their endowments grows enough to cross the "subsistence level." At the precise point where the poor farmers enter the market, there will be a convex kink in the aggregate supply curve. The reason is that, at that point, the slope of the poor farmers' supply curve switches from zero to strictly positive.

Economically, there is a form of "increasing return" to price increases at the point where poor farmers, who were previously operating in autonomy, enter the market and start providing a positive supply of tradeable goods. In consequence, one intuition for the shape of the aggregate supply curve (and of the drivers of this shape) is that, in societies with very high inequality of income, this type of price regions with "increasing returns" will be present. Tipping points will exist which, when surpassed, suddenly large numbers of previously autarkic farmers enter the market with supply.

1.6 Exporter Solution

We look for a equilibrium for the exporters' oligopsony game. Exporters correctly understand and anticipate that the market price p depends on their own actions, other exporters' actions, and aggregate supply behavior from farmers. Let $Q \equiv \sum_{j=1}^{n} q_j$ denote aggregate demand from exporters, then a given exporter perceives the following problem:

$$\Pi(q_{k \neq j}, P, c_j^p) = \max_{q_j}(P - p - c_j^p) \cdot q_j \quad \text{such that } Q \equiv q_j + \sum_{k \neq j} q_k.$$

The state variables are the international price P, and other exporters' actions $q_{k \neq j}$. It can be shown that a sufficient condition for the problem to be concave is that the aggregate supply function $S(p)$ be concave as well, so that $S''(p) < 0$. As discussed before, this is not guaranteed by concavity of the individual supply functions $s(e; p)$. In other words, when the aggregate supply function is concave, the exporters' profit-maximization problem will be concave in their choice variable. If the aggregate supply function is not concave, then the problem may not be concave as well.

If the problem is concave, then the first-order condition $\partial \pi / \partial q_j = 0$ will of course be necessary and sufficient. Moreover, by the Maximum Theorem under convexity (Stokey and Lucas 1989; Sundaram 1996), the function $q_j(Q)$ is well defined and continuous.

We now turn to the first-order conditions. With n exporters, we have

$$q_j = (1 - \alpha)(P - p^s(Q) - c_j^p) \frac{(1 - F(\hat{e}(p^s(Q)))) \hat{e}(p^s(Q))}{p^s(Q)}$$

$$\Rightarrow \quad Q = (1 - \alpha) \left(nP - np^s(Q) - \sum_{j=1}^{n} c_j^p \right) \frac{(1 - F(\hat{e}(p^s(Q)))) \hat{e}(p^s(Q))}{p^s(Q)}.$$

2   THE SIMULATIONS

The equations that characterize the equilibrium are a set of the best responses of the firms and, given the aggregate supply of the farmers, market clearance (total farm supply of raw inputs equal to total firm demand of raw inputs). The solution to this problem has to be found numerically and we used MATLAB routines to do this.

The first step in the analysis is the calibration of the parameters of the farmer model. Note that we need to perform a different calibration for each of the country–crop case studies. We calibrate α, the parameter of the utility function, the farm supply parameters, and the subsistence cutoff. To do this, we assume that the distribution of endowments follows a lognormal distribution with mean μ and standard deviation σ. Then, we use the household survey data (see Chapter 2) and choose the parameters in order to match (as closely as possible) the observed aggregate shares of income derived from the production of the export crop. The calibrated parameters are in Table A4.1.[2]

As for the solution of the model, we work with aggregate farm supply,

$$S(p) = (1 - \alpha) \int_{\hat{e}}^{\bar{e}} e_i f(e) \, de - \hat{e}(p)(1 - F(\hat{e}(p))),$$

and the first-order conditions of the oligopsony game. Firms incur different costs of manufacturing, c_j^p. In equilibrium, given P, market shares differ across firms. In consequence, we search for farm-gate prices and a structure of firms' costs so as to match the number of firms and the distribution of market shares observed in the data. These market shares were described in detail in Chapter 3. To summarize, the search procedure comprises the following steps:

1. Given Q, we find an equilibrium price $p^s(Q)$ from the aggregate supply equation.
2. We know the market shares for each firm, sh_j, so $q_j = sh_j \cdot Q$ is identified.
3. Finally, we solve for c_j^p using the best response function of each firm.

This algorithm delivers the solution to the model, given the calibrated parameters. The solution comprises exogenous parameters, the firm costs, and an endogenous quantity, farm-gate prices. Now, given the calibrated parameters *and* the structure of costs associated with the solution, we can simulate comparative static results numerically.

We carry out thirty-five simulations for each case study (country–crop pair, as in Chapter 2). The main component of our simulation is a hypothetical change in the structure of the supply chain. To cover different types of changes in market structure, we explore the following seven cases:

1. Leader split (with equal marginal costs).
2. Small entrant (with marginal costs equal to smaller firm).

---

[2]Note that we calibrate a different set of parameters for each case study. This means that we use different parameters for different crops, even in a given country (such as cotton and tobacco in Zambia, for instance). We do this for consistency with the fact that our model is designed to describe one market in isolation. This assumption makes sense if, for instance, different crops are produced by different farmers (because of geography). A model with multiple choice of export crops could be an interesting extension of our work.

3. Leaders merge and small entrant (with costs equal to that of the most efficient merger and that of the smaller incumbent, respectively).
4. Leaders merge (with cost of the most efficient merger).
5. Exit of largest firm.
6. Equal market shares (all firms have the cost of the leader).
7. Perfect competition ($p^s(Q)$ equal to P less marginal cost of the most efficient firm).

Moreover, for each of these "competition" simulations we also allow for changes in complementary policies. We consider three complementary factors:

1. Complementary policies that affect farmers: 2 percent increase in μ.
2. Complementary policies that affect firms: 2 percent reduction of costs c_j^p.
3. Complementary policies that affect farmers and firms simultaneously: 2 percent increase in μ and 2 percent cost reduction.

Finally, we also study simulations where we interact the changes in competition with a 10 percent increase in international prices.

These simulations are performed with the following algorithm. In each of the simulations, there is a change in the number of firms, n, and/or a change in the baseline structure of costs, c_j^p. To find the solution, we need to find Q and $p^s(Q)$ that solve the first-order condition for each firm subject to aggregate farm supply. That is, we solve

$$q_j = (1 - \alpha)(P - p^s(Q) - c_j^p)\frac{(1 - F(\hat{e}(p^s(Q))))\hat{e}(p^s(Q))}{p^s(Q)} \quad \forall j \in n$$

subject to

$$Q = S(p), \quad \sum_{j=1}^{n} q_j = (1 - \alpha)\int_{\hat{e}}^{\bar{e}} e_i f(e)\,\mathrm{d}e - \hat{e}(p)(1 - F(\hat{e}(p))).$$

As a result, we calculate a new q_j for firm $j \in n$ (now the number of firms can be different from that in the baseline case, depending on the simulation performed).

The simulations are designed to compute different changes in farm-gate prices in different scenarios. These price changes feed into the poverty analysis of Chapter 5. However, the theoretical model can be used to preliminary assess changes in farmer's utility and in industry profits. To explore changes in utility, note that the individual indirect utility function is

$$e \leqslant \hat{e}(p) \quad \Rightarrow \quad V_{\mathrm{NP}}(e; p) = e^\alpha c^{1-\alpha},$$

$$e \geqslant \hat{e}(p) \quad \Rightarrow \quad V_{\mathrm{P}}(e; p) = \frac{\alpha^\alpha(1 - \alpha)^{1-\alpha}}{p^\alpha}(pe + c).$$

So, average utility is

$$\bar{V} = \int_{\underline{e}}^{\tilde{e}} V(e,p)f(e)\,de$$

$$= \int_{\underline{e}}^{\hat{e}} V_{NP}(e;p)f(e)\,de + \int_{\hat{e}}^{\tilde{e}} V_P(e;p)f(e)\,de$$

$$= \int_{\underline{e}}^{\hat{e}} e^{\alpha}c^{1-\alpha}f(e)\,de + \int_{\hat{e}}^{\tilde{e}} \frac{\alpha^{\alpha}(1-\alpha)^{1-\alpha}}{p^{\alpha}}(pe+c)f(e)\,de.$$

Individual profits are

$$\pi_j = (P - p^s(Q) - c_j^p)q_j.$$

Total profits are

$$\sum_{j=1}^{n} \pi_j,$$

thus average profits are equal to

$$\sum_{j=1}^{n} \frac{\pi_j}{n}.$$

3   SIMULATION RESULTS

We investigate twelve case studies in the book and, as previously explained, we run a total of thirty-five simulations for each case study.[3] Rather than discussing all the possible simulations, we focus on the case of cotton in Zambia and provide detailed explanations of the results for all the endogenous variables of the model. Then, we summarize the key findings from the remaining case studies, emphasizing both differences and similarities. We chose cotton in Zambia as our leading case because the cotton sector has undergone several of the transformations that our simulations aim to capture. Until 1994, the sector was controlled by a state monopoly. Immediately after the privatization, the sector was dominated by a duopoly, but over the years competition ensued. The Zambian cotton sector has also seen several outgrower schemes with variable degrees of success (see Sections 4 and 5).

3.1   Zambia Cotton

We begin with the baseline model (without any complementary changes) and we discuss results from the seven market structure simulations. The results are reported in Table A4.2 (in the appendix). The leader split simulation

---

[3]We have thirty-five additional simulations in the model with outgrower contracts. See Sections 4 and 5.

reveals an increase of both farm-gate prices and quantities because it raises competition among exporters. In the case of Zambia cotton, the increases in farm-gate prices and quantities are 8.92 and 5.32 percent, respectively. Figure A4.1 shows that prices and quantities increase in all twelve case studies. The largest price increase is observed in the case of cotton in Burkina Faso and this is because the leader absorbs around 85 percent of the market in the initial situation. In other cases, such as coffee in Uganda, the split of the leader does not boost competition by much and thus the changes in prices are small.

The impact of higher prices on welfare is positive, both for producers and for nonproducers (some of whom become producers). In Zambia, the average utility gain of cotton producers is equal to 1.56 percent. At the same time, the increase in prices makes cotton production more profitable for the marginal farmer and this triggers a supply response. This supply response is, however, small. In the end, the increase in utility for the average nonproducer is only 0.06 percent. However, those farmers that do switch enjoy very large gains. In the Zambian cotton case, the average gain of the switchers is 26.64 percent. The switchers, nevertheless, are a small group, and consequently the average impact on nonproducers is negligible. The unconditional change in total utility is a weighted average of changes in utility for producers and nonproducers. Given the low participation rate in cotton, this increase is equivalent to only 0.11 percent of pre-shock average utility.

In principle, the change in profits in the leader split simulation is ambiguous. There are three different discernable patterns (Figure A4.2). In the first case, total and average industry profits increase in the same proportion. This occurs when the leader is very efficient compared with its competitors, and the split into two efficient firms significantly increases total profits and average profits. In the case of Zambian cotton, for instance, average and total profits increase by 10.29 percent. In the second case, total industry profits increase but average industry profits decrease. This occurs when the leader is efficient enough to increase total profits as it splits, but not sufficiently efficient to maintain average profits unaffected. For instance, in the case of coffee in Uganda, total profits rise by 3.94 percent but average profits decline by 2.17 percent (Table A4.2(j)). Finally, there are cases where both total and average profits decline. This happens when the marginal cost of the leader is similar to the marginal costs of the competitors. In consequence, while the split of the leader does not enhance efficiency, the increase in competition brings average and total profits down. For instance, in the Rwandan coffee case, average and total profits declined by 3.94 percent (Table A4.2(i)).

The cases of Burkina–cotton, Malawi–tobacco, and Benin–cotton are intriguing (Tables A4.2(c), A4.2(k), and A4.2(b), respectively). In these cases, there are large differences between the market shares of the largest firm and the smaller competitors and this implies big differences in marginal costs. As a result, when the largest firm splits, some of the smaller and less efficient firms cannot compete and they must exit the market. This reduces the number of firms and, in the end, average profits can show a large increase. Note that this is a compositional effect.

Another market simulation that enhances competition, although on a very different scale, is the small entrant scenario. This means that the impacts on farm-gate prices, quantities, and average utility (of producers, nonproducers, and switchers) are qualitatively similar as in the leader split simulations, but much smaller in magnitude. In the case of Zambian cotton, for instance, prices and quantities increase by 1.01 and 0.62 percent, respectively; total average utility increases by only 0.1 percent, and the average utility of the producers increases by a meager 0.17 percent. These are, by and large, negligible impacts. Note, however, that while the utility of the switchers increases significantly, by over 26 percent, there are only very few switchers.

A small entrant causes profits to decline in all simulations (unlike in the leader split simulation). Recall that changes in market structure bring about a competition effect and an efficiency effect. A small entrant increases competition and this reduces total and average profits. But, since the small entrant is assumed to have the cost structure of the least efficient firm, the efficiency effect disappears. As a result, in all of the case studies, average and total profits are lower when a small firm enters. For example, in the Zambian cotton case study, total industry profits fall by 3.86 percent, and average industry profits fall by 19.88 percent.

We now discuss the results of the leaders merge simulation, which is the anticompetitive counterpart of the leader split model. Note that, in practical terms, this simulation is equivalent to the elimination of the second largest producer. Since competition among firms is now lower, farm-gate prices decline and, therefore, the producers' average utility also declines. The switchers are, in this scenario, farmers that were producing the export crop and retrench into subsistence agriculture as prices decline. The utility of the switchers decline significantly. Note, however, that nonproducers' utility remains unchanged because these farmers did not participate in the supply chain at the original prices and thus their decisions are unchanged by the lower price of the export crop. Total average utility is just a weighted average of these changes in utility. In the Zambia–cotton example, farm-gate prices fall by 8.59 percent, the average utility of cotton producers falls by 3.28 percent, the average utility of the switchers falls by 20.24 percent, and total average utility is reduced by only 0.10 percent.

Due to the coexistence of the competition and efficiency effects, profits can either increase or decrease. Since competition is actually less intense when the leaders merge, the competition effect tends to increase profits. However, the "elimination" of the second largest producer can entail relative efficiency gains or losses. If, for instance, the second firm is relatively efficient (with marginal costs that are close to those of the leader), then its elimination by the merger can decrease aggregate efficiency (when a lot of its output is diverted to smaller firms). This pushes industry profits down. In contrast, if the second largest producer is relatively inefficient (compared with the leader), then the resulting output reallocation may entail efficiency gains and higher industry profits. It is therefore unsurprising to observe that profits increase in cases such as Burkina Faso–cotton or Benin–cotton, where the leader is significantly more efficient than its merged partner. In contrast, in cases such as Malawi–tobacco, Rwanda–coffee, or Côte d'Ivoire–coffee (Table A4.2(h)), both mergers are relatively similar in efficiency and thus profits tends to decline.

We now turn to the leaders merge and small entrant simulation, which is, in fact, a combination of the two previous cases. There are, nevertheless, some interesting results to highlight. As we explained before, the leaders merge simulation eliminates the second largest firm from the market, and the small entrant simulation just duplicates the smaller and less efficient firm. Therefore, there are no efficiency gains because, in practice, in this exercise we are replacing the second most efficient firm with the least efficient one. This means that the efficiency effect is negative. Additionally, the extent of competition is necessarily lower because the anticompetitive effect of the merger (in practice, the elimination of the second largest firm) more than compensates for the procompetitive effect of a small entrant. It follows that the impact on prices, quantities, and profits are negative.[4] For instance, in the Zambian cotton case, prices fall by 6.22 percent and total average utility decline by 0.07 percent. However, the utility of cotton producers drops by 2.38 percent and the utility of the switchers drops by 20.24 percent. Since prices are going down, the utility of nonproducers is not affected.

This simulation delivers interesting results when we look at profits. In three cases, average and total profits increase. This is because the incumbent firm that merges with the leader is actually similar (in terms of costs and market shares) as the third largest firm (which now becomes the second firm in terms of market shares). This implies a relatively small efficiency effect so that the impact of the decline in competition prevails. In the other eight cases, average and total profits decline. In these cases, the competition effect (which increases profits) is not large enough to compensate for the efficiency losses caused by the merge. In the Zambian cotton case, both total and average profits fall by 7.71 percent. Instead, in Benin–cotton, both increase by 2.79 percent.

In the next simulation, the exit of the largest firm, we study the effects that would take place if the leader leaves the market. Thus, the most efficient firm, with the smallest marginal cost, disappears and the market is covered by the remaining (more inefficient) firms. Farm-gate prices and quantities fall because the total demand of farm output shrinks—in the Zambian cotton case, they fall by 11.84 and 7.58 percent, respectively. Total average utility, the average utility of the producers, and the average utility of the switcher

---

[4]Note that the effect of this simulation is not the sum of leader split and small entrant.

decline (by 0.14, 4.51, and 20.25 percent, respectively, in the Zambian cotton case). The utility of the nonproducers remains unchanged.

Surprisingly, there is heterogeneity in the response of profits. In principle, profits should decline because the most efficient firm leaves the market. In fact, this is the case in five case studies. For example, in Zambia–cotton, total profits decline by 22.37 percent and average profits decline by 2.96 percent. However, in two cases, total profits fall but average profits increase, probably because the effect of lower competition is enough to compensate for the efficiency losses caused by the exit of the largest company, though not large enough to cause average profits to fall. For example, in Zambia–tobacco (Table A4.2(l)), total profits fall by 21.7 percent but average profits increase by 5.10 percent. Finally, in the case of Rwanda–coffee, for instance, we find increases in average and total profits (by 2.17 and 27.72 percent, respectively). In this particular case, the anticompetitive effect is very strong (because only four firms remain and two of them have similar marginal costs to the one that left the market) and thus it compensates for the efficiency losses.

We now turn to study more extreme pro-competitive simulations. The first scenario that we consider is one in which the existing firms are all equally efficient (and as efficient as the leader). This is the equal market shares simulation. In this model, competition is enhanced and efficiency improves, and both channels cause large increases in price and quantities. In turn, this has a positive effect in the average utility of all farmers, both producers and nonproducers. A summary of results is reported in Figure A4.3. For example, in the Zambia cotton case, prices increase by 27.21 percent, total average utility increases by 0.34 percent, the average utility of the producers increases by 4.89 percent, and the average utility of the switchers increases by 26.78 percent. In the majority of the case studies, profits fall because the competition effect is stronger than the efficiency effect (as the number of firms remains unchanged, average and total profits show the same proportional change). In our leading-case, Zambia–cotton, profits decline by 1.33 percent.[5]

We end with a discussion of the perfect competition simulation, where we impose the marginal cost of the larger firms on all incumbents, as in equal market shares, and we set farm-gate prices at the difference between the international prices and the marginal cost. Clearly, profits drop to zero, while prices and quantities significantly increase. As a result, utility increases significantly as well. While this scenario can only be hypothetically realized, it nevertheless provides an interesting baseline for comparison purposes.

3.2 Complementarities

In this section, we summarize the impacts complementary factors to the proposed supply chain changes. As we mentioned above, we consider factors and

---

[5] There is only one case, Zambia–tobacco, where the efficiency effect is stronger and total and average profits increase by 11.26 percent.

policies that affect farmers and firms separately and jointly. Moreover, we also explore the role of complementary increases in international prices. We are interested not so much in the direct impact of the complementary factors but rather in the complementarities between the changes in competition and the provision of supplementary factors. In other words, we want to assess whether the impacts of a given change in competition along the supply chain can be boosted by those complementary factors. All the results are reported in Table A4.2. The column "respect to original" shows the impact of the complementary factors given the initial market structure (that is, without any of the simulated competition policies). Figure A4.4 summarizes the effects on farm-gate prices.

Complementary factors that affect farmers make export crop adoption more profitable and hence they trigger a positive supply response. Since market conditions are kept constant and thus the demand for the crop is also constant, the increase in supply brings farm-gate prices down. Note that the drop in prices does not entail a utility loss, because the complementary factors allow for productivity gains that are, in the end, welfare enhancing. When the complementary factors affect firms, the productivity of the incumbents increases and thus marginal costs decline. This causes an increase in the demand for the export crop, with farm-gate prices rising as a result. Finally, when there are complementary factors that affect both farmers and firms, prices tend to increase because the increase in demand is not matched by the increase in supply. Note that this is not a general result: if the complementarities affecting farmers were bigger or the complementarities affecting firms were smaller, equilibrium farm-gate prices could in fact decline. As before, lower prices do not necessarily entail welfare losses for the farmers if they are generated by productivity enhancements (due to complementary policies).

It is important to note that, in our model, an increase in international prices has a large impact on farm-gate prices. In Figure A4.4(b), we see that a 10 percent increase in international prices brings about increases in farm-gate prices ranging from 15 percent to 25 percent. In principle, we observe that the increase in farm-gate prices is proportionally higher when the market structure is characterized by tighter competition among firms. Changes in international prices affect farm-gate prices via changes in the derived demand for the export crop. Note that our results imply large pass-through rates (larger than expected at least). This happens because in the calibrations the ratio of farm-gate prices to international prices is fairly small and thus even small changes in the absolute level of farm-gate prices can generate large proportional changes.[6]

Finally, we turn to explore the magnitude of the complementarities between these complementary factors and the changes in competition along the supply

---

[6]In practice, the pass-through rate could be smaller if, for instance, the change in international prices is seen as transitory.

chain. The results are reported in Table A4.2 (where each column shows the implications of piling up complementary changes with market structure changes). As before, we focus on the case of farm-gate prices in Zambia–cotton to illustrate the results. In Figure A4.5, we plot the difference between the impact resulting from a simultaneous change in complementary factors and market structure and the impacts resulting from separate simulations of complementary factors and market structure. Overall, while we do find traces of complementarities, these are relatively small. In fact, the complementarities with policies and factors that affect farms and firms (separately and jointly) are negligible. One reason behind this result is that the complementary policies affect all farmers in the same fashion.[7] There are larger complementarities with international prices and, interestingly, the larger the extent of competition among firms the larger these complementarities become.

4   OUTGROWER CONTRACTS: THEORY

In this section, we extend our standard model to include outgrower contracts. We first solve the model with this addition and we later explain how to adapt the simulations to deal with these issues. To allow for the possibility of a liquidity constraint affecting the home-market decision, we rewrite the farmer's problem as follows:

$$V(e_i; p, r) = \max_{h,m} h^\alpha (m + c)^{1-\alpha}$$

$$\text{subject to } m + ph \leqslant (p - \lambda r)e_i, \ h \geqslant 0, \ m \geqslant 0.$$

As explained above, the liquidity constraint is parameterized by λ. For our purposes, the distinctive feature of the model is that the farmer pays an interest rate r on any loan taken from the firms. This interest rate r depends on the structure of the market.

The model behaves as before, except that we now add a function that determines the interest rate

$$r = r(r^*, \text{sh}_1, \ldots, \text{sh}_n, J).$$

The interest rate depends on the exogenous cost of funds for the firms r^*, the number of firms n, the share of each firm sh_j and a parameter J (the "legal" system) that captures how good "institutions" are. For instance, a country with a given market structure (say, three firms) may have a well-functioning outgrower scheme because of good rules of law, while another country with the same market structure may suffer from a collapse of outgrower schemes because of bad institutions. Given these assumptions, we can write

$$r = r^* + \varphi(\text{sh}_1, \ldots, \text{sh}_n, J).$$

---

[7]It would be possible to simulate policies that, for instance, only affect nonproducers (thus triggering a large supply response).

Ideally, the form of the function $\varphi(\cdot)$ should be determined as part of the equilibrium game. However, this entails a much more complicated dynamic game-theoretic oligopsonistic game. Since developing such a model is outside the scope of our analysis, we will work with functional form assumptions. While this is a shortcoming, we believe we can still illustrate the main economic phenomena that we want to explore.

To operationalize the model, we proceed as follows. First, to capture the notion that the equilibrium interest rate depends on both the number of firms and the structure of competition, we assume that $\varphi(\text{sh}_1, \ldots, \text{sh}_n, J)$ is a function of the Herfindahl index

$$H = \sum_{j=1}^{n} (\text{sh}_j)^2.$$

H ranges from $1/n$ to 1, where n is the number of firms—if there are n firms and they are symmetric, then each has a share equal to $1/n$ and thus $H = 1/n$.

Also, we want $\varphi(\cdot)$ to depend on the institutional framework. If the market does not have good "institutions," it could be hard for firms to collect loans. This will be more difficult as n increases. So, we need φ to be close to zero when there is, say, a monopolist and/or when J is low. At the other extreme, φ can be very high when the market tends to perfect competition (if J is not good enough). Note that φ should also depend on N; in other words, even in the case of symmetry, it matters if there are two firms, three firms, and so on.

In the end, we assume that

$$r = r^* + (1 - H)\frac{2r^*}{\max(1 - H_0)},$$

where $\max(1 - H_0)$ is the higher value that $(1 - H)$ could have before the simulations are performed. That is,

$$r = r^* + (1 - H)\frac{2r^*}{1 - 1/n_0}.$$

Note that the role of the second parenthesis is a sort of normalization for the value that r can get. In our normalization, the maximum spread over r^* is just $2r^*$ (so that, in the worst scenario, the interest rate charged to the farmers will be thrice as high as the cost of capital to the firms).

A key issue to note is that, in the model with outgrower contract, the supply of the farmer depends on r. This makes sense: if the interest rate that the farmer pays while producing for the market goes up, then the choice of market production may be affected. This fact requires that we modify the model.

Given $r = r^* + \varphi$ and given λ, the fraction of the investment that is financed with a loan, the modified cutoff is

$$\hat{e}(p) \equiv \frac{\alpha(1 + \lambda r)}{1 - \alpha}\frac{c}{p}.$$

and this gives a "new" supply function

$$S(p) = (1 - \alpha) \int_{\hat{e}}^{\bar{e}} e_i f(e) \, de - \hat{e}(p)(1 - F(\hat{e}(p))).$$

Note that, in the end, the formula is the same as before. The difference is that, now, $\hat{e}(p)$ depends on r and λ and, importantly, r depends among other things on the number of firms and on the market shares. In consequence, when we do the simulations and the number of firms n and the shares sh respond endogenously, this affects farm-gate prices and the interest rate and, in turn, both affect the supply of the farmers. This means that the model with outgrower contract cannot be solved in the same way as the standard model. Instead, we need to solve simultaneously

$$H = \sum_{j=1}^{n} \left(\frac{q_j}{\sum_{j=1}^{n} q_j} \right)^2, \tag{4.1}$$

$$r = r^* + (1 - H) \frac{2r^*}{1 - 1/n_0}, \tag{4.2}$$

$$\hat{e}(p) = \frac{\alpha(1 + \lambda r)}{1 - \alpha} \frac{c}{p}, \tag{4.3}$$

$$\sum_{j=1}^{n} q_j = (1 - \alpha) \int_{\hat{e}}^{\bar{e}} e_i f(e) \, de - \hat{e}(p)(1 - F(\hat{e}(p))), \tag{4.4}$$

$$q_j = (1 - \alpha)(P - p^s(Q) - c_j^p) \frac{(1 - F(\hat{e}(p^s(Q))))\hat{e}(p^s(Q))}{p^s(Q)} \quad \forall j \in n. \tag{4.5}$$

By using this system of nonlinear equations all variables are identified at the same time. With this model in mind, we run again the simulations and complementary changes to see how simulation results are affected by the existence of outgrower contracts. We discuss these results next.

5   SIMULATION RESULTS WITH OUTGROWER CONTRACTS

The main purpose of the model with outgrower contracts is to assess the poverty impacts of the interrelationship between the provision of services to the farmers (access to credit, seeds, and so on) and the level of competition. We are particularly interested in identifying situations where increases in competition can jeopardize the market by hindering the success of the outgrower contracts. For this reason, in this section we briefly focus on how different market structures affect farm-gate prices and interest rates. Results are reported in Table A4.3 for all the endogenous variables of the model (in the Appendix). As before, here we use summary graphs to illustrate the results.

In Figure A4.6, we plot the differences in the proportional change in farm-gate prices between the standard model and the model with outgrower contracts for the leader split simulation. Interestingly, we find that the differences in the price effects are tiny. Specifically, they are never larger than 0.2 percentage points. In most cases, the differences are negative, thus suggesting that the increase in farm-gate prices is slightly larger in the model with outgrower contracts. The reason is that when the leader splits, competition increases. While this pushes prices up, the interest rate increases too, and this reduces farm supply. In the end, the increase in prices is slightly higher than in the standard model. Note that there are cases were the leader split simulation produces a more fragmented market and the interest rate falls, so the opposite result holds. For example, in the Burkina Faso–cotton case, farm-gate prices increase by 0.17 percent more in the outgrower contract model. As can be seen in Table A4.3, the changes in farm-gate prices are very similar in all the market structure simulations.

In the outgrower contract model, the change in the interest rate is one of the main channels through which farmers are affected. To see the kind of impacts delivered by our model, in Figure A4.7 we plot the percentage change in the interest rate for the small entrant and leaders merge and small entrant simulations. Here, whereas the standard and the outgrower contract models generate quite similar changes in farm-gate prices, there are sizeable changes in the interest rate. In the Zambian cotton case, the interest rate would increase by slightly less than 2 percent in the small entrant simulation and would decrease by over 1 percent in the leaders merge/small entrant case. For our purposes, an increase in the interest rate is akin to a decline in farm-gate prices (or, in other words, to a lower increase in prices). The poverty implications of these mechanisms are explored in Chapter 5.

APPENDIX: TABLES AND FIGURES

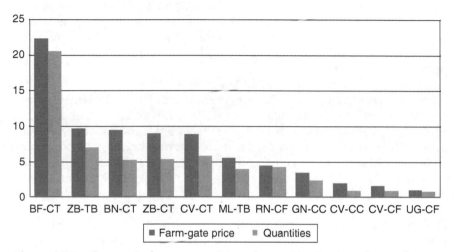

Figure A4.1: *Changes in farm-gate prices and quantities: leader split simulations.*

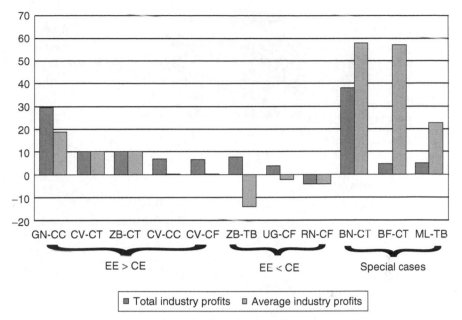

Figure A4.2: *Changes in total and average profits: leader split simulation.*

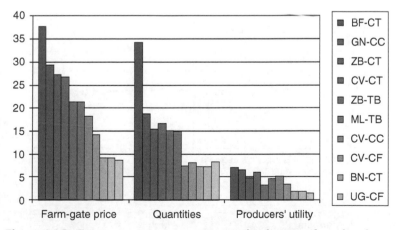

Figure A4.3: *Farm-gate prices, quantities, and utility: equal market shares.*

Supply Chains in Sub-Saharan Africa

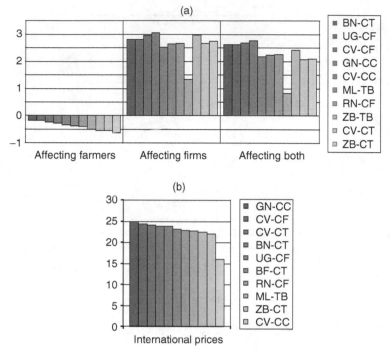

Figure A4.4: *Farm-gate prices and complementary factors.*

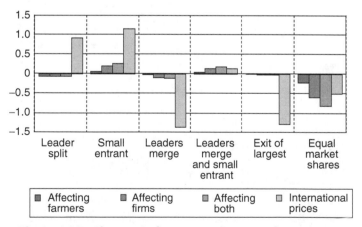

Figure A4.5: *Changes in farm-gate prices: complementarities.*

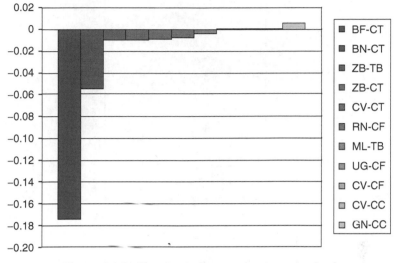

Figure A4.6: *Changes in farm-gate prices: standard model and outgrower contract model.*

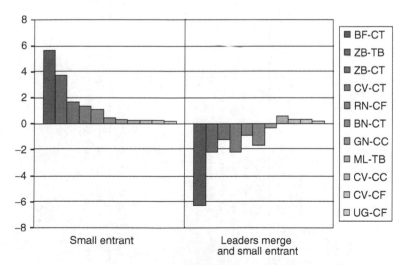

Figure A4.7: *Changes in the interest rate.*

Table A4.1: *Model calibration.*

Case	Income share	Producers' utility/ total utility	μ	σ	p_f	c	α
Burkina Faso, cotton	1.31	1.31	6.020	2	31.8	10,000,000	0.43
Zambia, tobacco	0.73	0.73	4.633	2.1	47.4	10,000,000	0.16
Uganda, coffee	2.40	2.40	5.216	2	41.6	3,600,000	0.36
Côte d'Ivoire, cotton	4.24	4.24	4.623	2	32.2	1,000,000	0.30
Zambia, cotton	2.97	2.98	4.236	2	33.7	1,200,000	0.16
Malawi, tobacco	3.82	3.82	4.985	2	38.2	1,800,000	0.37
Benin, cotton	6.59	6.59	4.188	2	41.9	600,000	0.25
Rwanda, coffee	0.88	0.88	6.071	2.1	37.7	25,000,000	0.45
Malawi, cotton	0.47	0.47	6.015	2.1	31.4	30,000,000	0.37
Côte d'Ivoire, cocoa	17.12	17.12	3.867	2	40.7	150,000	0.30
Ghana, cocoa	4.15	4.14	4.740	2	37.2	1,300,000	0.32
Côte d'Ivoire, coffee	6.81	6.81	4.355	2	38.8	600,000	0.30

The income share comes from the household surveys. μ denotes mean endowment (lognormal distribution), σ denotes standard deviation (lognormal distribution), p_f denotes farm-gate price, and c and α denote utility function parameters (see text).

Table A4.2: *Impact of supply chain changes on the standard model: (a) Zambia, cotton (percentage changes).*

	Respect to original	Leader split	Small entrant	Leaders merge	Leaders merge and small entrant	Exit of largest	Equal market shares	Perfect competition
(A) Basic model								
Farm-gate price	0.00	8.92	1.01	-8.59	-6.22	-11.84	27.21	71.64
Quantities	0.00	5.32	0.62	-5.44	-3.90	-7.58	15.35	35.91
Total utility	0.00	0.11	0.01	-0.10	-0.07	-0.14	0.34	0.91
Producers' utility	0.00	1.56	0.17	-3.28	-2.38	-4.51	4.89	13.48
Nonproducers' utility	0.00	0.06	0.01	0.00	0.00	0.00	0.19	0.50
Switchers' utility	0.00	26.64	26.65	-20.24	-20.24	-20.25	26.78	27.40
Total industry profits	0.00	10.29	-3.86	-0.36	-7.71	-22.37	-1.33	-100.00
Average industry profits	0.00	10.29	-19.88	24.55	-7.71	-2.96	-1.33	-100.00
(B) Complementary policies (farmers)								
Farm-gate price	-0.56	8.29	0.51	-9.17	-6.73	-12.39	26.43	71.64
Quantities	14.20	20.12	14.93	8.08	9.85	5.69	31.26	54.53
Total utility	1.44	1.56	1.45	1.33	1.36	1.28	1.81	2.46
Total industry profits	14.71	26.53	10.05	14.48	5.88	-10.39	14.25	-100.00
Average industry profits	14.71	26.53	-8.29	43.10	5.88	12.01	14.25	-100.00

Table A4.2: *(a) Continued.*

	Respect to original	Leader split	Small entrant	Leaders merge	Leaders merge and small entrant	Exit of largest	Equal market shares	Perfect competition
(C) Complementary policies (firms)								
Farm-gate price	2.65	11.50	3.85	-6.04	-3.42	-9.21	29.26	74.62
Quantities	1.62	6.80	2.34	-3.78	-2.13	-5.84	16.41	37.13
Total utility	0.03	0.14	0.05	-0.07	-0.04	-0.11	0.36	0.95
Producers' utility	0.46	2.02	0.67	-2.31	-1.32	-3.51	5.28	14.07
Nonproducers' utility	0.02	0.08	0.03	-0.07	-0.07	-0.07	0.20	0.53
Total industry profits	1.09	10.87	-3.44	1.31	-6.65	-19.72	1.67	-100.00
Average industry profits	1.09	-7.61	-19.53	26.63	-6.65	0.35	1.67	-100.00
(D) Complementary policies (farmers – firms)								
Farm-gate price	2.07	10.92	3.34	-6.63	-3.96	-9.78	28.47	74.62
Quantities	16.00	21.82	16.85	9.92	11.83	7.63	32.43	55.89
Total utility	1.48	1.60	1.49	1.36	1.39	1.32	1.84	2.51
Total industry profits	16.01	26.84	10.59	16.43	7.14	-7.32	17.69	-100.00
Average industry profits	16.01	5.70	-7.84	45.54	7.14	15.85	17.69	-100.00
(E) International prices								
Farm-gate price	22.39	32.23	24.56	12.44	16.30	9.27	49.10	103.73
Quantities	12.81	17.92	13.96	7.34	9.50	5.52	26.06	48.29
Total utility	0.28	0.40	0.30	0.15	0.20	0.11	0.62	1.34
Producers' utility	4.00	5.84	4.40	2.19	2.88	1.62	9.06	19.88
Nonproducers' utility	0.16	0.22	0.17	0.09	0.11	0.06	0.34	0.74
Total industry profits	24.22	31.42	16.12	27.05	15.20	6.56	32.59	-100.00
Average industry profits	24.22	9.52	-3.24	58.81	15.20	33.20	32.59	-100.00

Table A4.2: *(b) Benin, cotton (percentage changes).*

	Respect to original	Leader split	Small entrant	Leaders merge	Leaders merge and small entrant	Exit of largest	Equal market shares	Perfect competition
(A) Basic model								
Farm-gate price	0.00	9.49	0.25	−1.90	−1.44	−10.52	57.34	97.39
Quantities	0.00	5.19	0.14	−1.08	−0.82	−6.20	27.04	41.43
Total utility	0.00	0.26	0.01	−0.05	−0.04	−0.29	1.63	2.78
Producers' utility	0.00	2.21	0.06	−0.78	−0.59	−4.26	13.86	23.81
Nonproducers' utility	0.00	0.12	0.00	0.00	0.00	0.00	0.73	1.24
Switchers' utility	0.00	27.23	27.38	−20.30	−20.28	−20.25	27.99	28.96
Total industry profits	0.00	38.10	−0.95	4.47	2.79	−63.93	−14.77	−100.00
Average industry profits	0.00	57.83	−11.96	19.40	2.79	−58.78	−14.77	−100.00
(B) Complementary policies (farmers)								
Farm-gate price	−0.44	8.94	−0.15	−2.37	−1.87	−10.94	56.51	97.39
Quantities	13.67	19.38	13.85	12.44	12.76	6.77	43.50	59.68
Total utility	2.36	2.65	2.37	2.30	2.31	2.03	4.16	5.47
Total industry profits	13.11	55.94	11.88	18.29	16.20	−58.24	−1.74	−100.00
Average industry profits	13.11	78.22	−0.55	35.19	16.20	−52.28	−1.74	−100.00

Table A4.2: *(b) Continued.*

	Respect to original	Leader split	Small entrant	Leaders merge	Leaders merge and small entrant	Exit of largest	Equal market shares	Perfect competition
(C) Complementary policies (firms)								
Farm-gate price	2.09	11.26	2.42	0.11	0.67	−8.32	58.22	98.57
Quantities	1.17	6.12	1.36	0.06	0.38	−4.86	27.39	41.81
Total utility	0.06	0.31	0.07	0.00	0.02	−0.23	1.65	2.82
Producers' utility	0.48	2.63	0.56	0.03	0.16	−3.37	14.08	24.10
Nonproducers' utility	0.03	0.15	0.03	0.00	0.01	−0.11	0.74	1.26
Total industry profits	−1.96	35.10	−3.21	2.63	0.61	−62.42	−13.90	−100.00
Average industry profits	−1.96	54.41	−13.97	17.29	0.61	−57.06	−13.90	−100.00
(D) Complementary policies (farmers − firms)								
Farm-gate price	1.64	10.70	2.01	−0.37	0.23	−8.75	57.39	98.57
Quantities	14.97	20.41	15.20	13.71	14.09	8.26	43.88	60.10
Total utility	2.42	2.71	2.43	2.36	2.38	2.10	4.19	5.51
Total industry profits	10.97	52.63	9.39	16.26	13.80	−56.50	−0.75	−100.00
Average industry profits	10.97	74.44	−2.77	32.87	13.80	−50.29	−0.75	−100.00
(E) International prices								
Farm-gate price	19.78	28.80	20.53	17.28	18.35	8.80	76.41	123.03
Quantities	10.45	14.78	10.82	9.20	9.74	4.82	34.24	49.35
Total utility	0.55	0.81	0.58	0.48	0.51	0.25	2.18	3.52
Producers' utility	4.66	6.85	4.85	4.06	4.32	2.05	18.60	30.16
Nonproducers' utility	0.25	0.37	0.26	0.22	0.24	0.11	0.97	1.58
Total industry profits	6.70	43.74	3.94	12.55	8.79	−49.03	4.84	−100.00
Average industry profits	6.70	43.74	−7.61	28.63	8.79	−41.75	4.84	−100.00

Table A4.2: *(c) Burkina Faso, cotton (percentage changes).*

	Respect to original	Leader split	Small entrant	Leaders merge	Leaders merge and small entrant	Exit of largest	Equal market shares	Perfect competition
(A) Basic model								
Farm-gate price	0.00	22.26	1.00	-3.22	-1.23	-27.68	37.66	89.38
Quantities	0.00	20.57	0.95	-3.07	-1.17	-27.30	34.15	76.26
Total utility	0.00	0.13	0.01	-0.02	-0.01	-0.15	0.22	0.55
Producers' utility	0.00	4.12	0.18	-1.34	-0.52	-11.01	7.09	17.22
Nonproducers' utility	0.00	0.07	0.00	0.00	0.00	0.00	0.13	0.33
Switchers' utility	0.00	25.61	25.43	-20.24	-20.28	-20.52	25.90	27.20
Total industry profits	0.00	4.71	-2.57	7.28	2.39	-66.36	-10.24	-100.00
Average industry profits	0.00	57.06	-26.93	60.92	2.39	-49.54	-10.24	-100.00
(B) Complementary policies (farmers)								
Farm-gate price	-0.64	21.19	0.47	-4.01	-1.86	-28.23	36.70	89.38
Quantities	25.55	50.37	26.85	21.57	24.12	-8.15	67.11	119.27
Total utility	5.43	5.59	5.44	5.41	5.42	5.25	5.70	6.11
Total industry profits	25.36	32.66	21.77	34.96	28.29	-56.85	13.90	-100.00
Average industry profits	25.36	99.00	-8.67	102.43	28.29	-35.28	13.90	-100.00

Supply Chains in Sub-Saharan Africa

Table A4.2: (c) Continued.

	Respect to original	Leader split	Small entrant	Leaders merge	Leaders merge and small entrant	Exit of largest	Equal market shares	Perfect competition
(C) Complementary policies (firms)								
Farm-gate price	2.75	23.96	4.08	-0.97	1.54	-24.88	39.60	92.21
Quantities	2.60	22.10	3.86	-0.92	1.47	-24.44	35.82	78.43
Total utility	0.02	0.14	0.02	-0.01	0.01	-0.13	0.23	0.57
Producers' utility	0.49	4.44	0.73	-0.40	0.28	-9.96	7.47	17.77
Nonproducers' utility	0.01	0.08	0.01	-0.04	0.01	-0.04	0.14	0.34
Total industry profits	0.20	7.82	-3.21	8.53	2.41	-63.43	-7.55	-100.00
Average industry profits	0.20	61.74	-27.40	62.79	2.41	-45.15	-7.55	-100.00
(D) Complementary policies (farmers – firms)								
Farm-gate price	2.09	22.87	3.53	-1.79	0.90	-25.45	38.62	92.21
Quantities	28.73	52.22	30.41	24.20	27.34	-4.64	69.14	121.89
Total utility	5.45	5.60	5.46	5.42	5.44	5.27	5.72	6.13
Total industry profits	25.64	36.57	21.01	36.55	28.35	-53.14	17.28	-100.00
Average industry profits	25.64	104.85	-9.24	104.82	28.35	-29.71	17.28	-100.00
(E) International prices								
Farm-gate price	23.05	42.33	25.92	16.88	21.84	-7.10	60.20	122.48
Quantities	21.28	38.16	23.84	15.71	20.20	-6.82	53.12	100.81
Total utility	0.13	0.25	0.15	0.10	0.13	-0.04	0.36	0.77
Producers' utility	4.27	8.00	4.82	3.10	4.04	-2.94	11.51	23.61
Nonproducers' utility	0.08	0.15	0.09	0.06	0.07	-0.30	0.21	0.46
Total industry profits	22.29	42.16	14.55	36.81	24.18	-41.85	23.38	-100.00
Average industry profits	22.29	42.16	-14.09	105.21	24.18	-12.77	23.38	-100.00

Table A4.2: *(d) Côte d'Ivoire, cotton (percentage changes).*

	Respect to original	Leader split	Small entrant	Leaders merge	Leaders merge and small entrant	Exit of largest	Equal market shares	Perfect competition
(A) Basic model								
Farm-gate price	0.00	8.85	0.76	−7.37	−5.43	−11.46	26.78	67.20
Quantities	0.00	5.77	0.51	−5.05	−3.69	−7.95	16.63	37.82
Total utility	0.00	0.16	0.01	−0.13	−0.10	−0.21	0.49	1.26
Producers' utility	0.00	1.94	0.16	−3.02	−2.23	−4.68	6.01	15.46
Nonproducers' utility	0.00	0.08	0.01	0.00	0.00	0.00	0.24	0.61
Switchers' utility	0.00	26.20	26.28	−20.25	−20.23	−20.26	26.41	27.27
Total industry profits	0.00	10.34	−3.21	3.23	−3.60	−24.57	−0.54	−100.00
Average industry profits	0.00	10.34	−19.34	29.04	−3.60	−5.72	−0.54	−100.00
(B) Complementary policies (farmers)								
Farm-gate price	−0.55	8.23	0.27	−7.95	−5.93	−12.01	26.03	67.20
Quantities	16.18	22.72	16.81	10.39	12.00	7.10	34.97	59.37
Total utility	2.98	3.17	3.00	2.83	2.87	2.75	3.54	4.43
Total industry profits	16.75	28.85	12.73	20.68	12.48	−11.27	17.25	−100.00
Average industry profits	16.75	28.85	−6.06	50.85	12.48	10.91	17.25	−100.00

Table A4.2: *(d) Continued.*

	Respect to original	Leader split	Small entrant	Leaders merge	Leaders merge and small entrant	Exit of largest	Equal market shares	Perfect competition
(C) Complementary policies (firms)								
Farm-gate price	2.98	11.63	3.94	-4.52	-2.33	-8.52	29.17	70.57
Quantities	1.98	7.53	2.60	-3.07	-1.57	-5.86	18.00	39.41
Total utility	0.05	0.21	0.07	-0.08	-0.04	-0.15	0.54	1.33
Producers' utility	0.65	2.57	0.86	-1.86	-0.96	-3.48	6.56	16.26
Nonproducers' utility	0.03	0.10	0.04	-0.11	-0.11	-0.11	0.26	0.64
Total industry profits	1.60	12.07	-2.40	5.36	-2.24	-21.24	3.06	-100.00
Average industry profits	1.60	12.07	-18.67	31.70	-2.24	-1.54	3.06	-100.00
(D) Complementary policies (farmers – firms)								
Farm-gate price	2.41	10.99	3.43	-5.12	-2.86	-9.08	28.39	70.57
Quantities	18.42	24.70	19.19	12.64	14.41	9.48	36.51	61.16
Total utility	3.05	3.22	3.07	2.89	2.94	2.81	3.59	4.51
Total industry profits	18.67	30.92	13.73	23.21	14.12	-7.34	21.46	-100.00
Average industry profits	18.67	30.92	-5.22	54.01	14.12	15.83	21.46	-100.00
(E) International prices								
Farm-gate price	24.09	33.61	26.01	15.30	18.76	11.30	50.40	100.74
Quantities	15.07	20.50	16.18	9.80	11.91	7.32	29.49	52.78
Total utility	0.44	0.62	0.48	0.28	0.34	0.21	0.94	1.91
Producers' utility	5.39	7.59	5.83	3.39	4.18	2.49	11.51	23.36
Nonproducers' utility	0.22	0.30	0.23	0.14	0.17	0.10	0.46	0.93
Total industry profits	27.79	36.04	19.74	34.63	22.45	8.45	37.54	-100.00
Average industry profits	27.79	13.37	-0.22	68.28	22.45	35.56	37.54	-100.00

Table A4.2: *(e) Malawi, cotton (percentage changes).*

	Respect to original	Three firms	Four firms	Small entrant with half of the benefits
(A) Basic model				
Farm-gate price	0.00	12.15	19.64	6.09
Quantities	0.00	11.62	18.62	5.86
Total utility	0.00	0.03	0.04	0.01
Producers' utility	0.00	2.18	3.58	1.08
Nonproducers' utility	0.00	0.02	0.03	0.01
Switchers' utility	0.00	25.43	25.52	25.38
Total industry profits	0.00	−14.67	−26.52	−16.05
Average industry profits	0.00	−43.11	−63.26	−44.03
(B) Complementary policies (farmers)				
Farm-gate price	−0.75	11.49	19.06	5.47
Quantities	25.66	40.13	48.86	33.07
Total utility	4.62	4.66	4.68	4.64
Total industry profits	27.48	8.92	−6.11	6.94
Average industry profits	27.48	−27.39	−53.06	−28.70
(C) Complementary policies (firms)				
Farm-gate price	2.42	14.91	22.60	8.39
Quantities	2.34	14.21	21.36	8.05
Total utility	0.01	0.03	0.05	0.02
Producers' utility	0.42	2.69	4.14	1.49
Nonproducers' utility	0.00	0.02	0.03	0.01
Total industry profits	5.30	−10.12	−22.59	−11.23
Average industry profits	5.30	40.08	61.29	40.82
(D) Complementary policies (farmers − firms)				
Farm-gate price	1.65	14.23	22.00	7.76
Quantities	28.53	43.30	52.21	35.76
Total utility	4.63	4.66	4.68	4.65
Total industry profits	34.16	14.67	−1.14	13.00
Average industry profits	34.16	−23.55	−50.57	−24.66
(E) International prices				
Farm-gate price	21.33	36.44	45.81	26.42
Quantities	20.18	33.93	42.22	24.86
Total utility	0.05	0.08	0.10	0.06
Producers' utility	3.90	6.81	8.65	4.87
Nonproducers' utility	0.03	0.05	0.06	0.03
Total industry profits	51.40	29.49	11.70	32.17
Average industry profits	51.40	−13.67	−44.15	−11.89

Table A4.2: (f) Côte d'Ivoire, cocoa (percentage changes).

	Respect to original	Leader split	Small entrant	Leaders merge	Leaders merge and small entrant	Exit of largest	Equal market shares	Perfect competition
(A) Basic model								
Farm-gate price	0.00	1.95	0.37	-1.88	-1.38	-2.18	18.24	37.21
Quantities	0.00	0.85	0.16	-0.83	-0.61	-0.97	7.44	14.10
Total utility	0.00	0.14	0.03	-0.14	-0.10	-0.16	1.33	2.70
Producers' utility	0.00	0.55	0.10	-0.78	-0.58	-0.91	5.22	10.69
Nonproducers' utility	0.00	0.05	0.01	0.00	0.00	0.00	0.50	0.99
Switchers' utility	0.00	30.12	30.24	-20.24	-20.35	-20.29	30.23	30.55
Total industry profits	0.00	6.96	-2.91	-3.54	-7.10	-8.65	-1.24	-100.00
Average industry profits	0.00	0.28	-8.98	3.35	-7.10	-2.13	-1.24	-100.00
(B) Complementary policies (farmers)								
Farm-gate price	-0.34	1.62	0.04	-2.23	-1.72	-2.53	17.80	37.21
Quantities	11.57	12.51	11.76	10.66	10.91	10.51	19.63	27.03
Total utility	2.92	3.08	2.95	2.77	2.81	2.75	4.38	5.92
Total industry profits	12.76	20.25	9.40	9.02	4.94	3.43	12.51	-100.00
Average industry profits	12.76	12.73	2.56	16.81	4.94	10.82	12.51	-100.00

Table A4.2: *(f) Continued.*

	Respect to original	Leader split	Small entrant	Leaders merge	Leaders merge and small entrant	Exit of largest	Equal market shares	Perfect competition
(C) Complementary policies (firms)								
Farm-gate price	2.53	4.48	2.93	0.64	1.17	0.34	20.38	39.81
Quantities	1.10	1.94	1.27	0.28	0.51	0.15	8.24	14.95
Total utility	0.18	0.33	0.21	0.05	0.09	0.03	1.48	2.89
Producers' utility	0.72	1.27	0.83	0.18	0.33	0.10	5.83	11.44
Nonproducers' utility	0.07	0.12	0.08	0.02	0.03	0.01	0.55	1.06
Total industry profits	1.71	7.96	-1.44	-1.28	-5.07	-6.11	1.94	-100.00
Average industry profits	1.71	1.21	-7.60	5.77	-5.07	0.60	1.94	-100.00
(D) Complementary policies (farmers – firms)								
Farm-gate price	2.17	4.13	2.59	0.28	0.83	-0.02	19.93	39.81
Quantities	12.77	13.68	12.96	11.87	12.13	11.73	20.50	27.95
Total utility	3.13	3.28	3.16	2.97	3.02	2.95	4.55	6.13
Total industry profits	14.76	21.46	11.13	11.63	7.29	6.35	16.12	-100.00
Average industry profits	14.76	13.87	4.19	19.61	7.29	13.95	16.12	-100.00
(E) International prices								
Farm-gate price	22.05	24.22	22.66	19.93	20.69	19.63	40.05	63.94
Quantities	8.85	9.64	9.07	8.07	8.35	7.96	15.02	22.11
Total utility	1.61	1.76	1.65	1.45	1.51	1.43	2.91	4.61
Producers' utility	6.32	6.94	6.49	5.71	5.92	5.62	11.51	18.38
Nonproducers' utility	0.60	0.66	0.61	0.54	0.56	0.53	1.06	1.67
Total industry profits	26.67	30.85	21.98	25.58	20.17	21.20	33.17	-100.00
Average industry profits	26.67	22.68	14.36	34.55	20.17	29.85	33.17	-100.00

Supply Chains in Sub-Saharan Africa

Table A4.2: *(g) Ghana, cocoa (percentage changes).*

	Respect to original	Leader split	Small entrant	Leaders merge	Leaders merge and small entrant	Exit of largest	Equal market shares	Perfect competition
(A) Basic model								
Farm-gate price	0.00	3.43	0.28	-1.46	-1.05	-4.02	29.27	47.48
Quantities	0.00	2.35	0.20	-1.02	-0.72	-2.81	18.71	29.05
Total utility	0.00	0.06	0.01	-0.03	-0.02	-0.07	0.53	0.86
Producers' utility	0.00	0.74	0.06	-0.60	-0.43	-1.65	6.56	10.77
Nonproducers' utility	0.00	0.03	0.00	0.00	0.00	0.00	0.26	0.42
Switchers' utility	0.00	26.05	26.15	-20.26	-20.32	-20.24	26.33	26.70
Total industry profits	0.00	29.47	-2.17	3.68	0.66	-37.56	-7.07	-100.00
Average industry profits	0.00	18.68	-10.32	14.05	0.66	-31.32	-7.07	-100.00
(B) Complementary policies (farmers)								
Farm-gate price	-0.29	3.15	0.02	-1.77	-1.33	-4.31	28.86	47.48
Quantities	17.07	19.77	17.31	15.89	16.24	13.84	38.36	50.38
Total utility	3.30	3.37	3.31	3.27	3.28	3.22	3.91	4.30
Total industry profits	17.42	51.06	14.73	21.84	18.14	-25.55	10.76	-100.00
Average industry profits	17.42	38.47	5.17	34.02	18.14	-18.10	10.76	-100.00

Table A4.2: *(g) Continued.*

	Respect to original	Leader split	Small entrant	Leaders merge	Leaders merge and small entrant	Exit of largest	Equal market shares	Perfect competition
(C) Complementary policies (firms)								
Farm-gate price	3.06	6.48	3.39	1.56	2.04	-0.94	31.71	50.37
Quantities	2.10	4.40	2.32	1.08	1.40	-0.65	20.15	30.61
Total utility	0.05	0.11	0.06	0.03	0.04	-0.02	0.57	0.92
Producers' utility	0.66	1.41	0.74	0.34	0.44	-0.39	7.12	11.44
Nonproducers' utility	0.03	0.06	0.03	0.01	0.02	-0.11	0.28	0.45
Total industry profits	0.99	28.56	-1.55	4.93	1.53	-34.18	-3.66	-100.00
Average industry profits	0.99	17.85	-9.75	15.42	1.53	-27.60	-3.66	-100.00
(D) Complementary policies (farmers – firms)								
Farm-gate price	2.76	6.19	3.11	1.25	1.74	-1.24	31.29	50.37
Quantities	19.46	22.10	19.74	18.28	18.67	16.31	39.99	52.15
Total utility	3.37	3.44	3.37	3.33	3.34	3.28	3.96	4.36
Total industry profits	18.67	50.10	15.55	23.40	19.25	-21.53	14.78	-100.00
Average industry profits	18.67	37.59	5.92	35.73	19.25	-13.69	14.78	-100.00
(E) International prices								
Farm-gate price	24.89	28.60	25.48	23.08	23.86	20.56	53.89	76.66
Quantities	16.09	18.32	16.45	14.99	15.46	13.44	32.49	43.97
Total utility	0.45	0.52	0.46	0.41	0.43	0.37	0.98	1.41
Producers' utility	5.55	6.40	5.69	5.14	5.32	4.57	12.26	17.57
Nonproducers' utility	0.22	0.25	0.22	0.20	0.21	0.18	0.48	0.69
Total industry profits	25.06	49.34	20.45	30.95	25.23	-6.18	29.65	-100.00
Average industry profits	25.06	36.89	10.42	44.05	25.23	3.20	29.65	-100.00

Table A4.2: *(h) Côte d'Ivoire, coffee (percentage changes).*

	Respect to original	Leader split	Small entrant	Leaders merge	Leaders merge and small entrant	Exit of largest	Equal market shares	Perfect competition
(A) Basic model								
Farm-gate price	0.00	1.52	0.29	-1.47	-1.08	-1.71	14.25	27.57
Quantities	0.00	0.90	0.17	-0.88	-0.64	-1.02	8.08	15.00
Total utility	0.00	0.04	0.01	-0.04	-0.03	-0.05	0.41	0.81
Producers' utility	0.00	0.36	0.07	-0.60	-0.44	-0.70	3.40	6.66
Nonproducers' utility	0.00	0.02	0.00	0.00	0.00	0.00	0.19	0.36
Switchers' utility	0.00	26.85	27.12	-20.25	-20.32	-20.23	26.91	27.09
Total industry profits	0.00	6.78	-2.95	-3.22	-6.89	-8.25	-5.87	-100.00
Average industry profits	0.00	0.11	-9.02	3.69	-6.89	-1.69	-5.87	-100.00
(B) Complementary policies (farmers)								
Farm-gate price	-0.25	1.27	0.05	-1.73	-1.33	-1.97	13.95	27.57
Quantities	14.66	15.67	14.86	13.67	13.94	13.51	23.68	31.58
Total utility	2.91	2.96	2.92	2.86	2.88	2.86	3.38	3.83
Total industry profits	15.88	23.34	12.36	12.42	8.09	6.77	10.18	-100.00
Average industry profits	15.88	15.63	5.34	20.45	8.09	14.39	10.18	-100.00

Table A4.2: *(h) Continued.*

	Respect to original	Leader split	Small entrant	Leaders merge	Leaders merge and small entrant	Exit of largest	Equal market shares	Perfect competition
(C) Complementary policies (firms)								
Farm-gate price	2.95	4.47	3.27	1.48	1.90	1.24	16.90	30.62
Quantities	1.74	2.62	1.92	0.87	1.12	0.74	9.51	16.51
Total utility	0.09	0.13	0.09	0.04	0.05	0.04	0.49	0.90
Producers' utility	0.70	1.06	0.77	0.35	0.45	0.29	4.05	7.41
Nonproducers' utility	0.04	0.06	0.04	0.02	0.03	0.02	0.22	0.40
Total industry profits	2.55	8.58	−0.69	−0.07	−4.02	−4.82	−1.75	−100.00
Average industry profits	2.55	1.80	−6.89	7.06	−4.02	1.98	−1.75	−100.00
(D) Complementary policies (farmers – firms)								
Farm-gate price	2.69	4.22	3.02	1.20	1.64	0.97	16.59	30.62
Quantities	16.60	17.59	16.82	15.62	15.91	15.47	25.26	33.26
Total utility	3.01	3.06	3.02	2.96	2.97	2.95	3.46	3.93
Total industry profits	18.90	25.51	15.06	16.13	11.47	10.79	14.97	−100.00
Average industry profits	18.90	17.66	7.87	24.42	11.47	18.70	14.97	−100.00
(E) International prices								
Farm-gate price	24.36	26.06	24.84	22.68	23.29	22.45	38.48	55.59
Quantities	13.38	14.24	13.63	12.53	12.84	12.41	20.28	27.93
Total utility	0.71	0.76	0.73	0.66	0.68	0.65	1.13	1.64
Producers' utility	5.87	6.29	5.99	5.46	5.61	5.40	9.36	13.61
Nonproducers' utility	0.32	0.34	0.33	0.30	0.31	0.29	0.50	0.73
Total industry profits	33.07	36.86	27.98	32.61	26.68	28.20	34.58	−100.00
Average industry profits	33.07	28.30	19.98	42.08	26.68	37.36	34.58	−100.00

Table A4.2: *(i) Rwanda, coffee (percentage changes).*

	Respect to original	Leader split	Small entrant	Leaders merge	Leaders merge and small entrant	Exit of largest	Equal market shares	Perfect competition
(A) Basic model								
Farm-gate price	0.00	4.44	0.56	−5.84	−4.25	−6.08	8.71	31.91
Quantities	0.00	4.21	0.54	−5.61	−4.07	−5.84	8.21	29.28
Total utility	0.00	0.02	0.00	−0.02	−0.02	−0.02	0.03	0.12
Producers' utility	0.00	0.79	0.10	−2.42	−1.76	−2.52	1.57	5.93
Nonproducers' utility	0.00	0.01	0.00	0.00	0.00	0.00	0.02	0.07
Switchers' utility	0.00	25.39	25.46	−20.22	−20.24	−20.25	25.41	25.74
Total industry profits	0.00	−3.93	−3.92	3.84	−5.05	2.17	−4.32	−100.00
Average industry profits	0.00	−3.93	−19.94	29.80	−5.05	27.72	−4.32	−100.00
(B) Complementary policies (farmers)								
Farm-gate price	−0.40	4.03	0.21	−6.29	−4.63	−6.52	8.26	31.91
Quantities	26.11	31.30	26.84	19.12	21.10	18.83	36.21	62.64
Total utility	5.71	5.73	5.71	5.68	5.69	5.68	5.75	5.87
Total industry profits	27.57	22.86	22.20	32.69	21.10	30.61	22.76	−100.00
Average industry profits	27.57	2.38	1.83	65.87	21.10	63.27	22.76	−100.00

Table A4.2: *(i) Continued.*

	Respect to original	Leader split	Small entrant	Leaders merge	Leaders merge and small entrant	Exit of largest	Equal market shares	Perfect competition
(C) Complementary policies (firms)								
Farm-gate price	2.67	7.12	3.37	-3.26	-1.49	-3.50	11.19	35.02
Quantities	2.53	6.72	3.20	-3.12	-1.43	-3.34	10.52	32.02
Total utility	0.01	0.03	0.01	-0.01	-0.01	-0.01	0.04	0.14
Producers' utility	0.47	1.28	0.60	-1.36	-0.62	-1.45	2.02	6.52
Nonproducers' utility	0.01	0.02	0.01	-0.02	-0.02	-0.02	0.02	0.08
Total industry profits	3.73	-0.47	-1.14	8.39	-1.47	6.77	0.40	-100.00
Average industry profits	3.73	-17.06	-17.62	35.49	-1.47	33.46	0.40	-100.00
(D) Complementary policies (farmers – firms)								
Farm-gate price	2.25	6.74	3.01	-3.72	-1.89	-3.95	10.73	35.02
Quantities	29.23	34.45	30.11	22.18	24.35	21.91	39.04	66.01
Total utility	5.72	5.74	5.73	5.70	5.70	5.69	5.76	5.88
Total industry profits	32.33	26.79	25.77	38.49	25.67	36.47	28.76	-100.00
Average industry profits	32.33	5.65	4.81	73.11	25.67	70.59	28.76	-100.00
(E) International prices								
Farm-gate price	22.90	28.06	24.26	16.01	18.69	15.77	31.53	60.68
Quantities	21.23	25.86	22.46	14.97	17.41	14.75	28.94	53.91
Total utility	0.09	0.11	0.09	0.06	0.07	0.06	0.12	0.25
Producers' utility	4.21	5.19	4.47	2.92	3.42	2.87	5.85	11.48
Nonproducers' utility	0.05	0.06	0.05	0.04	0.04	0.04	0.07	0.14
Total industry profits	43.09	34.95	32.94	52.51	36.23	50.79	43.29	-100.00
Average industry profits	43.09	12.46	10.78	90.64	36.23	88.49	43.29	-100.00

Table A4.2: (i) Uganda, coffee (percentage changes).

	Respect to original	Leader split	Small entrant	Leaders merge	Leaders merge and small entrant	Exit of largest	Equal market shares	Perfect competition
(A) Basic model								
Farm-gate price	0.00	0.96	0.13	-0.96	-0.76	-1.08	9.16	17.89
Quantities	0.00	0.77	0.11	-0.77	-0.61	-0.87	7.18	13.76
Total utility	0.00	0.01	0.00	-0.01	-0.01	-0.01	0.10	0.19
Producers' utility	0.00	0.19	0.03	-0.40	-0.32	-0.45	1.85	3.66
Nonproducers' utility	0.00	0.01	0.00	0.00	0.00	0.00	0.05	0.10
Switchers' utility	0.00	25.65	25.71	-20.28	-20.22	-20.22	25.68	25.76
Total industry profits	0.00	3.94	-2.10	-1.67	-4.51	-4.71	-14.38	-100.00
Average industry profits	0.00	-2.17	-7.86	4.89	-4.51	1.65	-14.38	-100.00
(B) Complementary policies (farmers)								
Farm-gate price	-0.18	0.79	-0.04	-1.15	-0.94	-1.27	8.96	17.89
Quantities	20.35	21.26	20.48	19.44	19.63	19.32	28.76	36.65
Total utility	3.91	3.92	3.91	3.89	3.90	3.89	4.02	4.13
Total industry profits	21.57	26.04	18.90	19.80	16.22	16.22	5.28	-100.00
Average industry profits	21.57	18.63	11.90	27.78	16.22	23.96	5.28	-100.00

Table A4.2: *(j) Continued.*

	Respect to original	Leader split	Small entrant	Leaders merge	Leaders merge and small entrant	Exit of largest	Equal market shares	Perfect competition
(C) Complementary policies (firms)								
Farm-gate price	2.81	3.78	2.96	1.84	2.06	1.72	11.78	20.77
Quantities	2.23	2.99	2.35	1.47	1.64	1.37	9.18	15.88
Total utility	0.03	0.04	0.03	0.02	0.02	0.02	0.12	0.22
Producers' utility	0.56	0.76	0.59	0.37	0.41	0.34	2.39	4.27
Nonproducers' utility	0.02	0.02	0.02	0.01	0.01	0.01	0.07	0.12
Total industry profits	2.70	6.09	0.29	1.51	-1.64	-1.38	-10.17	-100.00
Average industry profits	2.70	-0.15	-5.61	8.28	-1.64	5.20	-10.17	-100.00
(D) Complementary policies (farmers – firms)								
Farm-gate price	2.62	3.59	2.78	1.65	1.88	1.53	11.57	20.77
Quantities	22.96	23.86	23.12	22.06	22.27	21.95	31.10	39.13
Total utility	3.94	3.95	3.94	3.93	3.93	3.93	4.05	4.17
Total industry profits	24.92	28.72	21.86	23.72	19.76	20.31	10.41	-100.00
Average industry profits	24.92	21.15	14.69	31.97	19.76	28.33	10.41	-100.00
(E) International prices								
Farm-gate price	23.81	24.89	24.07	22.71	23.05	22.59	32.92	44.07
Quantities	18.09	18.88	18.28	17.30	17.54	17.21	24.57	32.19
Total utility	0.25	0.26	0.26	0.24	0.24	0.24	0.35	0.48
Producers' utility	4.91	5.15	4.97	4.68	4.75	4.66	6.86	9.27
Nonproducers' utility	0.13	0.14	0.14	0.13	0.13	0.13	0.19	0.25
Total industry profits	36.02	37.55	31.71	36.81	31.58	34.00	27.22	-100.00
Average industry profits	36.02	29.46	23.96	45.93	31.58	42.93	27.22	-100.00

Table A4.2: (k) Malawi, tobacco (percentage changes).

	Respect to original	Leader split	Small entrant	Leaders merge	Leaders merge and small entrant	Exit of largest	Equal market shares	Perfect competition
(A) Basic model								
Farm-gate price	0.00	5.45	0.14	−5.12	−4.37	−6.00	21.39	46.12
Quantities	0.00	3.96	0.10	−3.82	−3.26	−4.49	14.96	30.52
Total utility	0.00	0.09	0.00	−0.08	−0.07	−0.10	0.35	0.77
Producers' utility	0.00	1.16	0.03	−2.09	−1.79	−2.45	4.64	10.18
Nonproducers' utility	0.00	0.04	0.00	0.00	0.00	0.00	0.18	0.38
Switchers' utility	0.00	25.84	26.10	−20.23	−20.23	−20.25	26.00	26.48
Total industry profits	0.00	5.00	−0.88	−6.50	−10.34	−15.93	−14.54	−100.00
Average industry profits	0.00	22.50	−13.27	9.09	−10.34	−1.92	−14.54	−100.00
(B) Complementary policies (farmers)								
Farm-gate price	−0.40	4.97	−0.22	−5.54	−4.75	−6.42	20.87	46.12
Quantities	18.46	22.99	18.62	14.00	14.70	13.23	35.69	53.99
Total utility	3.92	4.02	3.92	3.82	3.84	3.81	4.33	4.82
Total industry profits	18.89	25.32	17.56	11.53	6.73	0.53	3.00	−100.00
Average industry profits	18.89	46.20	2.86	30.12	6.73	17.28	3.00	−100.00

Table A4.2: *(k) Continued.*

	Respect to original	Leader split	Small entrant	Leaders merge	Leaders merge and small entrant	Exit of largest	Equal market shares	Perfect competition
(C) Complementary policies (firms)								
Farm-gate price	2.64	7.84	2.89	-2.50	-1.63	-3.36	23.58	48.87
Quantities	1.94	5.67	2.11	-1.85	-1.21	-2.50	16.41	32.15
Total utility	0.04	0.13	0.05	-0.04	-0.03	-0.05	0.39	0.81
Producers' utility	0.56	1.67	0.61	-1.02	-0.67	-1.38	5.12	10.80
Nonproducers' utility	0.02	0.06	0.02	-0.09	-0.09	-0.09	0.19	0.41
Total industry profits	0.91	6.93	-0.59	-4.78	-9.20	-13.79	-11.49	-100.00
Average industry profits	0.91	24.75	-13.02	11.09	-9.20	0.58	-11.49	-100.00
(D) Complementary policies (farmers – firms)								
Farm-gate price	2.23	7.34	2.51	-2.93	-2.02	-3.79	23.05	48.87
Quantities	20.70	24.95	20.94	16.28	17.06	15.53	37.36	55.86
Total utility	3.97	4.07	3.97	3.87	3.89	3.86	4.37	4.87
Total industry profits	20.04	27.67	17.97	13.63	8.15	3.13	6.64	-100.00
Average industry profits	20.04	48.95	3.22	32.56	8.15	20.32	6.64	-100.00
(E) International prices								
Farm-gate price	22.70	27.97	23.41	16.92	18.38	16.05	43.85	74.50
Quantities	15.83	19.27	16.30	11.96	12.95	11.37	29.16	46.52
Total utility	0.37	0.46	0.39	0.28	0.30	0.26	0.73	1.26
Producers' utility	4.93	6.10	5.09	3.65	3.97	3.46	9.66	16.58
Nonproducers' utility	0.19	0.23	0.19	0.14	0.15	0.13	0.36	0.63
Total industry profits	24.65	31.55	20.12	21.53	13.81	12.73	19.02	-100.00
Average industry profits	24.65	15.11	5.11	41.79	13.81	31.52	19.02	-100.00

Table A4.2: *(1) Zambia, tobacco (percentage changes).*

	Respect to original	Leader split	Small entrant	Leaders merge	Leaders merge and small entrant	Exit of largest	Equal market shares	Perfect competition
(A) Basic model								
Farm-gate price	0.00	9.63	2.20	-7.33	-3.44	-13.90	21.42	64.45
Quantities	0.00	6.95	1.62	-5.52	-2.56	-10.64	15.05	41.40
Total utility	0.00	0.03	0.01	-0.02	-0.01	-0.04	0.07	0.21
Producers' utility	0.00	1.46	0.33	-2.89	-1.36	-5.40	3.33	10.64
Nonproducers' utility	0.00	0.02	0.00	0.00	0.00	0.00	0.04	0.13
Switchers' utility	0.00	25.62	25.62	-20.24	-20.22	-20.25	25.69	26.23
Total industry profits	0.00	7.64	-7.98	12.08	-0.05	-21.17	11.26	-100.00
Average industry profits	0.00	-13.89	-26.38	49.44	-0.05	5.10	11.26	-100.00
(B) Complementary policies (farmers)								
Farm-gate price	-0.52	9.13	1.74	-7.91	-3.93	-14.42	20.75	64.45
Quantities	16.95	24.97	18.87	10.54	14.02	4.68	34.13	64.71
Total utility	1.51	1.54	1.51	1.48	1.49	1.46	1.58	1.75
Total industry profits	17.90	26.52	8.33	32.16	17.72	-6.49	31.74	-100.00
Average industry profits	17.90	1.22	-13.34	76.21	17.72	24.68	31.74	-100.00

Table A4.2: *(I) Continued.*

	Respect to original	Leader split	Small entrant	Leaders merge	Leaders merge and small entrant	Exit of largest	Equal market shares	Perfect competition
(C) Complementary policies (firms)								
Farm-gate price	1.34	10.96	3.68	-6.10	-2.02	-12.53	22.32	65.74
Quantities	0.99	7.88	2.69	-4.58	-1.50	-9.55	15.64	42.12
Total utility	0.00	0.03	0.01	-0.02	-0.01	-0.04	0.07	0.22
Producers' utility	0.20	1.66	0.55	-2.41	-0.81	-4.88	3.47	10.86
Nonproducers' utility	0.00	0.02	0.01	-0.01	-0.01	-0.01	0.04	0.14
Total industry profits	0.92	7.79	-7.48	13.25	0.67	-18.93	12.86	-100.00
Average industry profits	0.92	-13.76	-25.98	51.00	0.67	8.10	12.86	-100.00
(D) Complementary policies (farmers − firms)								
Farm-gate price	0.81	10.45	3.21	-6.69	-2.53	-13.06	21.64	65.74
Quantities	18.08	26.03	20.10	11.62	15.23	5.92	34.81	65.53
Total utility	1.51	1.55	1.52	1.49	1.50	1.46	1.59	1.76
Total industry profits	19.01	26.74	8.94	33.56	18.60	-3.84	33.62	-100.00
Average industry profits	19.01	1.39	-12.84	78.08	18.60	28.22	33.62	-100.00
(E) International prices								
Farm-gate price	16.05	26.60	19.24	7.37	12.66	0.90	37.24	87.33
Quantities	11.41	18.47	13.58	5.35	9.07	0.66	25.27	53.77
Total utility	0.05	0.08	0.06	0.02	0.04	0.00	0.12	0.30
Producers' utility	2.46	4.17	2.97	1.11	1.93	0.13	5.94	14.71
Nonproducers' utility	0.03	0.05	0.04	0.01	0.02	0.00	0.07	0.18
Total industry profits	24.05	28.71	12.25	39.74	22.92	6.41	41.05	-100.00
Average industry profits	24.05	2.97	-10.20	86.32	22.92	41.88	41.05	-100.00

Table A4.3: *Impact of supply chain changes on the outgrower contract model: (a) Zambia, cotton (percentage changes).*

	Respect to original	Leader split	Small entrant	Leaders merge	Leaders merge and small entrant	Exit of largest	Equal market shares	Perfect competition
(A) Basic model								
Farm-gate price	0.00	8.93	1.01	−8.62	−6.22	−11.84	27.28	71.64
Quantities	0.00	5.24	0.54	−5.21	−3.85	−7.59	14.85	35.32
Total utility	0.00	0.09	0.01	−0.08	−0.06	−0.12	0.26	0.74
Producers' utility	0.00	1.59	0.09	−2.57	−2.03	−4.03	4.64	13.83
Nonproducers' utility	0.00	0.04	0.00	0.00	0.00	0.00	0.12	0.33
Switchers' utility	0.00	18.56	18.54	−14.89	−14.86	−14.92	18.11	18.89
Total industry profits	0.00	10.19	−3.93	−0.10	−7.65	−22.38	−1.93	−100.00
Average industry profits	0.00	10.19	−19.94	24.87	−7.65	−2.98	−1.93	−100.00
Interest rate	0.00	1.82	1.67	−5.36	−1.26	0.38	11.01	11.01
(B) Complementary policies (farmers)								
Farm-gate price	−0.56	8.30	0.52	−9.20	−6.73	−12.39	26.51	71.64
Quantities	14.18	20.01	14.83	8.31	9.89	5.66	30.70	53.88
Total utility	1.42	1.52	1.43	1.34	1.36	1.29	1.71	2.26
Total industry profits	14.69	26.40	9.95	14.75	5.92	−10.42	13.57	−100.00
Average industry profits	14.69	26.40	−8.38	43.44	5.92	11.98	13.57	−100.00
Interest rate	0.37	2.13	2.10	−5.00	−0.85	0.56	11.01	11.01

Table A4.3: *(a) Continued.*

	Respect to original	Leader split	Small entrant	Leaders merge	Leaders merge and small entrant	Exit of largest	Equal market shares	Perfect competition
(C) Complementary policies (firms)								
Farm-gate price	2.32	11.16	3.51	−6.38	−3.76	−9.52	29.01	74.14
Quantities	1.37	6.48	2.00	−3.81	−2.34	−6.09	15.73	36.35
Total utility	0.02	0.11	0.03	−0.06	−0.04	−0.10	0.27	0.76
Producers' utility	0.37	1.97	0.48	−1.88	−1.29	−3.30	4.99	14.36
Nonproducers' utility	0.01	0.05	0.02	−0.06	−0.06	−0.06	0.13	0.35
Total industry profits	0.71	10.45	−3.84	1.13	−6.96	−20.16	0.57	−100.00
Average industry profits	0.71	−7.96	−19.86	26.42	−6.96	−0.20	0.57	−100.00
Interest rate	1.04	2.78	2.88	−4.22	−0.02	0.98	11.01	11.01
(D) Complementary policies (farmers − firms)								
Farm-gate price	1.74	10.59	3.00	−6.97	−4.29	−10.09	28.22	74.14
Quantities	15.70	21.43	16.45	9.87	11.57	7.34	31.68	55.02
Total utility	1.45	1.55	1.46	1.36	1.38	1.31	1.73	2.29
Total industry profits	15.55	26.34	10.12	16.21	6.76	−7.84	16.44	−100.00
Average industry profits	15.55	5.28	−8.23	45.27	6.76	15.20	16.44	−100.00
Interest rate	1.37	3.18	3.27	−3.89	0.34	1.15	11.01	11.01
(E) International prices								
Farm-gate price	20.76	30.53	22.84	10.87	14.65	7.72	47.56	101.32
Quantities	11.73	16.75	12.73	6.48	8.41	4.49	24.79	46.81
Total utility	0.21	0.30	0.22	0.11	0.14	0.07	0.47	1.07
Producers' utility	3.77	5.61	4.04	2.14	2.60	1.30	8.79	20.14
Nonproducers' utility	0.10	0.14	0.10	0.05	0.07	0.04	0.22	0.49
Total industry profits	21.97	29.31	14.08	24.84	13.08	4.05	29.16	−100.00
Average industry profits	21.97	7.76	−4.93	56.04	13.08	30.07	29.16	−100.00
Interest rate	4.23	6.31	6.58	−0.78	3.68	2.79	11.01	11.01

Table A4.3: *(b) Benin, cotton (percentage changes).*

	Respect to original	Leader split	Small entrant	Leaders merge	Leaders merge and small entrant	Exit of largest	Equal market shares	Perfect competition
(A) Basic model								
Farm-gate price	0.00	9.54	0.25	-1.91	-1.45	-10.46	57.47	97.39
Quantities	0.00	4.72	0.13	-0.99	-0.76	-6.83	26.25	40.56
Total utility	0.00	0.19	0.00	-0.04	-0.03	-0.33	1.37	2.41
Producers' utility	0.00	1.74	0.04	-0.58	-0.45	-4.95	13.68	24.04
Nonproducers' utility	0.00	0.08	0.00	0.00	0.00	0.00	0.51	0.89
Switchers' utility	0.00	19.87	20.64	-15.89	-15.84	-15.90	20.47	21.59
Total industry profits	0.00	37.56	-0.97	4.56	2.85	-64.27	-15.58	-100.00
Average industry profits	0.00	57.21	-11.97	19.50	2.85	-59.16	-15.58	-100.00
Interest rate	0.00	12.21	0.43	-2.49	-1.71	17.67	19.35	19.35
(B) Complementary policies (farmers)								
Farm-gate price	-0.43	9.00	-0.15	-2.38	-1.87	-10.88	56.65	97.39
Quantities	13.64	18.85	13.80	12.51	12.80	6.06	42.63	58.73
Total utility	2.33	2.54	2.34	2.29	2.30	1.97	3.87	5.05
Total industry profits	13.09	55.32	11.84	18.36	16.24	-58.62	-2.66	-100.00
Average industry profits	13.09	77.51	-0.59	35.27	16.24	-52.71	-2.66	-100.00
Interest rate	0.74	12.67	1.22	-1.73	-0.91	17.72	19.35	19.35

Table A4.3: *(b) Continued.*

	Respect to original	Leader split	Small entrant	Leaders merge	Leaders merge and small entrant	Exit of largest	Equal market shares	Perfect competition
(C) Complementary policies (firms)								
Farm-gate price	1.81	11.05	2.14	−0.16	0.39	−8.53	58.09	98.21
Quantities	0.95	5.48	1.12	−0.06	0.22	−5.67	26.50	40.83
Total utility	0.04	0.22	0.05	0.00	0.01	−0.28	1.39	2.43
Producers' utility	0.37	2.08	0.42	−0.01	0.09	−4.24	13.83	24.25
Nonproducers' utility	0.02	0.09	0.02	−0.09	0.00	−0.09	0.51	0.90
Total industry profits	−2.08	34.46	−3.33	2.56	0.54	−62.97	−14.98	−100.00
Average industry profits	−2.08	53.67	−14.07	17.21	0.54	−57.68	−14.98	−100.00
Interest rate	1.60	13.01	2.14	−0.80	0.06	17.77	19.35	19.35
(D) Complementary policies (farmers − firms)								
Farm-gate price	1.37	10.49	1.74	−0.64	−0.04	−8.96	57.26	98.21
Quantities	14.70	19.69	14.90	13.55	13.89	7.36	42.90	59.02
Total utility	2.38	2.58	2.39	2.33	2.35	2.02	3.88	5.07
Total industry profits	10.79	51.90	9.23	16.16	13.70	−57.13	−1.97	−100.00
Average industry profits	10.79	73.60	−2.91	32.75	13.70	−51.00	−1.97	−100.00
Interest rate	2.28	13.43	2.86	−0.10	0.79	17.82	19.35	19.35
(E) International prices								
Farm-gate price	18.43	27.44	19.15	15.97	17.00	7.53	75.23	121.23
Quantities	9.49	14.03	9.82	8.35	8.82	3.42	32.96	47.94
Total utility	0.44	0.69	0.45	0.39	0.41	0.11	1.83	3.04
Producers' utility	4.28	6.84	4.42	3.77	3.98	0.93	18.29	30.20
Nonproducers' utility	0.17	0.26	0.17	0.15	0.16	0.06	0.67	1.12
Total industry profits	5.85	43.18	3.21	1.66	8.02	−50.61	2.46	−100.00
Average industry profits	5.85	43.18	−8.22	7.61	8.02	−43.55	2.46	−100.00
Interest rate	6.86	2.60	7.71	4.78	5.84	18.12	19.35	19.35

Table A4.3: *(c) Burkina Faso, cotton (percentage changes).*

	Respect to original	Leader split	Small entrant	Leaders merge	Leaders merge and small entrant	Exit of largest	Equal market shares	Perfect competition
(A) Basic model								
Farm-gate price	0.00	22.44	1.01	-3.28	-1.25	-27.59	37.93	89.38
Quantities	0.00	18.56	0.68	-2.25	-0.88	-28.65	30.40	71.41
Total utility	0.00	0.10	0.00	-0.01	0.00	-0.15	0.16	0.45
Producers' utility	0.00	3.24	0.03	-0.59	-0.25	-11.45	5.52	15.82
Nonproducers' utility	0.00	0.05	0.00	0.00	0.00	0.00	0.09	0.24
Switchers' utility	0.00	20.80	21.61	-17.89	-17.88	-18.36	20.27	21.79
Total industry profits	0.00	2.69	-2.81	8.22	2.68	-67.07	-13.19	-100.00
Average industry profits	0.00	54.04	-27.11	62.33	2.68	-50.60	-13.19	-100.00
Interest rate	0.00	39.28	5.63	-18.47	-6.28	38.82	67.13	67.13
(B) Complementary policies (farmers)								
Farm-gate price	-0.63	21.37	0.49	-4.07	-1.87	-28.14	36.97	89.38
Quantities	25.42	47.93	26.37	22.48	24.32	-9.82	62.57	113.40
Total utility	5.43	5.54	5.43	5.42	5.42	5.24	5.62	5.98
Total industry profits	25.23	30.17	21.33	36.00	28.50	-57.74	10.24	-100.00
Average industry profits	25.23	95.25	-9.01	103.99	28.50	-36.61	10.24	-100.00
Interest rate	2.35	39.28	8.47	-16.71	-3.72	38.83	67.13	67.13

Table A4.3: *(c) Continued.*

	Respect to original	Leader split	Small entrant	Leaders merge	Leaders merge and small entrant	Exit of largest	Equal market shares	Perfect competition
(C) Complementary policies (firms)								
Farm-gate price	2.53	23.93	3.85	-1.22	1.31	-25.00	39.64	91.87
Quantities	2.08	19.88	2.99	-0.51	1.21	-26.05	31.85	73.28
Total utility	0.01	0.10	0.01	0.00	0.01	-0.14	0.17	0.46
Producers' utility	0.30	3.54	0.35	0.04	0.23	-10.57	5.86	16.32
Nonproducers' utility	0.01	0.06	0.01	-0.03	0.00	-0.03	0.09	0.25
Total industry profits	-0.30	5.39	-3.92	8.94	2.17	-64.42	-10.90	-100.00
Average industry profits	-0.30	58.08	-27.94	63.41	2.17	-46.63	-10.90	-100.00
Interest rate	6.36	39.28	13.22	-13.49	0.76	38.87	67.13	67.13
(D) Complementary policies (farmers – firms)								
Farm-gate price	1.88	22.85	3.32	-2.03	0.67	-25.57	38.67	91.87
Quantities	27.98	49.53	29.20	24.61	26.89	-6.62	64.32	115.66
Total utility	5.44	5.55	5.44	5.43	5.43	5.26	5.63	6.00
Total industry profits	24.91	33.54	20.00	36.94	27.92	-54.38	13.12	-100.00
Average industry profits	24.91	100.31	-10.00	105.42	27.92	-31.57	13.12	-100.00
Interest rate	8.49	39.28	15.78	-11.88	3.08	38.88	67.13	67.13
(E) International prices								
Farm-gate price	21.97	41.33	24.75	15.87	20.74	-8.02	59.38	120.79
Quantities	18.90	34.88	20.81	14.69	18.01	-9.46	48.08	94.29
Total utility	0.10	0.20	0.11	0.08	0.10	-0.06	0.28	0.63
Producers' utility	3.55	7.02	3.81	3.04	3.42	-4.52	9.83	22.00
Nonproducers' utility	0.06	0.11	0.06	0.05	0.05	-0.27	0.15	0.35
Total industry profits	19.64	38.15	11.81	35.04	21.74	-44.40	17.65	-100.00
Average industry profits	19.64	38.15	-16.15	102.56	21.74	-16.59	17.65	-100.00
Interest rate	25.46	39.89	35.61	1.86	21.80	39.02	67.13	67.13

Table A4.3: *(d) Côte d'Ivoire, cotton (percentage changes).*

	Respect to original	Leader split	Small entrant	Leaders merge	Leaders merge and small entrant	Exit of largest	Equal market shares	Perfect competition
(A) Basic model								
Farm-gate price	0.00	8.86	0.76	-7.40	-5.44	-11.46	26.85	67.20
Quantities	0.00	5.68	0.44	-4.79	-3.59	-8.01	16.08	37.17
Total utility	0.00	0.14	0.01	-0.11	-0.08	-0.19	0.41	1.10
Producers' utility	0.00	2.01	0.11	-2.50	-1.96	-4.44	5.91	15.92
Nonproducers' utility	0.00	0.06	0.00	0.00	0.00	0.00	0.17	0.44
Switchers' utility	0.00	19.55	19.48	-15.86	-15.83	-15.92	19.34	20.43
Total industry profits	0.00	10.24	-3.27	3.54	-3.49	-24.63	-1.17	-100.00
Average industry profits	0.00	10.24	-19.39	29.43	-3.49	-5.79	-1.17	-100.00
Interest rate	0.00	1.85	1.35	-5.79	-2.17	1.29	10.84	10.84
(B) Complementary policies (farmers)								
Farm-gate price	-0.54	8.24	0.28	-7.97	-5.94	-12.00	26.09	67.20
Quantities	16.16	22.60	16.71	10.67	12.09	7.03	34.35	58.64
Total utility	2.97	3.13	2.98	2.84	2.87	2.75	3.44	4.24
Total industry profits	16.73	28.70	12.63	21.01	12.57	-11.34	16.52	-100.00
Average industry profits	16.73	28.70	-6.14	51.26	12.57	10.82	16.52	-100.00
Interest rate	0.39	2.18	1.81	-5.39	-1.71	1.45	10.84	10.84

Table A4.3: *(d) Continued.*

	Respect to original	Leader split	Small entrant	Leaders merge	Leaders merge and small entrant	Exit of largest	Equal market shares	Perfect competition
(C) Complementary policies (firms)								
Farm-gate price	2.62	11.28	3.56	-4.89	-2.70	-8.86	28.88	70.06
Quantities	1.68	7.17	2.23	-3.10	-1.78	-6.18	17.24	38.53
Total utility	0.04	0.18	0.05	-0.07	-0.04	-0.15	0.45	1.15
Producers' utility	0.56	2.56	0.71	-1.60	-0.99	-3.49	6.41	16.64
Nonproducers' utility	0.02	0.07	0.02	-0.09	-0.09	-0.09	0.18	0.47
Total industry profits	1.16	11.50	-2.84	5.18	-2.56	-21.78	1.87	-100.00
Average industry profits	1.16	11.50	-19.03	31.48	-2.56	-2.22	1.87	-100.00
Interest rate	1.09	2.68	2.65	-4.56	-0.79	1.82	10.84	10.84
(D) Complementary policies (farmers – firms)								
Farm-gate price	2.05	10.65	3.07	-5.48	-3.22	-9.42	28.11	70.06
Quantities	18.07	24.28	18.74	12.59	14.14	9.10	35.66	60.16
Total utility	3.01	3.17	3.03	2.89	2.92	2.80	3.47	4.29
Total industry profits	18.14	30.23	13.20	22.97	13.73	-7.98	20.07	-100.00
Average industry profits	18.14	30.23	-5.67	53.71	13.73	15.03	20.07	-100.00
Interest rate	1.43	2.97	3.07	-4.20	-0.38	1.96	10.84	10.84
(E) International prices								
Farm-gate price	22.32	31.77	24.16	13.61	16.98	9.62	48.72	98.22
Quantities	13.79	19.13	14.75	8.81	10.66	6.09	28.00	51.05
Total utility	0.36	0.51	0.38	0.23	0.27	0.15	0.78	1.65
Producers' utility	5.16	7.39	5.49	3.32	3.91	2.12	11.32	23.62
Nonproducers' utility	0.15	0.21	0.16	0.09	0.11	0.06	0.32	0.67
Total industry profits	25.19	33.63	17.41	32.09	20.05	5.54	33.69	-100.00
Average industry profits	25.19	11.36	-2.16	65.11	20.05	31.93	33.69	-100.00
Interest rate	4.34	6.16	6.52	-0.93	3.25	3.35	10.84	10.84

Table A4.3: *(e) Malawi, cotton (percentage changes).*

	Respect to original	Three firms	Four firms	Small entrant with half of the benefits
(A) Basic model				
Farm-gate price	0.00	12.25	19.77	6.16
Quantities	0.00	9.80	15.75	4.49
Total utility	0.00	0.01	0.02	0.01
Producers' utility	0.00	1.28	2.23	0.31
Nonproducers' utility	0.00	0.01	0.01	0.00
Switchers' utility	0.00	17.71	17.23	17.89
Total industry profits	0.00	−16.27	−28.59	−17.27
Average industry profits	0.00	−44.18	−64.29	−44.84
Interest rate	0.00	22.22	33.33	17.38
(B) Complementary policies (farmers)				
Farm-gate price	−0.75	11.59	19.19	5.55
Quantities	25.66	37.90	45.35	31.37
Total utility	4.62	4.64	4.65	4.63
Total industry profits	27.48	6.92	−8.70	5.41
Average industry profits	27.48	−28.72	−54.35	−29.73
Interest rate	0.00	22.22	33.33	17.54
(C) Complementary policies (firms)				
Farm-gate price	2.07	14.61	22.30	8.13
Quantities	2.00	11.98	18.05	6.38
Total utility	0.00	0.02	0.03	0.01
Producers' utility	0.41	1.76	2.75	0.73
Nonproducers' utility	0.00	0.01	0.02	0.01
Total industry profits	4.52	−12.46	−25.32	−13.18
Average industry profits	4.52	−41.64	−62.66	−42.12
Interest rate	0.00	22.22	33.33	16.97
(D) Complementary policies (farmers – firms)				
Farm-gate price	1.30	13.93	21.71	7.50
Quantities	28.11	40.58	48.16	33.69
Total utility	4.63	4.64	4.66	4.63
Total industry profits	33.18	11.73	− 4.57	10.54
Average industry profits	33.18	−25.51	−52.28	−26.31
Interest rate	0.00	22.22	33.33	17.14
(E) International prices				
Farm-gate price	19.58	34.57	43.82	24.82
Quantities	18.56	30.07	37.07	22.12
Total utility	0.04	0.06	0.07	0.04
Producers' utility	3.96	5.89	7.22	4.31
Nonproducers' utility	0.02	0.03	0.04	0.02
Total industry profits	46.79	23.24	5.31	26.35
Average industry profits	46.79	−17.84	−47.34	−15.77
Interest rate	0.00	22.22	33.33	13.63

Table A4.3: *(f) Côte d'Ivoire, cocoa (percentage changes).*

	Respect to original	Leader split	Small entrant	Leaders merge	Leaders merge and small entrant	Exit of largest	Equal market shares	Perfect competition
(A) Basic model								
Farm-gate price	0.00	1.95	0.37	-1.88	-1.38	-2.18	18.25	37.21
Quantities	0.00	0.86	0.15	-0.83	-0.62	-0.98	7.37	14.04
Total utility	0.00	0.14	0.02	-0.13	-0.10	-0.15	1.23	2.53
Producers' utility	0.00	0.61	0.10	-0.76	-0.58	-0.90	5.47	11.27
Nonproducers' utility	0.00	0.04	0.01	0.00	0.00	0.00	0.36	0.72
Switchers' utility	0.00	22.77	22.77	-15.49	-15.54	-15.45	22.89	23.36
Total industry profits	0.00	6.97	-2.92	-3.54	-7.11	-8.67	-1.34	-100.00
Average industry profits	0.00	0.29	-8.99	3.35	-7.11	-2.14	-1.34	-100.00
Interest rate	0.00	-0.22	0.23	0.01	0.31	0.33	1.77	1.77
(B) Complementary policies (farmers)								
Farm-gate price	-0.34	1.62	0.04	-2.23	-1.72	-2.53	17.81	37.21
Quantities	11.57	12.51	11.75	10.65	10.89	10.49	19.57	26.96
Total utility	2.89	3.04	2.91	2.74	2.78	2.72	4.24	5.71
Total industry profits	12.76	20.25	9.38	9.02	4.92	3.41	12.40	-100.00
Average industry profits	12.76	12.74	2.55	16.81	4.92	10.80	12.40	-100.00
Interest rate	0.08	-0.12	0.32	0.07	0.38	0.38	1.77	1.77

Table A4.3: *(f) Continued.*

	Respect to original	Leader split	Small entrant	Leaders merge	Leaders merge and small entrant	Exit of largest	Equal market shares	Perfect competition
(C) Complementary policies (firms)								
Farm-gate price	2.17	4.12	2.57	0.29	0.81	−0.01	20.03	39.38
Quantities	0.94	1.78	1.10	0.12	0.34	−0.02	8.04	14.74
Total utility	0.15	0.28	0.17	0.02	0.05	−0.01	1.35	2.68
Producers' utility	0.65	1.25	0.76	0.08	0.22	−0.03	6.01	11.93
Nonproducers' utility	0.04	0.08	0.05	0.01	0.02	−0.24	0.39	0.76
Total industry profits	1.30	7.61	−1.83	−1.73	−5.50	−6.58	1.31	−100.00
Average industry profits	1.30	0.88	−7.96	5.29	−5.50	0.09	1.31	−100.00
Interest rate	0.16	−0.01	0.41	0.15	0.45	0.43	1.77	1.77
(D) Complementary policies (farmers – firms)								
Farm-gate price	1.81	3.77	2.23	−0.08	0.47	−0.37	19.58	39.38
Quantities	12.59	13.51	12.78	11.69	11.94	11.54	20.29	27.73
Total utility	3.05	3.20	3.08	2.91	2.94	2.88	4.38	5.87
Total industry profits	14.29	21.05	10.68	11.12	6.80	5.81	15.40	−100.00
Average industry profits	14.29	13.49	3.77	19.06	6.80	13.37	15.40	−100.00
Interest rate	0.23	0.08	0.48	0.20	0.51	0.47	1.77	1.77
(E) International prices								
Farm-gate price	20.27	22.42	20.86	18.17	18.91	17.87	38.30	61.77
Quantities	8.17	8.97	8.38	7.39	7.66	7.27	14.39	21.44
Total utility	1.38	1.53	1.42	1.24	1.29	1.22	2.60	4.20
Producers' utility	6.16	6.82	6.32	5.52	5.73	5.42	11.60	18.74
Nonproducers' utility	0.40	0.44	0.41	0.36	0.37	0.35	0.74	1.19
Total industry profits	24.26	28.66	19.70	22.98	17.71	18.54	30.11	−100.00
Average industry profits	24.26	20.62	12.22	31.76	17.71	27.00	30.11	−100.00
Interest rate	0.69	0.67	0.96	0.57	0.89	0.76	1.77	1.77

Table A4.3: *(g) Ghana, cocoa (percentage changes).*

	Respect to original	Leader split	Small entrant	Leaders merge	Leaders merge and small entrant	Exit of largest	Equal market shares	Perfect competition
(A) Basic model								
Farm-gate price	0.00	3.43	0.28	-1.47	-1.05	-4.01	29.28	47.48
Quantities	0.00	2.49	0.18	-0.97	-0.71	-3.02	18.40	28.71
Total utility	0.00	0.06	0.00	-0.02	-0.02	-0.07	0.46	0.76
Producers' utility	0.00	0.95	0.05	-0.51	-0.38	-1.79	6.80	11.30
Nonproducers' utility	0.00	0.02	0.00	0.00	0.00	0.00	0.19	0.31
Switchers' utility	0.00	19.55	19.62	-15.83	-15.75	-15.78	19.56	20.05
Total industry profits	0.00	29.64	-2.19	3.73	0.68	-37.73	-7.41	-100.00
Average industry profits	0.00	18.84	-10.34	14.10	0.68	-31.50	-7.41	-100.00
Interest rate	0.00	-2.63	0.34	-0.83	-0.34	4.02	5.41	5.41
(B) Complementary policies (farmers)								
Farm-gate price	-0.29	3.15	0.02	-1.77	-1.33	-4.30	28.87	47.48
Quantities	17.06	19.90	17.27	15.93	16.25	13.60	38.00	49.99
Total utility	3.29	3.36	3.29	3.26	3.27	3.20	3.81	4.17
Total industry profits	17.41	51.22	14.69	21.88	18.15	-25.75	10.36	-100.00
Average industry profits	17.41	38.62	5.14	34.07	18.15	-18.32	10.36	-100.00
Interest rate	0.23	-2.26	0.58	-0.60	-0.10	4.05	5.41	5.41

Table A4.3: *(g) Continued.*

	Respect to original	Leader split	Small entrant	Leaders merge	Leaders merge and small entrant	Exit of largest	Equal market shares	Perfect competition
(C) Complementary policies (firms)								
Farm-gate price	2.67	6.07	3.00	1.17	1.65	-1.31	31.34	49.91
Quantities	1.80	4.23	2.00	0.82	1.12	-1.13	19.61	30.02
Total utility	0.04	0.10	0.05	0.02	0.03	-0.03	0.49	0.81
Producers' utility	0.60	1.54	0.66	0.29	0.38	-0.77	7.31	11.90
Nonproducers' utility	0.02	0.04	0.02	0.01	0.01	-0.09	0.20	0.33
Total industry profits	0.60	28.40	-1.91	4.56	1.17	-34.82	-4.56	-100.00
Average industry profits	0.60	17.70	-10.09	15.02	1.17	-28.30	-4.56	-100.00
Interest rate	0.55	-1.78	0.91	-0.27	0.25	4.09	5.41	5.41
(D) Complementary policies (farmers – firms)								
Farm-gate price	2.37	5.79	2.72	0.86	1.35	-1.62	30.92	49.91
Quantities	19.11	21.89	19.36	17.98	18.33	15.76	39.38	51.48
Total utility	3.33	3.40	3.34	3.31	3.32	3.25	3.85	4.22
Total industry profits	18.20	49.88	15.10	22.94	18.81	-22.29	13.73	-100.00
Average industry profits	18.20	37.39	5.51	35.23	18.81	-14.52	13.73	-100.00
Interest rate	0.75	-1.44	1.13	-0.06	0.47	4.12	5.41	5.41
(E) International prices								
Farm-gate price	22.95	26.63	23.51	21.17	21.91	18.65	51.98	74.36
Quantities	14.78	17.09	15.10	13.73	14.16	12.00	31.13	42.50
Total utility	0.37	0.43	0.37	0.34	0.35	0.29	0.84	1.22
Producers' utility	5.42	6.40	5.54	5.03	5.18	4.25	12.41	17.96
Nonproducers' utility	0.15	0.17	0.15	0.14	0.14	0.12	0.34	0.50
Total industry profits	22.68	47.44	18.26	28.44	22.90	-9.13	26.14	-100.00
Average industry profits	22.68	35.15	8.40	41.28	22.90	-0.04	26.14	-100.00
Interest rate	2.20	0.83	2.66	1.42	2.02	4.31	5.41	5.41

Table A4.3: *(h) Côte d'Ivoire, coffee (percentage changes).*

	Respect to original	Leader split	Small entrant	Leaders merge	Leaders merge and small entrant	Exit of largest	Equal market shares	Perfect competition
(A) Basic model								
Farm-gate price	0.00	1.52	0.29	-1.47	-1.08	-1.70	14.26	27.57
Quantities	0.00	0.91	0.16	-0.88	-0.66	-1.04	8.00	14.91
Total utility	0.00	0.04	0.01	-0.04	-0.03	-0.05	0.37	0.73
Producers' utility	0.00	0.40	0.06	-0.57	-0.44	-0.68	3.59	7.09
Nonproducers' utility	0.00	0.01	0.00	0.00	0.00	0.00	0.13	0.26
Switchers' utility	0.00	19.68	19.85	-15.46	-15.42	-15.44	19.72	20.00
Total industry profits	0.00	6.80	-2.97	-3.23	-6.90	-8.26	-5.98	-100.00
Average industry profits	0.00	0.12	-9.03	3.69	-6.90	-1.71	-5.98	-100.00
Interest rate	0.00	-0.25	0.23	0.03	0.33	0.34	1.77	1.77
(B) Complementary policies (farmers)								
Farm-gate price	-0.25	1.27	0.05	-1.73	-1.32	-1.97	13.95	27.57
Quantities	14.66	15.68	14.84	13.66	13.92	13.49	23.58	31.48
Total utility	2.89	2.93	2.90	2.84	2.85	2.84	3.30	3.72
Total industry profits	15.87	23.35	12.34	12.41	8.07	6.74	10.06	-100.00
Average industry profits	15.87	15.64	5.32	20.44	8.07	14.37	10.06	-100.00
Interest rate	0.08	-0.15	0.31	0.09	0.39	0.39	1.77	1.77

Table A4.3: *(h) Continued.*

	Respect to original	Leader split	Small entrant	Leaders merge	Leaders merge and small entrant	Exit of largest	Equal market shares	Perfect competition
(C) Complementary policies (firms)								
Farm-gate price	2.55	4.07	2.87	1.08	1.50	0.85	16.51	30.17
Quantities	1.50	2.39	1.67	0.63	0.86	0.48	9.21	16.19
Total utility	0.07	0.11	0.07	0.03	0.04	0.02	0.43	0.80
Producers' utility	0.64	1.05	0.71	0.27	0.36	0.19	4.18	7.78
Nonproducers' utility	0.02	0.04	0.03	0.01	0.01	0.01	0.16	0.29
Total industry profits	2.05	8.14	-1.17	-0.62	-4.55	-5.40	-2.48	-100.00
Average industry profits	2.05	1.38	-7.35	6.48	-4.55	1.36	-2.48	-100.00
Interest rate	0.18	-0.02	0.41	0.17	0.47	0.45	1.77	1.77
(D) Complementary policies (farmers – firms)								
Farm-gate price	2.29	3.82	2.62	0.81	1.24	0.58	16.20	30.17
Quantities	16.33	17.33	16.53	15.35	15.62	15.18	24.93	32.91
Total utility	2.96	3.01	2.97	2.92	2.93	2.91	3.37	3.79
Total industry profits	18.31	24.99	14.49	15.48	10.85	10.12	14.12	-100.00
Average industry profits	18.31	17.17	7.33	23.73	10.85	17.98	14.12	-100.00
Interest rate	0.25	0.07	0.49	0.23	0.53	0.50	1.77	1.77
(E) International prices								
Farm-gate price	22.39	24.08	22.86	20.73	21.32	20.50	36.53	53.31
Quantities	12.34	13.20	12.57	11.49	11.78	11.36	19.26	26.86
Total utility	0.59	0.64	0.60	0.55	0.56	0.54	0.97	1.42
Producers' utility	5.79	6.23	5.89	5.36	5.49	5.28	9.46	13.91
Nonproducers' utility	0.21	0.23	0.22	0.20	0.20	0.19	0.35	0.51
Total industry profits	30.06	34.09	25.14	29.38	23.62	24.92	30.93	-100.00
Average industry profits	30.06	25.71	17.31	38.62	23.62	33.84	30.93	-100.00
Interest rate	0.72	0.69	0.98	0.60	0.92	0.79	1.77	1.77

Table A4.3: *(i) Rwanda, coffee (percentage changes).*

	Respect to original	Leader split	Small entrant	Leaders merge	Leaders merge and small entrant	Exit of largest	Equal market shares	Perfect competition
(A) Basic model								
Farm-gate price	0.00	4.45	0.57	−5.85	−4.25	−6.09	8.72	31.91
Quantities	0.00	4.01	0.46	−5.33	−4.00	−5.58	7.88	28.87
Total utility	0.00	0.01	0.00	−0.02	−0.01	−0.02	0.03	0.11
Producers' utility	0.00	0.76	0.06	−2.05	−1.60	−2.15	1.54	6.26
Nonproducers' utility	0.00	0.01	0.00	0.00	0.00	0.00	0.01	0.06
Switchers' utility	0.00	19.83	20.00	−16.66	−16.66	−16.64	19.82	20.37
Total industry profits	0.00	−4.15	−4.01	4.18	−4.98	2.48	−4.67	−100.00
Average industry profits	0.00	−4.15	−20.00	30.22	−4.98	28.10	−4.67	−100.00
Interest rate	0.00	2.71	1.10	−3.95	−0.92	−3.68	4.34	4.34
(B) Complementary policies (farmers)								
Farm-gate price	−0.40	4.03	0.22	−6.30	−4.63	−6.53	8.28	31.91
Quantities	26.10	31.04	26.72	19.45	21.16	19.14	35.79	62.14
Total utility	5.71	5.72	5.71	5.68	5.69	5.68	5.74	5.85
Total industry profits	27.55	22.59	22.07	33.10	21.17	30.99	22.32	−100.00
Average industry profits	27.55	2.16	1.73	66.38	21.17	63.73	22.32	−100.00
Interest rate	0.16	2.79	1.34	−3.81	−0.73	−3.55	4.34	4.34

Table A4.3: *(i) Continued.*

	Respect to original	Leader split	Small entrant	Leaders merge	Leaders merge and small entrant	Exit of largest	Equal market shares	Perfect competition
(C) Complementary policies (firms)								
Farm-gate price	2.30	6.75	2.99	-3.62	-1.86	-3.85	10.84	34.57
Quantities	2.16	6.14	2.71	-3.20	-1.75	-3.44	9.84	31.21
Total utility	0.01	0.02	0.01	-0.01	-0.01	-0.01	0.03	0.12
Producers' utility	0.43	1.20	0.52	-1.20	-0.70	-1.31	1.96	6.81
Nonproducers' utility	0.00	0.01	0.00	-0.02	-0.02	-0.02	0.02	0.06
Total industry profits	3.07	-1.27	-1.80	8.00	-2.04	6.35	-0.66	-100.00
Average industry profits	3.07	-17.72	-18.17	35.00	-2.04	32.94	-0.66	-100.00
Interest rate	0.39	3.03	1.67	-3.59	-0.43	-3.34	4.34	4.34
(D) Complementary policies (farmers – firms)								
Farm-gate price	1.89	6.37	2.63	-4.08	-2.25	-4.31	10.38	34.57
Quantities	28.75	33.71	29.50	22.07	23.95	21.77	38.21	65.01
Total utility	5.72	5.73	5.72	5.69	5.70	5.69	5.75	5.86
Total industry profits	31.48	25.76	24.91	37.97	24.93	35.92	27.41	-100.00
Average industry profits	31.48	4.80	4.09	72.46	24.93	69.90	27.41	-100.00
Interest rate	0.54	3.19	1.89	-3.46	-0.25	-3.22	4.34	4.34
(E) International prices								
Farm-gate price	21.09	26.20	22.40	14.28	16.88	14.04	29.74	58.40
Quantities	19.46	23.82	20.48	13.58	15.67	13.35	26.96	51.56
Total utility	0.07	0.09	0.08	0.05	0.06	0.05	0.10	0.21
Producers' utility	4.17	5.09	4.35	2.96	3.33	2.91	5.82	11.74
Nonproducers' utility	0.04	0.05	0.04	0.03	0.03	0.03	0.05	0.11
Total industry profits	39.16	31.14	29.36	48.56	32.50	46.82	38.69	-100.00
Average industry profits	39.16	9.29	7.80	85.70	32.50	83.53	38.69	-100.00
Interest rate	1.60	4.30	3.40	-2.49	1.07	-2.32	4.34	4.34

Table A4.3: *(i) Uganda, coffee (percentage changes).*

	Respect to original	Leader split	Small entrant	Leaders merge	Leaders merge and small entrant	Exit of largest	Equal market shares	Perfect competition
(A) Basic model								
Farm-gate price	0.00	0.96	0.14	-0.96	-0.76	-1.08	9.17	17.89
Quantities	0.00	0.78	0.10	-0.77	-0.62	-0.88	7.06	13.63
Total utility	0.00	0.01	0.00	-0.01	-0.01	-0.01	0.08	0.17
Producers' utility	0.00	0.22	0.02	-0.37	-0.31	-0.43	1.94	3.92
Nonproducers' utility	0.00	0.00	0.00	0.00	0.00	0.00	0.04	0.07
Switchers' utility	0.00	19.14	19.22	-15.98	-15.85	-15.87	19.09	19.26
Total industry profits	0.00	3.95	-2.11	-1.67	-4.52	-4.72	-14.50	-100.00
Average industry profits	0.00	-2.16	-7.87	4.89	-4.52	1.64	-14.50	-100.00
Interest rate	0.00	-0.12	0.15	-0.02	0.19	0.16	1.79	1.79
(B) Complementary policies (farmers)								
Farm-gate price	-0.18	0.79	-0.04	-1.15	-0.94	-1.27	8.96	17.89
Quantities	20.34	21.26	20.47	19.43	19.61	19.31	28.62	36.50
Total utility	3.89	3.90	3.89	3.88	3.88	3.88	3.99	4.09
Total industry profits	21.57	26.05	18.88	19.79	16.20	16.20	5.13	-100.00
Average industry profits	21.57	18.63	11.88	27.78	16.20	23.94	5.13	-100.00
Interest rate	0.08	-0.02	0.24	0.05	0.26	0.22	1.79	1.79

Table A4.3: *(i) Continued.*

	Respect to original	Leader split	Small entrant	Leaders merge	Leaders merge and small entrant	Exit of largest	Equal market shares	Perfect competition
(C) Complementary policies (firms)								
Farm-gate price	2.42	3.39	2.57	1.46	1.67	1.34	11.40	20.34
Quantities	1.91	2.68	2.02	1.15	1.31	1.05	8.76	15.44
Total utility	0.02	0.03	0.02	0.01	0.02	0.01	0.10	0.19
Producers' utility	0.52	0.74	0.55	0.31	0.35	0.28	2.45	4.48
Nonproducers' utility	0.01	0.01	0.01	0.01	0.01	0.01	0.05	0.08
Total industry profits	2.15	5.59	−0.23	0.93	−2.21	−1.98	−10.92	−100.00
Average industry profits	2.15	−0.62	−6.10	7.66	−2.21	4.56	−10.92	−100.00
Interest rate	0.17	0.08	0.33	0.13	0.34	0.29	1.79	1.79
(D) Complementary policies (farmers – firms)								
Farm-gate price	2.23	3.21	2.40	1.26	1.49	1.14	11.19	20.34
Quantities	22.58	23.49	22.72	21.68	21.88	21.56	30.61	38.62
Total utility	3.92	3.93	3.92	3.91	3.91	3.91	4.02	4.12
Total industry profits	24.24	28.10	21.22	23.00	19.07	19.58	9.49	−100.00
Average industry profits	24.24	20.57	14.09	31.20	19.07	27.55	9.49	−100.00
Interest rate	0.24	0.17	0.41	0.19	0.41	0.34	1.79	1.79
(E) International prices								
Farm-gate price	21.88	22.96	22.13	20.79	21.12	20.67	31.00	41.95
Quantities	16.64	17.42	16.81	15.86	16.08	15.76	23.09	30.62
Total utility	0.21	0.22	0.21	0.20	0.20	0.19	0.29	0.40
Producers' utility	4.89	5.14	4.94	4.65	4.71	4.62	6.94	9.48
Nonproducers' utility	0.09	0.10	0.09	0.09	0.09	0.09	0.13	0.18
Total industry profits	32.73	34.46	28.59	33.32	28.28	30.48	23.39	−100.00
Average industry profits	32.73	26.55	21.03	42.21	28.28	39.18	23.39	−100.00
Interest rate	0.70	0.72	0.89	0.57	0.81	0.68	1.79	1.79

Table A4.3: *(k) Malawi, tobacco (percentage changes).*

	Respect to original	Leader split	Small entrant	Leaders merge	Leaders merge and small entrant	Exit of largest	Equal market shares	Perfect competition
(A) Basic model								
Farm-gate price	0.00	5.46	0.14	-5.12	-4.37	-6.00	21.43	46.12
Quantities	0.00	3.90	0.09	-3.78	-3.29	-4.55	14.36	29.94
Total utility	0.00	0.08	0.00	-0.07	-0.07	-0.09	0.29	0.68
Producers' utility	0.00	1.21	0.02	-1.93	-1.72	-2.36	4.51	10.49
Nonproducers' utility	0.00	0.03	0.00	0.00	0.00	0.00	0.13	0.29
Switchers' utility	0.00	19.77	19.85	-16.25	-16.25	-16.23	19.56	20.31
Total industry profits	0.00	4.93	-0.89	-6.45	-10.37	-15.98	-15.12	-100.00
Average industry profits	0.00	22.41	-13.28	9.14	-10.37	-1.98	-15.12	-100.00
Interest rate	0.00	1.14	0.24	-0.79	0.54	1.01	10.27	8.65
(B) Complementary policies (farmers)								
Farm-gate price	-0.40	4.97	-0.22	-5.54	-4.74	-6.41	20.91	46.12
Quantities	18.44	22.90	18.57	14.03	14.64	13.15	35.00	53.33
Total utility	3.90	3.99	3.91	3.82	3.83	3.80	4.24	4.70
Total industry profits	18.86	25.22	17.52	11.56	6.67	0.45	2.30	-100.00
Average industry profits	18.86	46.09	2.83	30.15	6.67	17.19	2.30	-100.00
Interest rate	0.35	1.35	0.64	-0.51	0.89	1.23	10.28	8.65

Supply Chains in Sub-Saharan Africa

Table A4.3: *(k) Continued.*

	Respect to original	Leader split	Small entrant	Leaders merge	Leaders merge and small entrant	Exit of largest	Equal market shares	Perfect competition
(C) Complementary policies (firms)								
Farm-gate price	2.30	7.51	2.53	-2.84	-1.98	-3.70	23.28	48.44
Quantities	1.64	5.34	1.79	-2.10	-1.54	-2.84	15.58	31.32
Total utility	0.03	0.11	0.03	-0.04	-0.03	-0.06	0.32	0.71
Producers' utility	0.49	1.66	0.53	-1.09	-0.85	-1.51	4.95	11.04
Nonproducers' utility	0.01	0.05	0.02	-0.07	-0.07	-0.07	0.14	0.30
Total industry profits	0.52	6.39	-0.95	-5.17	-9.60	-14.27	-12.57	-100.00
Average industry profits	0.52	24.12	-13.33	10.64	-9.60	0.02	-12.57	-100.00
Interest rate	0.81	1.61	1.17	-0.09	1.37	1.55	10.27	8.65
(D) Complementary policies (farmers – firms)								
Farm-gate price	1.89	7.02	2.16	-3.27	-2.37	-4.12	22.75	48.44
Quantities	20.33	24.56	20.54	15.98	16.66	15.13	36.40	54.91
Total utility	3.94	4.03	3.94	3.85	3.87	3.84	4.28	4.74
Total industry profits	19.55	27.01	17.52	13.14	7.65	2.54	5.35	-100.00
Average industry profits	19.55	48.17	2.83	32.00	7.65	19.63	5.35	-100.00
Interest rate	1.13	1.80	1.54	0.17	1.69	1.75	10.28	8.65
(E) International prices								
Farm-gate price	20.98	26.22	21.66	15.25	16.66	14.38	42.19	72.32
Quantities	14.48	17.90	14.89	10.70	11.55	10.04	27.48	44.75
Total utility	0.31	0.38	0.31	0.22	0.24	0.21	0.61	1.09
Producers' utility	4.75	5.98	4.88	3.46	3.70	3.20	9.46	16.74
Nonproducers' utility	0.13	0.16	0.13	0.09	0.10	0.09	0.26	0.46
Total industry profits	22.32	29.45	18.04	19.02	11.50	10.11	15.51	-100.00
Average industry profits	22.32	13.27	3.29	38.86	11.50	28.46	15.51	-100.00
Interest rate	3.38	3.73	4.07	2.07	3.96	3.20	10.28	8.65

Table A4.3: *(I) Zambia, tobacco (percentage changes).*

	Respect to original	Leader split	Small entrant	Leaders merge	Leaders merge and small entrant	Exit of largest	Equal market shares	Perfect competition
(A) Basic model								
Farm-gate price	0.00	9.65	2.21	-7.38	-3.44	-13.90	21.46	64.45
Quantities	0.00	6.77	1.41	-5.03	-2.44	-10.54	14.60	40.86
Total utility	0.00	0.02	0.00	-0.01	-0.01	-0.03	0.05	0.17
Producers' utility	0.00	1.41	0.12	-1.82	-1.01	-4.54	3.19	11.12
Nonproducers' utility	0.00	0.01	0.00	0.00	0.00	0.00	0.03	0.09
Switchers' utility	0.00	17.25	17.16	-14.72	-14.73	-14.77	17.07	17.77
Total industry profits	0.00	7.44	-8.18	12.73	0.08	-21.07	10.72	-100.00
Average industry profits	0.00	-14.05	-26.54	50.30	0.08	5.23	10.72	-100.00
Interest rate	0.00	3.18	3.71	-9.50	-2.22	-1.90	7.52	7.52
(B) Complementary policies (farmers)								
Farm-gate price	-0.52	9.15	1.76	-7.95	-3.94	-14.42	20.79	64.45
Quantities	16.94	24.74	18.62	11.09	14.14	4.79	33.62	64.10
Total utility	1.50	1.53	1.51	1.49	1.49	1.46	1.56	1.70
Total industry profits	17.88	26.27	8.08	32.89	17.85	-6.38	31.12	-100.00
Average industry profits	17.88	1.02	-13.54	77.19	17.85	24.83	31.12	-100.00
Interest rate	0.23	3.48	3.98	-9.25	-1.93	-1.86	7.52	7.52

Table A4.3: *(I) Continued.*

	Respect to original	Leader split	Small entrant	Leaders merge	Leaders merge and small entrant	Exit of largest	Equal market shares	Perfect competition
(C) Complementary policies (firms)								
Farm-gate price	1.09	10.71	3.43	−6.38	−2.28	−12.76	22.11	65.38
Quantities	0.78	7.49	2.26	−4.29	−1.61	−9.65	15.04	41.39
Total utility	0.00	0.02	0.01	−0.01	0.00	−0.03	0.05	0.17
Producers' utility	0.15	1.56	0.29	−1.52	−0.66	−4.17	3.30	11.30
Nonproducers' utility	0.00	0.01	0.00	−0.01	−0.01	−0.01	0.03	0.09
Total industry profits	0.54	7.26	−8.01	13.46	0.43	−19.23	11.88	−100.00
Average industry profits	0.54	−14.20	−26.41	51.29	0.43	7.69	11.88	−100.00
Interest rate	0.49	3.75	4.29	−8.91	−1.57	−1.79	7.52	7.52
(D) Complementary policies (farmers – firms)								
Farm-gate price	0.56	10.20	2.97	−6.96	−2.79	−13.29	21.43	65.38
Quantities	17.83	25.56	19.59	11.94	15.10	5.82	34.12	64.70
Total utility	1.50	1.53	1.51	1.49	1.50	1.47	1.56	1.70
Producers' utility	18.55	26.09	8.31	33.78	18.30	−4.20	32.48	−100.00
Nonproducers' utility	18.55	0.87	−13.35	78.37	18.30	27.73	32.48	−100.00
Average industry profits	0.70	4.03	4.54	−8.68	−1.29	−1.76	7.52	7.52
(E) International prices								
Farm-gate price	14.83	25.32	17.96	6.20	11.42	−0.24	36.07	85.57
Quantities	10.44	17.27	12.33	4.92	8.17	−0.10	24.04	52.29
Total utility	0.04	0.06	0.04	0.02	0.03	0.00	0.09	0.23
Producers' utility	2.38	3.99	2.65	1.49	1.89	0.03	5.82	15.17
Nonproducers' utility	0.02	0.03	0.02	0.01	0.02	−0.11	0.05	0.12
Total industry profits	21.91	26.55	10.16	38.04	20.97	4.25	38.00	−100.00
Average industry profits	21.91	1.24	−11.87	84.06	20.97	39.00	38.00	−100.00
Interest rate	2.17	5.75	6.27	−6.91	0.67	−1.46	7.52	7.52

5

Supply Chain Simulations and Poverty Analysis in Sub-Saharan Africa

In this chapter, we estimate the impact on household income, at the farm level, of changes in the supply chain. In the previous chapter, using our theoretical model, we identified the farm-gate price changes generated by shocks to the level of competition in the value chain for our twelve case studies. We simulated seven alternative market configurations for the baseline model and we also allowed for complementary factors affecting farms, firms, or both and also for shocks to the international price of the crop. We also ran the same set of simulations under the extended model with outgrower contracts. In the end, we have seventy simulations with seventy corresponding changes in farm-gate prices, the main variable of interest for our analysis.

We now want to use these price changes and the household survey data described in Chapter 2 to carry out a comprehensive analysis of the impacts of changes in value chains on poverty and welfare. Using standard methods to approximate welfare changes with first-order effects (see Section 1), we estimate the impact on average household income for the total population as well as for the subset of export crop producers. Furthermore, the household data allows us to differentiate the effect among poor and nonpoor households, a distinction that will help us to understand under which circumstances commercial agriculture can work as an effective vehicle for poverty alleviation. We also explore gender issues by looking at results for male-headed and female-headed households and advance some explanations for any potential differential impacts.

In Section 2, we present the welfare implications of our simulations for each of the twelve country–crop case studies. Rather than providing a detailed discussion of the seventy simulations per case study, we focus, as in Chapter 4, on the case of cotton in Zambia. We then summarize the main findings and discrepancies for the other eleven cases grouped by crop to facilitate the comparison. We present all the tables with the simulation results for the interested reader.

1 THE METHODOLOGY

Our task is to estimate the welfare effects of the changes in farm-gate prices and in input costs due to complementary policies or changes in the conditions under which outgrower contracts are implemented. We adopt the standard first-order approach advanced by Deaton (1989).[1]

1.1 Calculation of Income Changes without Outgrower Contracts

To derive the formulas needed in the analysis, we start from the income–expenditure equation. This equation indicates that, in equilibrium, expenditures need to be covered with income (we can allow for transfers, savings, and so on). Suppose for simplicity that the farmer produces only two crops, the exportable crop q_1 and the subsistence crop q_2. Then we can write:

$$p \cdot c + r_1 v_1 = p_1 q_1 + p_2 q_2 + x_0. \tag{5.1}$$

In (5.1), $r_1 v_1$ is the "expenditure" in investment in sector 1 (we could also include a similar term for the second crop, but we do not need it for the analysis). The term $r_1 v_1$ includes expenditures in seeds, fertilizer, pesticides, and also interest payments on loans. The term $p \cdot c$ is total expenditure in goods and services. Finally, $p_1 q_1$ and $p_2 q_2$ are gross income from sales of product 1 and 2, respectively, and x_0 is an exogenous source of income.

We are first interested in studying the first-order effect assuming no changes in production costs. The welfare effect of a price change is defined as $-dx_0/y$, where $y = p_1 q_1 + p_2 q_2$. Assume that there is an increase in p_1, keeping v_1 and p_2 constant for the moment. We then have:

$$-\frac{dx_0}{y} = s_1 \, d \ln p_1.$$

This means that the proportional change in income dy/y is the product of the income share s_1 and the proportional change in prices (these are the price changes from the different simulations in the previous chapter). For example, if a household earns 50 percent of its income from cotton and the price of cotton increases by 10 percent, then the impact effect for the household would be equivalent to 5 percent of its initial income.

Assume now that the change in farm-gate price comes along with a change in the input cost due, for example, to complementary policies. Now, we have

$$-\frac{dx_0}{y} = s_1 \, d \ln p_1 - \frac{r_1 v_1}{y} \frac{dr_1}{r_1}.$$

One practical problem we face is that we do not observe input expenditures in the data. So, we will assume that the input expenditure is a constant fraction

---

[1] This approach has been extensively utilized in the literature. Early examples include Deaton (1989b), Budd (1993), Benjamin and Deaton (1993), Barret and Dorosh (1996), and Sahn and Sarris (1991). More recent examples include Ivanic and Martin (2008) and Wodon et al. (2008). Deaton (1997) provides an account of the early use of these techniques in distributional analysis of pricing policies.

of the total gross sales of the product $r_1 v_1 = \delta^* p_1 q_1$. In this case, we have that

$$-\frac{dx_0}{y} = s_1 \, d \ln p_1 - \delta s_1 \, d \ln r_1.$$

In practical terms, when simulating the impact of changes in the value chain together with complementary factors that affect farmers, we use $d \ln p_1$ calculated from the simulations, and we let $d \ln r_1 = -0.02$ (a decline of 2 percent in production costs). We assume $\delta = 0.5$ in our numeric simulations.

There is an important caveat to this approach. Our framework works well for things like seeds, fertilizer, etc., but not for labor. Suppose that the increase in competition for output also increases wages in the sector. Are there additional welfare effects? The answer depends on how farmers allocate their labor supply and how we measure welfare. Suppose the farmer only works on her farm. If wages increase, we have a welfare effect because now she earns more money on wages, but this is just a cost of production in our model. In our analysis, we will not deal with these effects.

1.2 Calculation of Income Changes with Outgrower Contracts

The model is the same as above:

$$p \cdot c + r_1 v_1 = p_1 q_1 + p_2 q_2 + x_0.$$

The difference is that now when there is a change in the supply chains, there are effects on output prices p_1 and also on the interest rate charged on inputs. Input expenditures are $r_1 v_1$, which, in turn, we assume equals a fraction δ of sales $p_1 q_1$

$$r_1 v_1 = \delta p_1 q_1.$$

As in the theoretical model, we will now assume that farmers finance a fraction λ of their expenditures in inputs with outgrower contracts. This means that the amount being financed is

$$\lambda r_1 v_1 = \lambda \delta p_1 q_1.$$

The farmer needs to pay interest on this equal to $r^* \lambda \delta p_1 q_1$. Hence,

$$p \cdot c + r_1 v_1 + r^* \lambda r_1 v_1 = p_1 q_1 + p_2 q_2 + x_0.$$

To calculate the welfare effects, allow changes in p_1 and in r

$$-\frac{dx_0}{y} = s_1 \, d \ln p_1 - \delta \lambda s_1 \, d \ln r.$$

As before, we also want to consider the case of changes in farm-gate prices that come along with a change in the input cost due, for example, to complementary policies. Taking this and the outgrower scheme into consideration, we have

$$-\frac{dx_0}{y} = s_1 \, d \ln p_1 - \delta \lambda s_1 \, d \ln r - \delta s_1 \, d \ln r_1.$$

Once again we assume $\delta = 0.5$ for our calculations.

2   WELFARE SIMULATIONS

Using the price changes generated by each of the seventy simulations of Chapter 4 and the methodology described in the previous section, here we study the effects of changes in the value chain on farmers' income for our twelve case studies. We explore the Zambian cotton case in detail and then we summarize the major findings from the remaining eleven case studies.

2.1   Cotton in Zambia

Most of the cotton seeds in Zambia are devoted to the exports of cotton lint. Atomistic farmers produce cotton which is purchased by the ginneries to produce cotton lint that later is exported to world markets. While two ginneries control 72 percent of the market and therefore can exercise monopsonistic power over farmers, their share in the world market is insignificant and consequently take the international price as given.

Baseline Model

Table A5.1(a) presents the simulation results for changes in household income for each of the seven market configurations and five scenarios in our leading case. The outcomes are also presented for different rural population groups. The exercise in the previous chapter showed that the change in farm-gate cotton prices ranged from −12 percent (in the case of exit of the largest firm under complementary policies for the farmers) to 104 percent (in the case of perfect competition under an increase of 10 percent in international prices). The overall impact of these prices changes on average household income depends on the share of cotton on total household income. In Chapter 2 we showed that most households in the survey do not produce cotton, or, when they do, in general they do not specialize in its production. For the average rural household in Zambia, cotton generates less than 3 percent of its total income. Among producers, the cotton share in income increases to 23 percent.

The main conclusion from the simulations is that, in our baseline model, competition among ginneries is good for the cotton farmers because they fetch a higher farm-gate price and therefore enjoy a higher level of income. For example, if Dunavant (the leader firm) splits, the increase in income for the average producer would be equivalent to 2.4 percent of its initial income. On the other hand, if the two largest firms (Dunavant and Cargill) were to merge, the income of the average producer would decline by 2.3 percent. The largest possible gain for the farmers comes under perfect competition, where farmers would enjoy an income gain of 19.3 percent. The upper bound increase in income under imperfect competition is 7.3 percent, and this takes place in the equal market share simulation. Another evident conclusion from our basic model is that small changes in the level of competition among ginneries are not likely to generate important impacts on farmers' income. For instance, a small firm entering the market would generate only an increase of one quarter of a percentage point in producers' income.

One concern often encountered in practice is to understand the implications of exit, in particular of the largest firm. The exit of Dunavant would imply a reduction in competition among the remaining firms that would impact negatively in the farm-gate price for cotton in Zambia. In addition, in our model, the largest firm is also the most efficient one (smallest marginal cost) so the exit would imply a reduction in the total demand for cotton, further depressing the farm-gate price. In our basic simulation, this is the worst scenario for producers, with an average income loss of 3.2 percent.

We also estimate the income effect under different complementary policies.[2] Figure A5.1 shows the income effect for producers in Zambia under the five different scenarios when we increase competition (leader split) and when we reduce it (leaders merge). The implementation of complementary policies and the positive international price shock intensify the positive effects of more competition and moderate the negative effects of a reduction in the level of competition among ginneries. The original increase of 2.4 percent in income for producers following the split of the leader becomes 2.8 percent under complementary policies for farmers, 3.1 percent when these policies affect firms, and 3.5 percent when they affect both farmers and firms. If the split of the leader takes place concurrently with an increase of 10 percent in international prices, the average producer earns 8.7 percent more income. On the other hand, if the leaders merge, a complementary policy affecting both farmers and firms will cut the income loss for producer households from 2.32 percent to 1.25 percent.

It should be noted that we are estimating only the first-order effects of the price changes and, in consequence, only farmers that were initially producers are affected. The nonproducers are in fact isolated from the changes in the supply chain, meaning both that they do not enjoy the benefits of increased competition, if any, or the losses from higher oligopsony power. In Table A5.1(a), we report the income changes for households that produce some cotton versus the whole population of rural households. Figure A5.2 illustrates the difference in income impacts for the two groups for different shocks to the level of competition for our basic model. For instance, in the case of equal market shares, producers would enjoy a gain of 7.3 percent while the gain for the whole rural population is only 0.8 percent. The qualitative results are the same for the complementary policies and increase in the international price scenarios.

Nonproducers are not affected because we are not incorporating estimates of second-order effects. The main reason to do this is that we do not have

---

[2]The literature on complementary policies to trade shocks includes Deininger and Olinto (2000), Eswaran and Kotwal (1986), Balat and Porto (2007), Key et al. (2000), and McKay et al. (1997).

a model to estimate those effects that can be convincingly utilized with sub-Saharan data. Estimates of second-order effects require estimates of supply responses, which in turn require some evidence on farm supply elasticities. Even if these elasticities were available, the estimated second-order welfare impacts would nevertheless be small because, in the margin, the returns to different economic activities are equalized. This may not necessarily be the case in the presence of distortions or market imperfection that generate a wedge between the marginal return to factors allocated to export crops and to subsistence crops. This type of effect can be seen in the model of Chapter 4, because there is discrete increase in utility for those farmers that switch activities and adopt export crops when prices increase. But, as we also showed in Chapter 4, these welfare effects are very small, on average. This is mostly because initial farmer participation in the export supply chain is very limited and thus the majority of households are nonproducers. In consequence, even if the switchers enjoy sizeable gains, there are only a few of them in any given simulation. In the end, these gains are averaged out across many nonparticipants, thereby creating negligible welfare effects. In short, the addition of those supply responses is unlikely to affect our welfare and poverty analysis. This feature of the analysis is a general result, not a property of our data (see, for example, Cadot et al. 2009; McMillan et al. 2003; Heltberg and Tarp 2002; Key et al. 2000; Lopez et al. 1995).

With the household survey data, we can also distinguish differential effects for poor and nonpoor rural households. Given a farm-gate price change, the results among the two groups will depend entirely on the initial income incidence of cotton across groups of households. Our microdata shows that, among cotton producers, cotton is relatively more important for poor than for nonpoor households. However, for the whole rural population, the opposite happens. Parts (a) and (b) of Figure A5.3 show these two results. For instance, in panel (a), an increase in competition represented by the split of the leader increases the income of poor producers by 2.6 percent, and of nonpoor producers by 2.3 percent. For the sample of all households (panel (b)), the increase in the income of the average poor household is only 0.23 percent and the increase in the average of the nonpoor is 0.29 percent. Once again, we do not discuss the differential impact for the poor and the nonpoor across different market and policy configurations because the result is proportional to the change in price and this change is the same for all households. This is a limitation of the model (it could well be the case that a particular complementary policy has a differentiated effect on farm-gate prices received by poor versus nonpoor farmers because different access to markets, information, technologies, or inputs) that is partially driven by the restriction imposed by the available data.

An important result to discuss is the presence of gender-specific impacts, that is, differential impacts for male-headed and female-headed households. As before, since our theoretical model delivers a common price change that applies to all producers, the differences in the poverty impacts will be driven by the share of cotton in total income across households. Figures A5.4(a) and A5.4(b) display the effects of different shocks to the level of competition in the ginning sector among male-headed and female-headed households both for the sample of producers and for the total population. For producers, the share of income among male-headed and female-headed households is similar and therefore the results of the simulations do not differ significantly across genders. In the case of equal market shares, the average income of a male-headed producer household increases by 7.36 percent, while it increases by 7.17 percent in the case of the average female-headed producer household. If we consider all households, the income effects are negligible, but the difference between male-headed and female-headed households is proportionally larger than in the case of the producers' subsample. For the equal market share simulation, male-headed household income increases on average by 0.87 percent, while it only increases by 0.57 percent for the female-headed counterparts. It should be mentioned that we are not considering second-order effects, nor are we allowing the complementary policies to have a different impact based on gender considerations.[3]

Outgrower Contracts

In the previous analysis we assumed that farmers have access to working capital and that the structure of the market does not affect the cost of those inputs. However, in the absence of enforcement mechanisms, processors may be reticent to advance the inputs needed for production, or, if they do, charge a premium to compensate for the possibility that the contracts are not honored. In our analysis, we have assumed that the borrowing cost for the farmers increases with the level of competition. This modification to the basic model does not generate important effects in the equilibrium farm-gate price but it changes the production cost for the farmers and therefore affects their income. The results from the simulations are reported in parts (a)–(l) of Table A5.1.

---

[3] This is a simplification of the model, which, once again, it is driven by data constraints. Note that the literature points out several constraints that particularly affect female farmers and their ability to improve yield, profit, and efficiency in agriculture production. Some of these constraints are women's legal and cultural status, which affects the degree of control women have over productive resources, inputs, and the benefits which flow from them (Olawoye 1989); property rights and inheritance laws, which govern access to and use of land and other natural resources (Jiggins 1989a); the relationship among ecological factors such as the seasonality of rainfall and availability of fuelwood, economic factors such as product market failures, and gender-determined responsibilities such as feeding the family, which trade off basic household self-provisioning goals and care of the family against production for the market (Jiggins 1989b; Horenstein 1989); and the way that agricultural services are staffed, managed, and designed (FAO 1993; Saito and Weidemann 1990; Gittinger et al. 1990). Given these constraints, changes in the level of competition and complementary policies may have different effects among female farmers.

Figure A5.5 illustrates the effects on producing farmers' income of the intro-duction of outgrower contracts and liquidity constraints. We plot the change in average income for cotton producers due to changes in market configura-tion in the models with and without outgrower contracts. Despite the fact that the differences in levels seems to be minor, the percentage changes among the two models are economically important. All the simulations where mar-ket competition increases show lower gains for farmers in the model with outgrower contracts. These gains are reduced to 5.8 percent in the leader split case, 11.9 percent in the equal market shares, and to almost half in the small entrant simulation. On the other hand, in the simulations generating market concentration, the losses under outgrower contracts are smaller due to a reduction in the borrowing costs (for instance, 18.5 percent lower in the leaders merge simulation). The exit of the largest firm is an interesting case as it reduces market competition but nevertheless increases the borrowing costs for the farmers and their income falls further.

In the simulations that we implemented above, the presence of outgrower contracts affects the magnitude of the impacts, but it does not affect the sign. In principle, however, it could happen that an increase in competition breaks down the whole contractual agreement, leading to a collapse of the market. The case of the cotton sector in Zambia in the early 2000s is an example of this type of effect (see, for example, Brambilla and Porto 2011) and these implications should thus be taken into account when designing competition policies in the sub-Saharan cash-crop sector.

Now we move to analyze the effects of outgrower contracts under the differ-ent scenarios of complementary policies and exogenous increase in interna-tional prices. Figure A5.6(a) shows the average income change for producers in the event of an increase in competition (leader split) in the basic model, the three scenarios with complementary policy, and the increase of 10 per-cent in the international price of cotton for the model with and without out-grower contracts. Figure A5.6(b) presents the same simulations for the case of a reduction in the level of competition (leaders merge). When the leader splits, the results under outgrower contracts are qualitatively the same but the level of income gains is lower. This is due to the additional cost for the farmers of a higher interest rate. This additional cost is increasing in the size of the gain generated by the complementary policy. While the interest rate paid by the farmers is 2.13 percent higher in the case of complementary policies support-ing farmers, it increases to 3.18 percent in the case of policies assisting both farmers and firms. Despite having the highest interest rate, this last policy still maximizes the gains for the household producing cotton in Zambia. The average income effect is 3.13 percent, while, in the model without outgrower contracts, it was 3.48 percent, which implies a reduction of 10 percent. In the case of leaders merging, the reduction in competition reduces the inter-est costs for farmers, partially compensating the reduction of income due to a lower farm-gate price. This offsetting factor varies across the different complementary policies. The average income losses are 20.7 percent lower when complementary policies focus on farmers, while they are only 15.3 percent lower when the policies center on the firms. In the case of an increase in international prices, the existence of outgrower contracts reduces the average income gain for farmers at about the same order of magnitude for both an increase and a reduction in the competition level among ginneries.

2.2   Other Case Studies

Cotton

Besides our lead case of Zambia, we study the effects of competition among cotton processors on farm-gate prices and household income for another four sub-Saharan African countries. For Benin, Burkina Faso, and Côte d'Ivoire we run the same set of simulation we had for Zambia. In the case of Malawi, we follow a different approach as the country currently has two ginneries each controlling 50 percent of the market. For that reason some of our simulations do not make much sense and we decided to study the effect of splitting the market among three and later four firms, and we also allow for the entrance of a small firm. We apply the model both with and without outgrower contracts and we study the effect of complementary policies and exogenous variation in the international price of cotton.

Qualitatively, we found the same result that we found in the Zambian case: competition is good for the farmers. The income effects, as expected, are much larger for those households producing the crop than for the typical rural household that may or may not produce cotton (five times larger in Benin and more than forty times in the case of Burkina Faso). For that reason, we discuss mainly the result of the income simulation for cotton producers. The income effect depends both on the magnitude of the price change and on the importance of cotton in the total income of the average producer-household. Figure A5.7(a) displays the effect of increased competition (leader split) under the five different scenarios. The income effects are, on average, 3.3 percent in Benin, 4.6 percent in Côte d'Ivoire, and 12.4 percent in Burkina Faso (all these impacts are larger than in the case of Zambia, which was slightly over 2 percent). In the Burkina Faso case, part of the result is due to the fact that the leader, SOFITEX, controls 85 percent of the market. In the other countries, the differences in income impact are mainly driven by income shares as the farm-gate price changes when the leader splits is of the same order of magnitude (around 9 percent) for the three countries. In the case of Malawi, moving from two to three firms in the market causes income gains of only 1.9 percent, while moving to four firms causes income gains of 3 percent. Complementary policies also have a positive impact on farmers' income, with larger impacts in cases where those policies affect both farmers and firms. For instance, the income gains with both types of complementary policies are 12 percent in Burkina Faso, 34 percent in Benin, and 47 percent in

Côte d'Ivoire—higher than under the baseline scenario. In Figure A5.7(b) we show the income effects of a merger between the two leading companies. This type of competition simulations brings about welfare losses for the farmers. The largest losses are observed in Côte d'Ivoire, where the average producer household would lose 3.9 percent of income in comparison with 2.3 percent in Zambia, 1.8 in Burkina Faso, and only 0.7 in Benin. On the positive side, the implementation of complementary policies can reduce these negative impacts and sometimes even can attain an overall positive effect, as in the case of Burkina Faso and Benin. In the case of Burkina Faso this only happens when we combine complementary policies supporting firms and farmers. Instead, in the case of Benin, it would be enough with firms' oriented complementary policies to obtain a positive (but negligible) effect on farmers' income under this scenario. The overall effect of the complementary policies on farmers' welfare depends on the combined farm-gate price and quantity effect. Typically, farmer support would depress the farm-gate price but would increase the supply of crops while complementary policies supporting firms would have a positive impact in farm-gate price but a minor impact in the overall supply from farmers. Policies affecting both farmers and firms would generate a price effect that lies in between the previous two cases and a quantity effect that would be higher than the combination of the two individual supply effects.

The analysis of the impact on poor versus nonpoor households shows a different pattern than in the case of Zambia. As we can see in Figure A5.8 nonpoor households benefit more than poor household from an increase in competition (equal market shares in this case) in Benin, Burkina Faso, and Côte d'Ivoire. (This also happens in Malawi, not shown in the graph). The differences, however, are very small. For instance, in our baseline case, under equal market shares, nonpoor households in Burkina Faso will earn 21.4 percent more than under the actual market configuration, while poor households would see their income rise by 20.1 percent.

Turning now to gender issues, we find that male-headed households benefit relatively more than female-headed households in Burkina Faso and Malawi, while the opposite happens in Benin and Côte d'Ivoire. The gender differences are not trivial. For example, in the case of perfect competition in Burkina Faso, male-headed households would earn 50.4 percent more, while female-headed households would earn 15.9 more (see Figure A5.9). On the contrary, female-headed households in Benin would benefit from a 34.7 percent increase in income increases versus a 22 percent for the average male-headed household.

The last issue we want to discuss for the cotton sector is the analysis of the plausible negative effects of competition when we introduce the need of outgrower contracts that may not be perfectly enforceable. The cases of Benin, Côte d'Ivoire, and Malawi are similar to the Zambia case. In general, competition is still good in our calibrations but the benefits for farmers are slightly offset by increasing borrowing cost. On the other hand, the case of Burkina

Faso merits a thorough discussion. Figure A5.10 displays the seven shocks to the level of competition in cotton processors in Burkina Faso for the basic model. Contrary to what we found in the other cotton case studies, the benefits of tighter competition are greatly offset by the increasing costs of funds in the model with outgrower contracts. While farm-gate prices and quantities changes are about the same in the model with and without outgrower contracts, the interest rate greatly increases in the model with outgrower contracts. For example, a leader split situation would generate an increase in the interest rate of 39.3 percent in Burkina Faso but only 1.8 percent in the case of Zambia. That would reduce gains for producing households in Burkina Faso from 12.4 percent to 6.5 percent in the baseline case with outgrower contracts. Figures A5.11(a) and 5.11b show that the gap between the income effects in the two models does not shrink when we bring in the possibility of complementary policy. The 40 percent difference in income gains between the two models in the baseline case slightly increases to 41 percent when we introduce complementary variations aiming to reduce costs for both firms and farmers. If the two leading companies were to merge in the model without outgrower contracts, households would lose 1.8 percent of their income but would actually win an extra 1.3 percent in the model with outgrower contracts. This is a case where the reduction in competition generates savings in borrowing costs that are larger than the reduction in the price paid to the farmers. Another interesting feature of this simulation, and a difference with the previous cases, is that, with outgrower contracts, the complementary policy applied only to firms results in a worse outcome for farmers than the one applied only to the farmers.

Cocoa

We now study the effects of competition in farm-gate prices and rural household income in the two largest cocoa producers, Côte d'Ivoire and Ghana. Like our previous cases, increase in competition among exporting companies benefits producers and a decrease in competition reduces the price paid to farmers. Figure A5.12(a) represents this last case, where a reduction in competition due to the exit of the largest firm decreases the income received by producing households in both countries. However, the effect is small in comparison with other case studies, with the typical Ivorian producing household losing 1.3 percent of its income and the Ghanaian counterpart receiving only 1 percent less. This result is both a combination of prices not varying much due to a relatively low market power concentration and a moderate share of cocoa in income due to producers' diversification. If the reduction in competition came along with the implementation of complementary policies, the reductions in income are partially compensated or even reverted in the case of policies benefiting both firms and farmers.

Figure A5.12(b) shows the effects of an increase in competition where we display the case of equal market shares. This would lead to an increase in farm-gate prices of 18.2 percent in Côte d'Ivoire and 29.3 percent in Ghana. Despite the significant price differential in favor of Ghanaian producers, the overall impact on income is larger in Côte d'Ivoire because the average rural household cocoa income share is around twice that of Ghana. In our standard scenario, equal market shares would lead to an increase in income of 10.5 percent in Côte d'Ivoire and 7.3 percent in Ghana. Once again, if combined with complementary policies, this increase would be larger with households receiving an extra 2.1 percent and 1 percent of income in Côte d'Ivoire and Ghana, respectively.

An increase in the international price of cocoa (Figure A5.12(c)) would have a larger effect on farmers' income in Côte d'Ivoire than in Ghana. Once again, this result is mainly driven by the differences in cocoa income shares among the two countries. In the current market configuration, producing households in Côte d'Ivoire would see their income increase by 12.7 percent against 6.2 percent in Ghana. This difference varies, however, with the level of competition. Increases in competition would make the income gains difference between the two countries larger, while reduction in competition would reduce the gap.

The income impact of more or less competition among exporters on poor and nonpoor cocoa-producing households (Figure A5.13) is about the same in both countries. In the simulation of perfect competition in our baseline model, poor Ivorian households would gain 21.6 percent while nonpoor households would witness an increase in income of 21.3 percent. On the other hand, in Ghana, nonpoor household are the ones that benefit the most. However, the income gain is only marginally higher than for poor households. In both countries, on average, male-headed households benefit more than female-headed households from an increase in competition (Figure A5.14 shows the case of leader split). The gender difference is slightly higher for Côte d'Ivoire.

The introduction of outgrower contracts does not generate important income effects in cocoa like in the previous case of cotton in Burkina Faso. In both countries the effects are modest, even in the extreme cases of equal market shares and perfect competition. The only significant difference with the cotton cases reviewed above is that, in the case of cocoa in both Ghana and Côte d'Ivoire, when the leader splits, the interest rate decreases instead of increasing and, therefore, households enjoy a larger income effect in the model that has outgrower contracts. This difference is important in the case of Ghana for the basic model, but the differential shrinks when we incorporate complementary policies (Figure A5.15). On the other hand, an increase in international prices generates higher income effects for rural producing households in the model without outgrower contracts than in the model with them.

Coffee

Increasing competition benefits coffee smallholder producers in Côte d'Ivoire, Rwanda, and Uganda. In Figure A5.16(a) we show the result of a leader split in the income of the average producing household. The effects are modest for the three countries, with a larger effect in Côte d'Ivoire and Rwanda than in Uganda. The increase is larger when accompanied with complementary policies and, as is the case in most simulations, policies focusing on firms have a higher impact than the ones supporting the farmers.

Figure A5.16(b) shows the simulation for the case of a reduction of competition due to the merging of the two leading firms. The farmers' income effects are again modest, with the most negative effect taking place in Rwanda, where the average producing household loses slightly more than half a percentage point of their income.

Another issue we are interested in studying is the effect of an increase in the international price of coffee. Figure A5.16(c) displays the effects of a 10 percent increase in the international price on the income received by the producing households. In the current market configuration, farmers in Côte d'Ivoire would receive 6.5 percent more, while in Rwanda and Uganda the increase would only be around 2 percent. Increasing competition among exporters would drive these income gains up, but only modestly for Rwanda and Uganda. Côte d'Ivoire producers would get 12 percent more income if the increase in international prices takes place in a market where all firms have the same market share.

Figures A5.17 and A5.18 show the income effects of more competition among processors on poor and nonpoor households (equal market share simulation) and on male-headed and female-headed households (perfect competition simulation). In Côte d'Ivoire and Rwanda, poor households benefit more on average than nonpoor households. These differences are significant since, in the first case, the income gain is 57.7 percent higher, and in the second case it is 43.3 percent higher. On the other hand, the effect is about the same for poor and nonpoor households in Uganda. Male-headed households benefit on average more in Côte d'Ivoire and Uganda, while female-headed household benefit more on average in Rwanda. Once again, the differences are significant as, for instance, in Côte d'Ivoire, the male-headed household income increase in the case of perfect competition is 67 percent larger than for the female-headed households.

The effects of outgrower contracts are similar to what was discussed above and therefore we do not report the simulations here. The interested reader can check the specific results in parts (h)–(j) of Table A5.1.

Tobacco

Tobacco is the last crop in our study and we perform the analysis for the cases of Malawi and Zambia. As before, we find positive effects of competition. We illustrate this with two of the multiple simulations. In Figure A5.19(a) we present the "exit of the largest" for our basic model and the different scenarios. The negative impact of the loss of competition is felt strongest by farmers in Zambia, where the average producing household loses 4.7 percent of its income in the baseline case. This is almost three times the effect in Malawi and is mostly due to the price effect. The largest firm in tobacco in Zambia controls almost half of the market while in Malawi the leading firm controls one-third of it. The introduction of complementary policies at the firm and the farm levels somehow reduces this negative impact but never turns it positive, as was the case in some of the previous cases. Figure A5.19(b) shows the case of equal market shares. This increase in competition generates sizeable increases in income in both countries. Producing households in Malawi obtain on average 5.7 percent more income, while in Zambia the increment is 7.2 percent. Complementary policies would enhance these income gains but the increase is not as substantial as it was in other cases.

Nonpoor households profit more than poor households from increases in competition among domestic tobacco buyers. Figure A5.20 presents the case of perfect competition. In this scenario, nonpoor farmers would gain 41 percent and 47 percent more in Malawi and Zambia, respectively, than poor producing households in the same countries. The income effect is larger in both countries for male-headed household. In Figure A5.21 we show the effects upon the income of households of the leader splitting simulation in the baseline scenarios for both genders. As can be seen from the figure, the gender difference is larger in Zambia, where male-headed households would profit from a 34 percent extra income increase, in comparison with female-headed households.

In both case studies for tobacco, the incorporation of outgrower contracts into the model reduces the farmers' income gains from further competition among exporters. Figure A5.22 illustrates the results of leader split with and without outgrower contracts in Malawi. In the basic model, the improvement in producing households' income is 44.8 percent lower in the model with outgrower contracts. This difference is reduced to 29.4 percent when we incorporate complementary policies affecting both farmers and firms.

3   SUMMARY OF FINDINGS

In this chapter we studied the effects on the income of households of increasing competition among processors in twelve case studies covering four cash crops in eight sub-Saharan African countries. The main conclusion of the analysis is that competition among processors is good for farmers as it increases the farm-gate price of the crop. Take, for instance, the case where the firm with the largest market share splits. This would lead to an average income increase for producing households of 2.8 percent in our case studies. This average, however, masks a great variability, with cotton-producing households as the top earners and the smallholders in the coffee sector with the lowest gains. For instance, in our baseline scenario, the leader split simulation would increase average households' income for cotton in Burkina Faso by 12.4 percent but only 0.1 percent in coffee in Uganda. This does not come as a surprise, however, as the leading firm in cotton in Burkina Faso controls 85 percent of the market but only 14.3 percent of the market in the case of coffee in Uganda. Another interesting simulation showing an increase in competition is the case of "equal market shares." This would give us the upper bound increase in income under imperfect competition. Here the average effect is much larger than in the case of leader split. The average producing household in our study would see their income grow by 9.1 percent, with cotton in Burkina Faso once again experiencing the largest impact with 20.9 percent, followed by Benin with 20.1 percent and Côte d'Ivoire with a 14 percent increase, both in cotton. At the other end of the spectrum, the average household gains less than 1 percent in the equal market shares simulation in coffee in Uganda and Rwanda.

The conclusion from the previous paragraph that an increase in competition among processors is good for the farmers needs to be put into perspective. One of the findings from our simulations is that small changes to the level of competition are unlikely to have significant effects on farmers' livelihoods. This is captured by the small entrant simulation. Under this scenario, the income of households only increases by an average of a quarter of a percentage point for our case studies. The largest effects for this simulation are observed in cotton in Malawi (0.94 percent) and tobacco in Zambia (0.74 percent).

We were also interested in assessing the effects on farmers' income of a reduction in competition among upstream firms. This was done by studying the effects of the merging of the largest two firms in the market and through the case of the exit of the largest (and most efficient) firm. In the first simulation, the average loss for producing households is 1.3 percent of their income, with the largest loss registered in the case of cotton in Côte d'Ivoire (3.8 percent), where the new firm would control three quarters of the market. In the exit of the largest firm simulation, the worst income loss for producing households would take place in the cotton sector of Burkina Faso, where the disappearance of SOFITEX, which controls 85 percent of the market, would lead to a reduction in income of 15.4 percent. On the other hand, the reduction in competition arising from these two simulations would affect the average producing household in the coffee sector in Uganda the least, where the loss would only be around a tenth of a percentage point in both simulations.

Another issue we wanted to incorporate into the analysis is the effects of complementary policies. We did so by comparing our baseline scenario with cases where we introduced a complementary policy affecting farmers (2 percent of increase in yields), affecting firms (2 percent reduction of processing cost), or both. The main finding here is that these policies help to increase the income of households when there is an increase in competition and can mitigate or even revert income loss when there is a loss because of a reduction in competition. In all cases, the effect is the largest when applied to both firms and farmers. In the case of only farmers versus only firms' complementary policies, the latter have the largest effect on the livelihood of farmers in all cases except tobacco in Zambia. The quantitative effects of these policies depend on the particular crop, country, and market structure but it goes from as little as an extra 0.2 percent more up to 2.7 percent extra income for the average producing household.

We also studied the effects on households' livelihood of a 10 percent exogenous increase in the international price of the crop under consideration. Given the current market configuration for each crop and country, that exogenous price increase leads to an average raise in producing households' income of 6.9 percent, with the largest effect taking place for cotton in Burkina Faso (12.8 percent) and the lowest for coffee in Rwanda (2 percent). We then allow for combinations of the international crop price increase with different changes to the level of competition among processors. Increasing competition will boost the positive effects of the price change, while a reduction in the competition will dampen its effects. For instance, in the case of perfect competition, the income gains for producing households would range between 68 percent (cotton in Burkina Faso) and 3.8 percent (coffee in Uganda), with an average effect across case studies of 29.6 percent. On the other hand, when the largest firm exits the market, the overall income effect of the international price increase would range between −3.9 percent (cotton in Burkina Faso) and 11.3 percent (cocoa in Côte d'Ivoire), with an average income effect of 3.4 percent for all the case studies.

The survey data allows us to distinguish the effect of the different simulations on poor versus nonpoor households and across gender groups. Here the results depend on the income share of the crop in each country for each group, as the price simulations are unique. A richer model could incorporate policies or market changes that affect poor or female-headed households in a different way from nonpoor and male-headed households, but this is not the case in our simulations. In nine out of the twelve simulations, the benefits of more competition have a larger income effect in male-headed households than in the female counterpart. The three exceptions were the case of cotton in Benin and Côte d'Ivoire, and coffee in Rwanda. The largest differences among genders were registered in Burkina Faso cotton, where male-headed households received 217 percent more income increase than female-headed households, and in Benin cotton, where female-headed households received 57 percent more than the male equivalent. In only four out of the twelve case studies, the increase in competition has been pro-poor. The income gains on average benefitted more poor households in the case of coffee and cocoa in Côte d'Ivoire, coffee in Rwanda, and cotton in Zambia.

We also present the results for a model that incorporates outgrower contracts. Small farmers can receive financing from processors in exchange for future output sales through outgrower schemes. We assume that the cost of enforcing these contracts increases with market competition and that those costs are transferred to producers through increasing borrowing costs. We therefore run the same set of simulations taking this feature into consideration and compare it with our original set of simulations. We find that, with outgrower contracts, the benefits of increasing competition and the negative effects of a more concentrated market are both reduced. The effect is, however, rather small except for the case of cotton in Burkina Faso. In this last case study, the merging of the largest two firms would reduce farmers' income by 1.8 percent in the basic model without outgrower contracts but it would actually increase it by 1.3 percent in the model with these types of contracts. This is an atypical case in which less competition is better for smallholders.

Three of the countries in our study have more than one case study. In Côte d'Ivoire we study cotton, coffee, and cocoa. In Malawi and Zambia we cover both cotton and tobacco. It is interesting, then, to describe how the same scenario and simulation has different effects across crops in the same country. For instance, in Côte d'Ivoire, an increase in competition has a larger effect on producing households' income in cotton than in cocoa and coffee. If the leader firm in cotton, cocoa, and coffee were to split, the effect on income would be a 4.6, 1.1, and 0.6 percent increase, respectively. In the case of equal market shares, the increase in the income of households would be 14, 10.5, and 5.4 percent, respectively. The effect is also different for poor versus nonpoor households, and across gender depending on the crop. Competition in coffee benefits more poor and male-headed households, while, in cotton, female-headed and nonpoor households are the ones that obtain larger gains. In cocoa, competition benefits male-headed households slightly more, while the effect is about the same among poor and nonpoor households. In Malawi we cannot directly compare the results from the cotton and the tobacco simulations, since the latter are slightly different to the standard simulation we run for all the other case studies. However, the overall effects seem to be of about the same order of magnitude and, in both crops, male and nonpoor households benefit the most from the increase in competition. Finally, in Zambia, the effect of competition has similar quantitative effects on cotton and tobacco. The leader split case would increase the income of households by 2.4 percent for cotton and by 3.2 percent for tobacco, while the equal market share case would generate a growth in income of 7.3 percent in cotton and 7.2 percent in tobacco. In both crops, male-headed households benefit the most, though only slightly in the case of cotton. Poor producing households gain more in cotton, while nonpoor benefit more in the case of increased competition among tobacco exporters.

APPENDIX: TABLES AND FIGURES

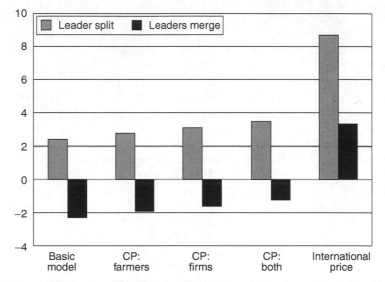

Figure A5.1: *Income effects under different scenarios for cotton in Zambia.*

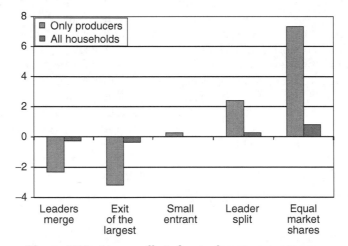

Figure A5.2: *Income effects for producers versus income effects for all households for cotton in Zambia.*

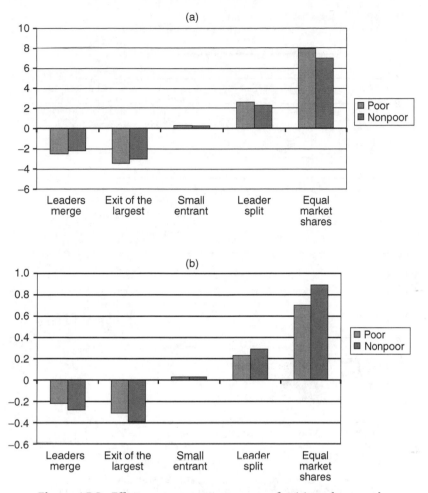

Figure A5.3: *Effects on poor versus nonpoor for (a) producers only and (b) all households for cotton in Zambia.*

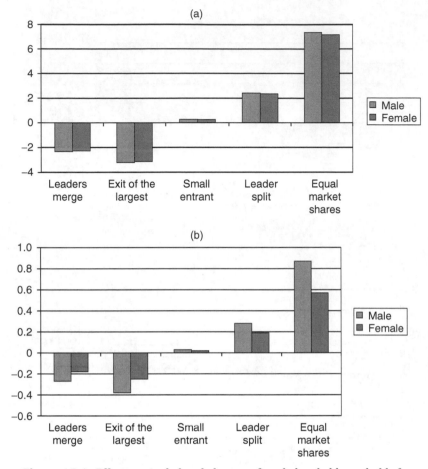

Figure A5.4: *Effects on male-headed versus female-headed households for (a) producers only and (b) all households for cotton in Zambia.*

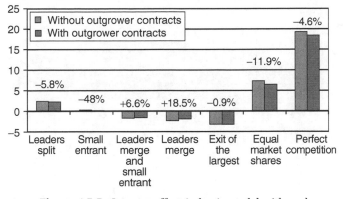

Figure A5.5: *Income effect in basic model with and without outgrower contracts for cotton in Zambia.*

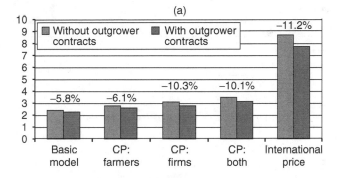

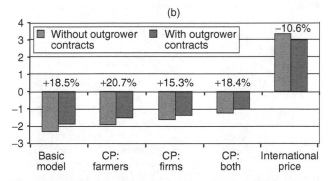

Figure A5.6: *Scenarios under (a) leader split and (b) leaders merge with and without outgrower contracts for cotton in Zambia.*

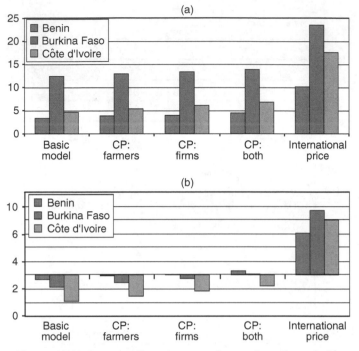

Figure A5.7: *Income effects in cotton for producer households under (a) leader split and (b) leaders merge.*

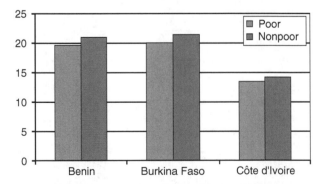

Figure A5.8: *Equal market shares income effects in cotton for poor and nonpoor producer households.*

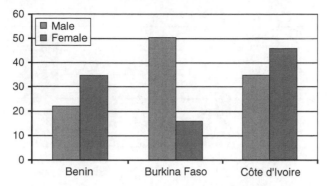

Figure A5.9: *Perfect competition income effects in cotton for male-headed and female-headed producer households.*

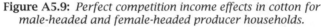

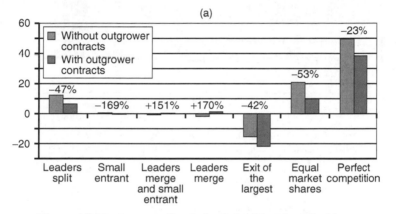

Figure A5.10: *Income effect in basic model with and without outgrower contracts in cotton–Burkina Faso.*

Supply Chains in Sub-Saharan Africa

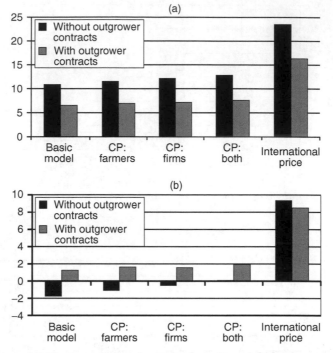

Figure A5.11: *Scenarios under (a) leader split and (b) leaders merge with and without outgrower contracts in cotton–Burkina Faso.*

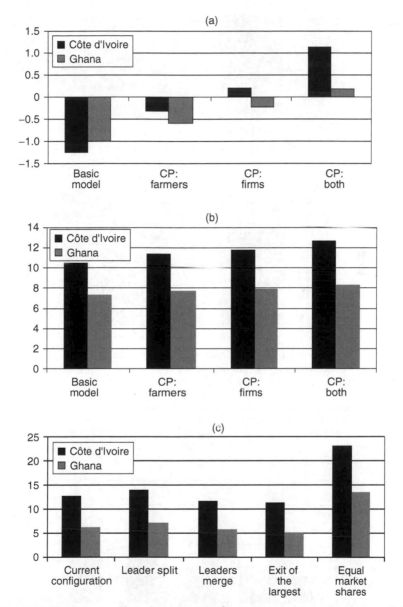

Figure A5.12: *Income effects for cocoa producer households under (a) exit of the leader, (b) equal market shares, and (c) increased international price.*

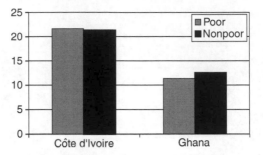

Figure A5.13: *Perfect competition income effects in cocoa for poor and nonpoor producer households.*

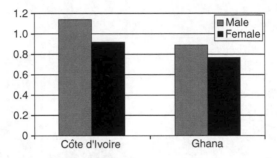

Figure A5.14: *Leader split income effects in cocoa for male-headed and female-headed producer households.*

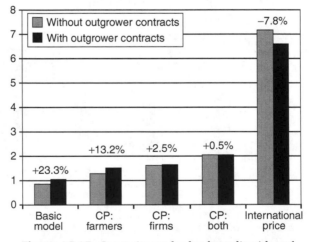

Figure A5.15: *Scenarios under leader split with and without outgrower contracts in cocoa–Ghana.*

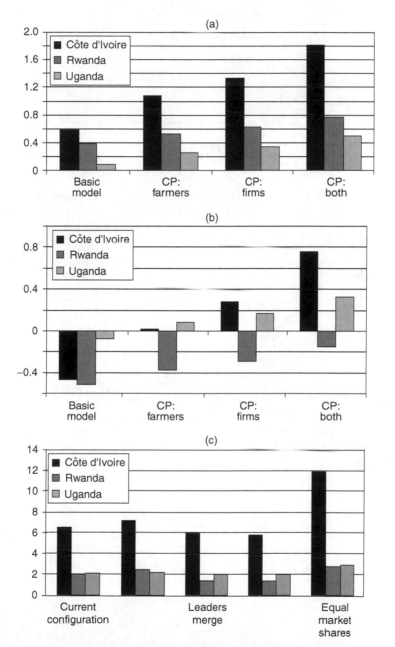

Figure A5.16: *Income effects for coffee producer households under (a) leader split, (b) leaders merge, and (c) increased international price.*

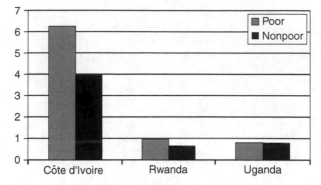

Figure A5.17: *Equal market shares income effects in coffee for poor and nonpoor producer households.*

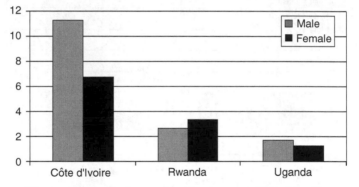

Figure A5.18: *Perfect competition income effects in coffee for male-headed and female-headed producer households.*

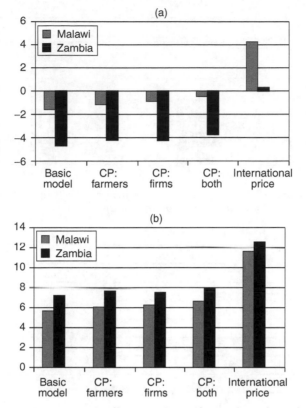

Figure A5.19: *Income effects in tobacco for producer households under (a) exit of the largest and (b) equal market shares.*

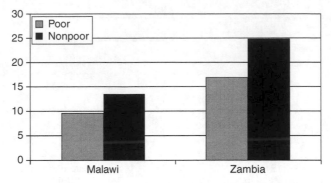

Figure A5.20: *Perfect competition income effects in tobacco for poor and nonpoor producer households.*

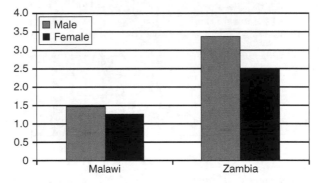

Figure A5.21: *Leader split income effects in tobacco for male-headed and female-headed producer households.*

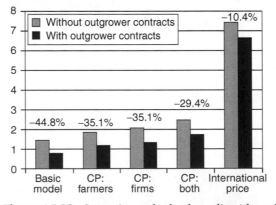

Figure A5.22: *Scenarios under leader split with and without outgrower contracts in tobacco–Malawi.*

Table A5.1: *Impact of supply chain changes on the standard model: (a) Zambia, cotton (household income percentage changes).*

		Respect to original	Leader split	Small entrant	Leaders merge and small entrant	Leaders merge	Exit of largest	Equal market shares	Perfect competition
(A) Basic model									
Only producers	Total	0.00	2.40	0.27	1.68	2.32	3.19	7.33	19.30
	Poor	0.00	2.60	0.29	1.82	2.51	3.46	7.95	20.92
	Nonpoor	0.00	2.29	0.26	1.60	2.21	3.04	6.99	18.40
	Male-headed	0.00	2.41	0.27	1.68	2.32	3.20	7.36	19.37
	Female-headed	0.00	2.35	0.26	1.64	2.26	3.12	7.17	18.87
All households	Total	0.00	0.27	0.03	0.18	0.26	0.35	0.81	2.13
	Poor	0.00	0.23	0.03	0.16	0.22	0.31	0.70	1.86
	Nonpoor	0.00	0.29	0.03	0.20	0.28	0.39	0.89	2.35
	Male-headed	0.00	0.28	0.03	0.20	0.27	0.38	0.87	2.28
	Female-headed	0.00	0.19	0.02	0.13	0.18	0.25	0.57	1.51
(B) Complementary policies (farmers)									
Only producers	Total	0.39	2.77	0.68	1.27	1.93	2.80	7.66	19.84
	Poor	0.42	3.00	0.73	1.38	2.09	3.03	8.30	21.51
	Nonpoor	0.37	2.64	0.64	1.22	1.84	2.67	7.30	18.91
	Male-headed	0.39	2.78	0.68	1.28	1.94	2.81	7.69	19.91
	Female-headed	0.38	2.71	0.66	1.25	1.89	2.74	7.49	19.39
All households	Total	0.04	0.31	0.07	0.14	0.21	0.31	0.85	2.19
	Poor	0.04	0.27	0.06	0.12	0.19	0.27	0.74	1.91
	Nonpoor	0.05	0.34	0.08	0.16	0.24	0.34	0.93	2.41
	Male-headed	0.05	0.33	0.08	0.15	0.23	0.33	0.91	2.34
	Female-headed	0.03	0.22	0.05	0.10	0.15	0.22	0.60	1.55

Table A5.1: *(a) Continued.*

	Respect to original	Leader split	Small entrant	Leaders merge and small entrant	Leaders merge	Exit of largest	Equal market shares	Perfect competition
(C) Complementary policies (firms)								
Only producers								
Total	0.71	3.10	1.04	0.92	1.63	2.48	7.88	20.11
Poor	0.77	3.36	1.13	1.00	1.76	2.69	8.55	21.80
Nonpoor	0.68	2.95	0.99	0.88	1.55	2.36	7.52	19.17
Male-headed	0.72	3.11	1.04	0.93	1.63	2.49	7.91	20.18
Female-headed	0.70	3.03	1.01	0.90	1.59	2.42	7.71	19.65
All households								
Total	0.08	0.34	0.11	0.10	0.18	0.27	0.87	2.22
Poor	0.07	0.30	0.10	0.09	0.16	0.24	0.76	1.93
Nonpoor	0.09	0.38	0.13	0.11	0.20	0.30	0.96	2.45
Male-headed	0.08	0.37	0.12	0.11	0.19	0.29	0.93	2.38
Female-headed	0.06	0.24	0.08	0.07	0.13	0.19	0.62	1.58
(D) Complementary policies (farmers – firms)								
Only producers								
Total	1.10	3.48	1.44	0.53	1.25	2.10	8.21	20.64
Poor	1.19	3.78	1.56	0.57	1.35	2.27	8.90	22.38
Nonpoor	1.05	3.32	1.37	0.50	1.19	2.00	7.83	19.68
Male-headed	1.10	3.50	1.44	0.53	1.25	2.10	8.24	20.72
Female-headed	1.07	3.40	1.41	0.52	1.22	2.05	8.02	20.18
All households								
Total	0.12	0.38	0.16	0.06	0.14	0.23	0.91	2.28
Poor	0.11	0.33	0.14	0.05	0.12	0.20	0.79	1.98
Nonpoor	0.13	0.42	0.17	0.06	0.15	0.25	1.00	2.51
Male-headed	0.13	0.41	0.17	0.06	0.15	0.25	0.97	2.44
Female-headed	0.09	0.27	0.11	0.04	0.10	0.16	0.64	1.62

Table A5.1: *(a) Continued.*

		Respect to original	Leader split	Small entrant	Leaders merge and small entrant	Leaders merge	Exit of largest	Equal market shares	Perfect competition
(E) International prices									
Only producers	Total	6.03	8.69	6.62	4.39	3.35	2.50	13.23	27.95
	Poor	6.54	9.42	7.17	4.76	3.63	2.71	14.34	30.30
	Nonpoor	5.75	8.28	6.31	4.19	3.19	2.38	12.61	26.64
	Male-headed	6.06	8.72	6.64	4.41	3.36	2.51	13.28	28.05
	Female-headed	5.90	8.49	6.47	4.29	3.28	2.44	12.93	27.32
All households	Total	0.67	0.96	0.73	0.48	0.37	0.28	1.46	3.08
	Poor	0.58	0.84	0.64	0.42	0.32	0.24	1.27	2.69
	Nonpoor	0.73	1.06	0.80	0.53	0.41	0.30	1.61	3.40
	Male-headed	0.71	1.03	0.78	0.52	0.40	0.29	1.56	3.30
	Female-headed	0.47	0.68	0.52	0.34	0.26	0.20	1.04	2.19

Table A5.1: *(b) Benin, cotton (household income percentage changes).*

	Respect to original	Leader split	Small entrant	Leaders merge and small entrant	Leaders merge	Exit of largest	Equal market shares	Perfect competition
(A) Basic model								
Only producers								
Total	0.00	3.33	0.09	0.51	0.67	3.69	20.11	34.16
Poor	0.00	3.25	0.09	0.49	0.65	3.60	19.64	33.36
Nonpoor	0.00	3.47	0.09	0.53	0.70	3.85	20.99	35.66
Male-headed	0.00	2.15	0.06	0.33	0.43	2.38	12.97	22.02
Female-headed	0.00	3.38	0.09	0.51	0.68	3.75	20.42	34.68
All households								
Total	0.00	0.63	0.02	0.10	0.13	0.69	3.78	6.42
Poor	0.00	0.79	0.02	0.12	0.16	0.87	4.75	8.07
Nonpoor	0.00	0.46	0.01	0.07	0.09	0.51	2.79	4.74
Male-headed	0.00	0.11	0.00	0.02	0.02	0.12	0.65	1.11
Female-headed	0.00	0.72	0.02	0.11	0.14	0.80	4.33	7.36
(B) Complementary policies (farmers)								
Only producers								
Total	0.55	3.84	0.65	0.05	0.13	3.13	20.52	34.86
Poor	0.54	3.75	0.63	0.04	0.13	3.06	20.04	34.04
Nonpoor	0.57	4.00	0.68	0.05	0.14	3.27	21.42	36.39
Male-headed	0.35	2.47	0.42	0.03	0.08	2.02	13.23	22.48
Female-headed	0.56	3.89	0.66	0.05	0.13	3.18	20.83	35.39
All households								
Total	0.10	0.72	0.12	0.01	0.02	0.59	3.86	6.55
Poor	0.13	0.91	0.15	0.01	0.03	0.74	4.85	8.24
Nonpoor	0.08	0.53	0.09	0.01	0.02	0.44	2.85	4.84
Male-headed	0.02	0.12	0.02	0.00	0.00	0.10	0.67	1.14
Female-headed	0.12	0.83	0.14	0.01	0.03	0.68	4.42	7.51

Table A5.1: *(b) Continued.*

	Respect to original	Leader split	Small entrant	Leaders merge and small entrant	Leaders merge	Exit of largest	Equal market shares	Perfect competition
(C) Complementary policies (firms)								
Only producers Total	0.73	3.95	0.85	0.24	0.04	2.92	20.42	34.58
Poor	0.71	3.86	0.83	0.23	0.04	2.85	19.94	33.76
Nonpoor	0.76	4.12	0.89	0.25	0.04	3.05	21.32	36.09
Male-headed	0.47	2.55	0.55	0.15	0.03	1.88	13.17	22.29
Female-headed	0.74	4.01	0.86	0.24	0.04	2.96	20.73	35.10
All households Total	0.14	0.74	0.16	0.04	0.01	0.55	3.84	6.50
Poor	0.17	0.93	0.20	0.06	0.01	0.69	4.82	8.17
Nonpoor	0.10	0.55	0.12	0.03	0.01	0.41	2.83	4.80
Male-headed	0.02	0.13	0.03	0.01	0.00	0.10	0.67	1.13
Female-headed	0.16	0.85	0.18	0.05	0.01	0.63	4.40	7.45
(D) Complementary policies (farmers – firms)								
Only producers Total	1.28	4.45	1.41	0.78	0.57	2.37	20.83	35.28
Poor	1.25	4.35	1.37	0.76	0.56	2.31	20.34	34.45
Nonpoor	1.33	4.65	1.47	0.82	0.60	2.47	21.74	36.82
Male-headed	0.82	2.87	0.91	0.50	0.37	1.53	13.43	22.74
Female-headed	1.29	4.52	1.43	0.79	0.58	2.40	21.15	35.81
All households Total	0.24	0.84	0.26	0.15	0.11	0.44	3.91	6.63
Poor	0.30	1.05	0.33	0.19	0.13	0.56	4.92	8.33
Nonpoor	0.18	0.62	0.20	0.11	0.08	0.33	2.89	4.90
Male-headed	0.04	0.15	0.05	0.03	0.02	0.08	0.68	1.15
Female-headed	0.27	0.96	0.30	0.17	0.12	0.51	4.49	7.60

Table A5.1: *(b) Continued.*

		Respect to original	Leader split	Small entrant	Leaders merge and small entrant	Leaders merge	Exit of largest	Equal market shares	Perfect competition
(E) International prices									
Only producers	Total	6.94	10.10	7.20	6.44	6.06	3.09	26.80	43.16
	Poor	6.77	9.86	7.03	6.29	5.92	3.01	26.17	42.14
	Nonpoor	7.24	10.54	7.52	6.72	6.33	3.22	27.97	45.04
	Male-headed	4.47	6.51	4.64	4.15	3.91	1.99	17.28	27.82
	Female-headed	7.04	10.25	7.31	6.53	6.15	3.13	27.20	43.81
All households	Total	1.30	1.90	1.35	1.21	1.14	0.58	5.03	8.11
	Poor	1.64	2.39	1.70	1.52	1.43	0.73	6.33	10.20
	Nonpoor	0.96	1.40	1.00	0.89	0.84	0.43	3.72	5.99
	Male-headed	0.23	0.33	0.23	0.21	0.20	0.10	0.87	1.41
	Female-headed	1.49	2.18	1.55	1.39	1.31	0.66	5.78	9.30

Table A5.1: *(c) Burkina Faso, cotton (household income percentage changes).*

		Respect to original	Leader split	Small entrant	Leaders merge and small entrant	Leaders merge	Exit of largest	Equal market shares	Perfect competition
(A) Basic model									
Only producers	Total	0.00	12.36	0.55	0.68	1.79	-15.36	20.91	49.61
	Poor	0.00	11.85	0.53	0.66	1.71	-14.74	20.05	47.59
	Nonpoor	0.00	12.67	0.57	0.70	1.83	-15.75	21.44	50.87
	Male-headed	0.00	12.55	0.56	0.69	1.81	-15.60	21.23	50.39
	Female-headed	0.00	3.95	0.18	0.22	0.57	4.91	6.68	15.86
All households	Total	0.00	0.29	0.01	0.02	0.04	0.36	0.49	1.17
	Poor	0.00	0.22	0.01	0.01	0.03	0.28	0.38	0.90
	Nonpoor	0.00	0.36	0.02	0.02	0.05	0.44	0.60	1.43
	Male-headed	0.00	0.31	0.01	0.02	0.04	0.39	0.52	1.24
	Female-headed	0.00	0.03	0.00	0.00	0.00	0.04	0.06	0.13
(B) Complementary policies (farmers)									
Only producers	Total	0.76	12.87	1.37	0.08	1.12	-14.56	21.48	50.72
	Poor	0.73	12.35	1.32	0.08	1.07	-13.96	20.61	48.65
	Nonpoor	0.78	13.20	1.41	0.08	1.14	-14.93	22.03	52.01
	Male-headed	0.77	13.07	1.39	0.08	1.13	-14.78	21.82	51.51
	Female-headed	0.24	4.12	0.44	0.03	0.36	4.65	6.87	16.22
All households	Total	0.02	0.30	0.03	0.00	0.03	0.34	0.51	1.20
	Poor	0.01	0.23	0.02	0.00	0.02	0.26	0.39	0.92
	Nonpoor	0.02	0.37	0.04	0.00	0.03	0.42	0.62	1.47
	Male-headed	0.02	0.32	0.03	0.00	0.03	0.37	0.54	1.27
	Female-headed	0.00	0.03	0.00	0.00	0.00	0.04	0.06	0.14

Table A5.1: *(c) Continued.*

		Respect to original	Leader split	Small entrant	Leaders merge and small entrant	Leaders merge	Exit of largest	Equal market shares	Perfect competition
(C) Complementary policies (firms)									
Only producers	Total	1.53	13.30	2.26	0.86	0.54	−13.81	21.98	51.18
	Poor	1.46	12.76	2.17	0.82	0.52	−13.25	21.09	49.10
	Nonpoor	1.56	13.64	2.32	0.88	0.55	−14.16	22.54	52.48
	Male-headed	1.55	13.51	2.30	0.87	0.55	−14.02	22.33	51.98
	Female-headed	0.49	4.25	0.72	0.27	0.17	4.41	7.03	16.36
All households	Total	0.04	0.31	0.05	0.02	0.01	0.33	0.52	1.21
	Poor	0.03	0.24	0.04	0.02	0.01	0.25	0.40	0.93
	Nonpoor	0.04	0.38	0.07	0.02	0.02	0.40	0.64	1.48
	Male-headed	0.04	0.33	0.06	0.02	0.01	0.35	0.55	1.28
	Female-headed	0.00	0.04	0.01	0.00	0.00	0.04	0.06	0.14
(D) Complementary policies (farmers – firms)									
Only producers	Total	2.27	13.80	3.07	1.61	0.12	−13.02	22.55	52.29
	Poor	2.18	13.24	2.95	1.54	0.11	−12.49	21.63	50.16
	Nonpoor	2.33	14.15	3.15	1.65	0.12	−13.35	23.12	53.62
	Male-headed	2.31	14.02	3.12	1.63	0.12	−13.22	22.90	53.11
	Female-headed	0.73	4.41	0.98	0.51	0.04	4.16	7.21	16.72
All households	Total	0.05	0.33	0.07	0.04	0.00	0.31	0.53	1.24
	Poor	0.04	0.25	0.06	0.03	0.00	0.24	0.41	0.95
	Nonpoor	0.07	0.40	0.09	0.05	0.00	0.38	0.65	1.51
	Male-headed	0.06	0.35	0.08	0.04	0.00	0.33	0.57	1.31
	Female-headed	0.01	0.04	0.01	0.00	0.00	0.04	0.06	0.14

Table A5.1: *(c) Continued.*

		Respect to original	Leader split	Small entrant	Leaders merge and small entrant	Leaders merge	Exit of largest	Equal market shares	Perfect competition
(E) International prices									
Only producers	Total	12.80	23.49	14.39	12.12	9.37	3.94	33.42	67.98
	Poor	12.27	22.53	13.80	11.63	8.99	3.78	32.05	65.21
	Nonpoor	13.12	24.09	14.75	12.43	9.61	4.04	34.27	69.71
	Male-headed	13.00	23.86	14.61	12.31	9.52	4.00	33.94	69.05
	Female-headed	4.09	7.51	4.60	3.88	3.00	1.26	10.68	21.73
All households	Total	0.30	0.56	0.34	0.29	0.22	0.09	0.79	1.61
	Poor	0.23	0.43	0.26	0.22	0.17	0.07	0.60	1.23
	Nonpoor	0.37	0.68	0.42	0.35	0.27	0.11	0.97	1.96
	Male-headed	0.32	0.59	0.36	0.30	0.24	0.10	0.84	1.71
	Female-headed	0.03	0.06	0.04	0.03	0.03	0.01	0.09	0.18

Table A5.1: *(d) Côte d'Ivoire, cotton (household income percentage changes).*

		Respect to original	Leader split	Small entrant	Leaders merge and small entrant	Leaders merge	Exit of largest	Equal market shares	Perfect competition
(A) Basic model									
Only producers	Total	0.00	4.62	0.40	2.84	3.85	5.99	13.99	35.11
	Poor	0.00	4.45	0.38	2.73	3.71	5.76	13.47	33.79
	Nonpoor	0.00	4.69	0.40	2.88	3.91	6.08	14.21	35.66
	Male-headed	0.00	4.58	0.39	2.81	3.82	5.94	13.87	34.80
	Female-headed	0.00	6.04	0.52	3.70	5.03	7.83	18.28	45.88
All households	Total	0.00	0.38	0.03	0.23	0.31	0.49	1.14	2.85
	Poor	0.00	0.20	0.02	0.12	0.17	0.26	0.61	1.53
	Nonpoor	0.00	0.56	0.05	0.35	0.47	0.73	1.71	4.29
	Male-headed	0.00	0.44	0.04	0.27	0.36	0.57	1.32	3.32
	Female-headed	0.00	0.08	0.01	0.05	0.07	0.11	0.25	0.62
(B) Complementary policies (farmers)									
Only producers	Total	0.76	5.35	1.19	2.06	3.11	5.23	14.64	36.16
	Poor	0.73	5.15	1.14	1.98	2.99	5.03	14.09	34.80
	Nonpoor	0.77	5.43	1.21	2.09	3.16	5.31	14.87	36.72
	Male-headed	0.75	5.30	1.18	2.04	3.08	5.18	14.51	35.83
	Female-headed	0.99	6.99	1.55	2.69	4.06	6.83	19.13	47.25
All households	Total	0.06	0.43	0.10	0.17	0.25	0.42	1.19	2.94
	Poor	0.03	0.23	0.05	0.09	0.14	0.23	0.64	1.58
	Nonpoor	0.09	0.65	0.15	0.25	0.38	0.64	1.79	4.42
	Male-headed	0.07	0.50	0.11	0.19	0.29	0.49	1.38	3.41
	Female-headed	0.01	0.09	0.02	0.04	0.05	0.09	0.26	0.64

Table A5.1: *(d) Continued.*

		Respect to original	Leader split	Small entrant	Leaders merge and small entrant	Leaders merge	Exit of largest	Equal market shares	Perfect competition
(C) Complementary policies (firms)									
Only producers	Total	1.56	6.07	2.06	1.22	2.36	4.45	15.24	36.87
	Poor	1.50	5.85	1.98	1.17	2.27	4.28	14.67	35.48
	Nonpoor	1.58	6.17	2.09	1.23	2.40	4.52	15.48	37.44
	Male-headed	1.54	6.02	2.04	1.21	2.34	4.41	15.10	36.54
	Female-headed	2.03	7.94	2.69	1.59	3.09	5.82	19.91	48.18
All households	Total	0.13	0.49	0.17	0.10	0.19	0.36	1.24	3.00
	Poor	0.07	0.26	0.09	0.05	0.10	0.19	0.66	1.61
	Nonpoor	0.19	0.74	0.25	0.15	0.29	0.54	1.86	4.51
	Male-headed	0.15	0.57	0.19	0.11	0.22	0.42	1.44	3.48
	Female-headed	0.03	0.11	0.04	0.02	0.04	0.08	0.27	0.65
(D) Complementary policies (farmers – firms)									
Only producers	Total	2.30	6.79	2.84	0.45	1.63	3.70	15.88	37.92
	Poor	2.22	6.53	2.73	0.43	1.57	3.56	15.28	36.49
	Nonpoor	2.34	6.89	2.88	0.45	1.66	3.76	16.13	38.50
	Male-headed	2.28	6.73	2.81	0.44	1.62	3.67	15.74	37.58
	Female-headed	3.01	8.87	3.71	0.58	2.13	4.84	20.75	49.54
All households	Total	0.19	0.55	0.23	0.04	0.13	0.30	1.29	3.08
	Poor	0.10	0.30	0.12	0.02	0.07	0.16	0.69	1.65
	Nonpoor	0.28	0.83	0.35	0.05	0.20	0.45	1.94	4.63
	Male-headed	0.22	0.64	0.27	0.04	0.15	0.35	1.50	3.58
	Female-headed	0.04	0.12	0.05	0.01	0.03	0.07	0.28	0.67

Table A5.1: *(d) Continued.*

		Respect to original	Leader split	Small entrant	Leaders merge and small entrant	Leaders merge	Exit of largest	Equal market shares	Perfect competition
(E) International prices									
Only producers	Total	12.59	17.56	13.59	9.80	7.99	5.90	26.33	52.64
	Poor	12.11	16.90	13.08	9.43	7.69	5.68	25.34	50.66
	Nonpoor	12.78	17.83	13.80	9.96	8.12	5.99	26.74	53.45
	Male-headed	12.47	17.40	13.47	9.72	7.92	5.85	26.10	52.17
	Female-headed	16.44	22.94	17.76	12.81	10.45	7.71	34.41	68.78
All households	Total	1.02	1.43	1.10	0.80	0.65	0.48	2.14	4.28
	Poor	0.55	0.77	0.59	0.43	0.35	0.26	1.15	2.30
	Nonpoor	1.54	2.15	1.66	1.20	0.98	0.72	3.22	6.43
	Male-headed	1.19	1.66	1.28	0.93	0.75	0.56	2.49	4.97
	Female-headed	0.22	0.31	0.24	0.17	0.14	0.10	0.46	0.93

Table A5.1: *(e) Malawi, cotton (household income percentage changes).*

		Respect to original	Three firms	Four firms	Small entrant with half of the benefits
(A) Basic model					
Only producers	Total	0.00	1.87	3.02	0.94
	Poor	0.00	1.49	2.40	0.75
	Nonpoor	0.00	2.12	3.43	1.06
	Male-headed	0.00	1.89	3.05	0.95
	Female-headed	0.00	1.68	2.72	0.84
All households	Total	0.00	0.06	0.09	0.03
	Poor	0.00	0.04	0.07	0.02
	Nonpoor	0.00	0.07	0.11	0.03
	Male-headed	0.00	0.07	0.11	0.03
	Female-headed	0.00	0.02	0.04	0.01
(B) Complementary policies (farmers)					
Only producers	Total	0.19	2.07	3.23	1.15
	Poor	0.15	1.65	2.58	0.91
	Nonpoor	0.22	2.36	3.68	1.31
	Male-headed	0.19	2.10	3.27	1.16
	Female-headed	0.17	1.87	2.92	1.04
All households	Total	0.01	0.06	0.10	0.04
	Poor	0.00	0.05	0.07	0.03
	Nonpoor	0.01	0.08	0.12	0.04
	Male-headed	0.01	0.08	0.12	0.04
	Female-headed	0.00	0.03	0.04	0.01
(C) Complementary policies (firms)					
Only producers	Total	0.37	2.29	3.47	1.29
	Poor	0.30	1.83	2.77	1.03
	Nonpoor	0.42	2.61	3.95	1.47
	Male-headed	0.38	2.32	3.51	1.30
	Female-headed	0.34	2.07	3.13	1.16
All households	Total	0.01	0.07	0.11	0.04
	Poor	0.01	0.05	0.08	0.03
	Nonpoor	0.01	0.09	0.13	0.05
	Male-headed	0.01	0.08	0.13	0.05
	Female-headed	0.00	0.03	0.04	0.02

Table A5.1: *(e) Continued.*

		Respect to original	Three firms	Four firms	Small entrant with half of the benefits
(D) Complementary policies (farmers – firms)					
Only producers	Total	0.56	2.49	3.69	1.50
	Poor	0.45	1.99	2.94	1.19
	Nonpoor	0.64	2.84	4.19	1.71
	Male-headed	0.57	2.52	3.73	1.52
	Female-headed	0.51	2.25	3.33	1.35
All households	Total	0.02	0.08	0.11	0.05
	Poor	0.01	0.06	0.08	0.03
	Nonpoor	0.02	0.09	0.14	0.06
	Male-headed	0.02	0.09	0.13	0.05
	Female-headed	0.01	0.03	0.05	0.02
(E) International prices					
Only producers	Total	3.28	5.60	7.04	4.06
	Poor	2.61	4.46	5.61	3.23
	Nonpoor	3.73	6.37	8.01	4.62
	Male-headed	3.32	5.67	7.12	4.11
	Female-headed	2.96	5.05	6.35	3.66
All households	Total	0.10	0.17	0.22	0.12
	Poor	0.07	0.12	0.16	0.09
	Nonpoor	0.12	0.21	0.26	0.15
	Male-headed	0.12	0.20	0.26	0.15
	Female-headed	0.04	0.07	0.09	0.05

Table A5.1: (f) *Côte d'Ivoire, cocoa (household income percentage changes).*

		Respect to original	Leader split	Small entrant	Leaders merge and small entrant	Leaders merge	Exit of largest	Equal market shares	Perfect competition
(A) Basic model									
Only producers	Total	0.00	1.13	0.21	0.64	0.91	1.26	10.53	21.49
	Poor	0.00	1.13	0.21	0.64	0.92	1.27	10.60	21.62
	Nonpoor	0.00	1.12	0.21	0.63	0.91	1.25	10.46	21.33
	Male-headed	0.00	1.14	0.22	0.55	0.92	1.27	10.64	21.70
	Female-headed	0.00	0.92	0.17	0.52	0.75	1.03	8.60	17.55
All households	Total	0.00	0.33	0.06	0.19	0.27	0.37	3.12	6.37
	Poor	0.00	0.35	0.07	0.20	0.29	0.40	3.31	6.75
	Nonpoor	0.00	0.31	0.06	0.18	0.25	0.35	2.92	5.96
	Male-headed	0.00	0.39	0.07	0.22	0.31	0.43	3.61	7.37
	Female-headed	0.00	0.08	0.02	0.05	0.07	0.09	0.75	1.53
(B) Complementary policies (farmers)									
Only producers	Total	0.96	2.09	1.18	0.32	0.04	0.31	11.44	22.65
	Poor	0.96	2.10	1.19	0.32	0.04	0.31	11.51	22.78
	Nonpoor	0.95	2.07	1.17	0.32	0.04	0.31	11.35	22.48
	Male-headed	0.97	2.11	1.19	0.33	0.04	0.31	11.55	22.87
	Female-headed	0.78	1.71	0.96	0.26	0.03	0.25	9.34	18.50
All households	Total	0.28	0.62	0.35	0.10	0.01	0.09	3.39	6.71
	Poor	0.30	0.66	0.37	0.10	0.01	0.10	3.59	7.11
	Nonpoor	0.27	0.58	0.33	0.09	0.01	0.09	3.17	6.28
	Male-headed	0.33	0.72	0.40	0.11	0.01	0.11	3.92	7.77
	Female-headed	0.07	0.15	0.08	0.02	0.00	0.02	0.82	1.62

Table A5.1: *(f) Continued.*

		Respect to original	Leader split	Small entrant	Leaders merge and small entrant	Leaders merge	Exit of largest	Equal market shares	Perfect competition
(C) Complementary policies (firms)									
Only producers	Total	1.46	2.59	1.69	0.83	0.54	0.20	11.77	22.99
	Poor	1.47	2.60	1.70	0.84	0.54	0.20	11.84	23.13
	Nonpoor	1.45	2.57	1.68	0.83	0.53	0.20	11.68	22.82
	Male-headed	1.47	2.61	1.71	0.84	0.54	0.20	11.88	23.22
	Female-headed	1.19	2.11	1.38	0.68	0.44	0.16	9.61	18.78
All households	Total	0.43	0.77	0.50	0.25	0.16	0.06	3.49	6.82
	Poor	0.46	0.81	0.53	0.26	0.17	0.06	3.70	7.22
	Nonpoor	0.40	0.72	0.47	0.23	0.15	0.05	3.26	6.37
	Male-headed	0.50	0.89	0.58	0.29	0.18	0.07	4.04	7.89
	Female-headed	0.10	0.18	0.12	0.06	0.04	0.01	0.84	1.64
(D) Complementary policies (farmers – firms)									
Only producers	Total	2.41	3.54	2.65	1.79	1.48	1.14	12.66	24.15
	Poor	2.42	3.56	2.67	1.80	1.49	1.15	12.74	24.30
	Nonpoor	2.39	3.52	2.63	1.77	1.47	1.13	12.57	23.97
	Male-headed	2.43	3.58	2.68	1.81	1.49	1.15	12.79	24.38
	Female-headed	1.97	2.89	2.17	1.46	1.21	0.93	10.34	19.72
All households	Total	0.71	1.05	0.79	0.53	0.44	0.34	3.75	7.16
	Poor	0.76	1.11	0.83	0.56	0.46	0.36	3.98	7.59
	Nonpoor	0.67	0.98	0.74	0.50	0.41	0.32	3.51	6.69
	Male-headed	0.83	1.22	0.91	0.61	0.51	0.39	4.34	8.29
	Female-headed	0.17	0.25	0.19	0.13	0.11	0.08	0.90	1.72

Table A5.1: *(f) Continued.*

	Respect to original	Leader split	Small entrant	Leaders merge and small entrant	Leaders merge	Exit of largest	Equal market shares	Perfect competition
(E) International prices								
Only producers Total	12.74	13.99	13.09	12.11	11.68	11.34	23.13	36.93
Poor	12.81	14.07	13.17	12.18	11.75	11.41	23.27	37.15
Nonpoor	12.64	13.88	12.99	12.02	11.59	11.25	22.96	36.65
Male-headed	12.86	14.12	13.21	12.22	11.79	11.45	23.35	37.29
Female-headed	10.40	11.42	10.69	9.89	9.54	9.26	18.89	30.16
All households Total	3.78	4.15	3.88	3.59	3.46	3.36	6.86	10.95
Poor	4.00	4.39	4.11	3.80	3.67	3.56	7.27	11.60
Nonpoor	3.53	3.88	3.63	3.36	3.24	3.14	6.41	10.24
Male-headed	4.37	4.80	4.49	4.15	4.01	3.89	7.94	12.67
Female-headed	0.91	1.00	0.93	0.86	0.83	0.81	1.65	2.63

Table A5.1: (g) Ghana, cocoa (household income percentage changes).

		Respect to original	Leader split	Small entrant	Leaders merge and small entrant	Leaders merge	Exit of largest	Equal market shares	Perfect competition
(A) Basic model									
Only producers	Total	0.00	0.86	0.07	0.26	0.37	1.01	7.33	11.90
	Poor	0.00	0.82	0.07	0.25	0.35	0.96	7.01	11.37
	Nonpoor	0.00	0.91	0.07	0.28	0.39	1.06	7.75	12.57
	Male-headed	0.00	0.89	0.07	0.27	0.38	1.04	7.56	12.26
	Female-headed	0.00	0.77	0.06	0.23	0.33	0.90	6.57	10.67
All households	Total	0.00	0.14	0.01	0.04	0.06	0.17	1.21	1.97
	Poor	0.00	0.14	0.01	0.04	0.06	0.16	1.19	1.94
	Nonpoor	0.00	0.14	0.01	0.04	0.06	0.17	1.24	2.01
	Male-headed	0.00	0.16	0.01	0.05	0.07	0.19	1.39	2.26
	Female-headed	0.00	0.09	0.01	0.03	0.04	0.11	0.81	1.31
(B) Complementary policies (farmers)									
Only producers	Total	0.43	1.29	0.50	0.17	0.06	0.58	7.73	12.40
	Poor	0.41	1.23	0.48	0.16	0.06	0.55	7.39	11.84
	Nonpoor	0.45	1.36	0.53	0.18	0.06	0.61	8.17	13.10
	Male-headed	0.44	1.33	0.52	0.17	0.06	0.60	7.97	12.78
	Female-headed	0.38	1.16	0.45	0.15	0.05	0.52	6.93	11.12
All households	Total	0.07	0.21	0.08	0.03	0.01	0.10	1.28	2.05
	Poor	0.07	0.21	0.08	0.03	0.01	0.09	1.26	2.02
	Nonpoor	0.07	0.22	0.09	0.03	0.01	0.10	1.30	2.09
	Male-headed	0.08	0.25	0.10	0.03	0.01	0.11	1.47	2.36
	Female-headed	0.05	0.14	0.06	0.02	0.01	0.06	0.85	1.37

Table A5.1: *(g) Continued.*

		Respect to original	Leader split	Small entrant	Leaders merge and small entrant	Leaders merge	Exit of largest	Equal market shares	Perfect competition
(C) Complementary policies (firms)									
Only producers	Total	0.77	1.62	0.85	0.51	0.39	0.23	7.95	12.62
	Poor	0.73	1.55	0.81	0.49	0.37	0.22	7.59	12.06
	Nonpoor	0.81	1.71	0.90	0.54	0.41	0.25	8.39	13.33
	Male-headed	0.79	1.67	0.88	0.53	0.40	0.24	8.19	13.01
	Female-headed	0.69	1.45	0.76	0.46	0.35	0.21	7.12	11.32
All households	Total	0.13	0.27	0.14	0.08	0.06	0.04	1.32	2.09
	Poor	0.12	0.26	0.14	0.08	0.06	0.04	1.29	2.06
	Nonpoor	0.13	0.27	0.14	0.09	0.07	0.04	1.34	2.13
	Male-headed	0.15	0.31	0.16	0.10	0.07	0.04	1.51	2.40
	Female-headed	0.08	0.18	0.09	0.06	0.04	0.03	0.88	1.39
(D) Complementary policies (farmers – firms)									
Only producers	Total	1.19	2.05	1.28	0.94	0.81	0.19	8.34	13.12
	Poor	1.14	1.96	1.22	0.90	0.78	0.18	7.97	12.53
	Nonpoor	1.26	2.17	1.35	0.99	0.86	0.20	8.81	13.86
	Male-headed	1.23	2.11	1.32	0.97	0.84	0.20	8.60	13.52
	Female-headed	1.07	1.84	1.15	0.84	0.73	0.17	7.48	11.76
All households	Total	0.20	0.34	0.21	0.16	0.13	0.03	1.38	2.17
	Poor	0.19	0.33	0.21	0.15	0.13	0.03	1.36	2.14
	Nonpoor	0.20	0.35	0.22	0.16	0.14	0.03	1.41	2.21
	Male-headed	0.23	0.39	0.24	0.18	0.15	0.04	1.58	2.49
	Female-headed	0.13	0.23	0.14	0.10	0.09	0.02	0.92	1.45

Table A5.1: *(g) Continued.*

		Respect to original	Leader split	Small entrant	Leaders merge and small entrant	Leaders merge	Exit of largest	Equal market shares	Perfect competition
(E) International prices									
Only producers	Total	6.24	7.17	6.38	5.98	5.78	5.15	13.50	19.21
	Poor	5.96	6.85	6.10	5.71	5.53	4.92	12.90	18.35
	Nonpoor	6.59	7.57	6.74	6.31	6.11	5.44	14.26	20.29
	Male-headed	6.43	7.38	6.58	6.16	5.96	5.31	13.92	19.80
	Female-headed	5.59	6.42	5.72	5.36	5.19	4.62	12.11	17.22
All households	Total	1.03	1.19	1.06	0.99	0.96	0.85	2.23	3.18
	Poor	1.02	1.17	1.04	0.97	0.94	0.84	2.20	3.13
	Nonpoor	1.05	1.21	1.08	1.01	0.98	0.87	2.28	3.24
	Male-headed	1.19	1.36	1.21	1.14	1.10	0.98	2.57	3.65
	Female-headed	0.69	0.79	0.70	0.66	0.64	0.57	1.49	2.12

Table A5.1: *(h) Côte d'Ivoire, coffee (household income percentage changes).*

		Respect to original	Leader split	Small entrant	Leaders merge and small entrant	Leaders merge	Exit of largest	Equal market shares	Perfect competition
(A) Basic model									
Only producers	Total	0.00	0.58	0.11	0.33	0.47	0.65	5.42	11.06
	Poor	0.00	0.67	0.13	0.38	0.54	0.75	6.26	12.77
	Nonpoor	0.00	0.42	0.08	0.24	0.34	0.48	3.97	8.10
	Male-headed	0.00	0.59	0.11	0.34	0.48	0.66	5.53	11.27
	Female-headed	0.00	0.35	0.07	0.20	0.29	0.40	3.31	6.75
All households	Total	0.00	0.13	0.03	0.08	0.11	0.15	1.24	2.53
	Poor	0.00	0.19	0.04	0.11	0.15	0.21	1.74	3.56
	Nonpoor	0.00	0.07	0.01	0.04	0.06	0.08	0.69	1.42
	Male-headed	0.00	0.16	0.03	0.09	0.13	0.17	1.46	2.97
	Female-headed	0.00	0.02	0.00	0.01	0.02	0.02	0.21	0.42
(B) Complementary policies (farmers)									
Only producers	Total	0.49	1.08	0.61	0.17	0.02	0.16	5.89	11.65
	Poor	0.57	1.24	0.70	0.19	0.02	0.18	6.79	13.45
	Nonpoor	0.36	0.79	0.44	0.12	0.01	0.12	4.31	8.53
	Male-headed	0.50	1.10	0.62	0.17	0.02	0.16	6.00	11.88
	Female-headed	0.30	0.66	0.37	0.10	0.01	0.10	3.59	7.11
All households	Total	0.11	0.25	0.14	0.04	0.00	0.04	1.35	2.67
	Poor	0.16	0.35	0.20	0.05	0.01	0.05	1.89	3.75
	Nonpoor	0.06	0.14	0.08	0.02	0.00	0.02	0.75	1.49
	Male-headed	0.13	0.29	0.16	0.04	0.01	0.04	1.58	3.13
	Female-headed	0.02	0.04	0.02	0.01	0.00	0.01	0.23	0.45

Table A5.1: *(h) Continued.*

		Respect to original	Leader split	Small entrant	Leaders merge and small entrant	Leaders merge	Exit of largest	Equal market shares	Perfect competition
(C) Complementary policies (firms)									
Only producers	Total	0.75	1.33	0.87	0.43	0.28	0.10	6.06	11.83
	Poor	0.87	1.54	1.01	0.50	0.32	0.12	6.99	13.66
	Nonpoor	0.55	0.97	0.64	0.31	0.20	0.07	4.43	8.66
	Male-headed	0.77	1.36	0.89	0.44	0.28	0.10	6.17	12.06
	Female-headed	0.46	0.81	0.53	0.26	0.17	0.06	3.70	7.22
All households	Total	0.17	0.30	0.20	0.10	0.06	0.02	1.39	2.71
	Poor	0.24	0.43	0.28	0.14	0.09	0.03	1.95	3.80
	Nonpoor	0.10	0.17	0.11	0.06	0.04	0.01	0.78	1.52
	Male-headed	0.20	0.36	0.23	0.12	0.07	0.03	1.63	3.18
	Female-headed	0.03	0.05	0.03	0.02	0.01	0.00	0.23	0.45
(D) Complementary policies (farmers – firms)									
Only producers	Total	1.24	1.82	1.36	0.92	0.76	0.59	6.52	12.43
	Poor	1.43	2.10	1.58	1.06	0.88	0.68	7.52	14.35
	Nonpoor	0.91	1.33	1.00	0.67	0.56	0.43	4.77	9.10
	Male-headed	1.26	1.86	1.39	0.94	0.78	0.60	6.64	12.67
	Female-headed	0.76	1.11	0.83	0.56	0.46	0.36	3.98	7.58
All households	Total	0.28	0.42	0.31	0.21	0.17	0.13	1.49	2.85
	Poor	0.40	0.59	0.44	0.30	0.24	0.19	2.10	4.00
	Nonpoor	0.16	0.23	0.17	0.12	0.10	0.08	0.84	1.59
	Male-headed	0.33	0.49	0.37	0.25	0.20	0.16	1.75	3.34
	Female-headed	0.05	0.07	0.05	0.04	0.03	0.02	0.25	0.48

Table A5.1: *(h) Continued.*

		Respect to original	Leader split	Small entrant	Leaders merge and small entrant	Leaders merge	Exit of largest	Equal market shares	Perfect competition
(E) International prices									
Only producers	Total	6.55	7.20	6.73	6.23	6.01	5.83	11.90	19.00
	Poor	7.57	8.31	7.77	7.19	6.94	6.73	13.74	21.94
	Nonpoor	4.80	5.27	4.93	4.56	4.40	4.27	8.72	13.92
	Male-headed	6.68	7.34	6.86	6.35	6.13	5.95	12.13	19.37
	Female-headed	4.00	4.39	4.11	3.80	3.67	3.56	7.26	11.60
All households	Total	1.50	1.65	1.54	1.43	1.38	1.34	2.73	4.35
	Poor	2.11	2.31	2.17	2.00	1.93	1.88	3.83	6.11
	Nonpoor	0.84	0.92	0.86	0.80	0.77	0.75	1.53	2.44
	Male-headed	1.76	1.93	1.81	1.67	1.61	1.57	3.20	5.10
	Female-headed	0.25	0.28	0.26	0.24	0.23	0.22	0.46	0.73

Table A5.1: *(i) Rwanda, coffee (household income percentage changes).*

		Respect to original	Leader split	Small entrant	Leaders merge and small entrant	Leaders merge	Exit of largest	Equal market shares	Perfect competition
(A) Basic model									
Only producers	Total	0.00	0.39	0.05	0.38	0.52	0.54	0.77	2.82
	Poor	0.00	0.49	0.06	0.47	0.64	0.67	0.96	3.51
	Nonpoor	0.00	0.34	0.04	0.33	0.45	0.47	0.67	2.47
	Male-headed	0.00	0.37	0.05	0.35	0.48	0.50	0.72	2.64
	Female-headed	0.00	0.47	0.06	0.45	0.61	0.64	0.91	3.35
All households	Total	0.00	0.04	0.00	0.04	0.05	0.05	0.08	0.28
	Poor	0.00	0.04	0.00	0.04	0.05	0.05	0.07	0.27
	Nonpoor	0.00	0.04	0.01	0.04	0.05	0.06	0.08	0.29
	Male-headed	0.00	0.04	0.01	0.04	0.05	0.06	0.08	0.29
	Female-headed	0.00	0.04	0.00	0.03	0.05	0.05	0.07	0.26
(B) Complementary policies (farmers)									
Only producers	Total	0.14	0.53	0.20	0.23	0.38	0.40	0.91	2.99
	Poor	0.18	0.66	0.24	0.29	0.47	0.50	1.13	3.73
	Nonpoor	0.12	0.47	0.17	0.20	0.33	0.35	0.79	2.62
	Male-headed	0.13	0.50	0.18	0.22	0.35	0.37	0.85	2.80
	Female-headed	0.17	0.63	0.23	0.28	0.45	0.48	1.08	3.56
All households	Total	0.01	0.05	0.02	0.02	0.04	0.04	0.09	0.30
	Poor	0.01	0.05	0.02	0.02	0.04	0.04	0.09	0.29
	Nonpoor	0.01	0.06	0.02	0.02	0.04	0.04	0.09	0.31
	Male-headed	0.01	0.06	0.02	0.02	0.04	0.04	0.09	0.31
	Female-headed	0.01	0.05	0.02	0.02	0.03	0.04	0.08	0.28

Table A5.1: *(i) Continued.*

		Respect to original	Leader split	Small entrant	Leaders merge and small entrant	Leaders merge	Exit of largest	Equal market shares	Perfect competition
(C) Complementary policies (firms)									
Only producers	Total	0.24	0.63	0.30	0.13	0.29	0.31	0.99	3.09
	Poor	0.29	0.78	0.37	0.16	0.36	0.38	1.23	3.85
	Nonpoor	0.21	0.55	0.26	0.12	0.25	0.27	0.87	2.71
	Male-headed	0.22	0.59	0.28	0.12	0.27	0.29	0.93	2.90
	Female-headed	0.28	0.75	0.35	0.16	0.34	0.37	1.18	3.68
All households	Total	0.02	0.06	0.03	0.01	0.03	0.03	0.10	0.31
	Poor	0.02	0.06	0.03	0.01	0.03	0.03	0.09	0.29
	Nonpoor	0.02	0.07	0.03	0.01	0.03	0.03	0.10	0.32
	Male-headed	0.02	0.07	0.03	0.01	0.03	0.03	0.10	0.32
	Female-headed	0.02	0.06	0.03	0.01	0.03	0.03	0.09	0.28
(D) Complementary policies (farmers – firms)									
Only producers	Total	0.38	0.77	0.44	0.01	0.15	0.17	1.12	3.27
	Poor	0.47	0.96	0.55	0.01	0.19	0.21	1.40	4.07
	Nonpoor	0.33	0.68	0.39	0.01	0.13	0.15	0.98	2.86
	Male-headed	0.35	0.72	0.41	0.01	0.14	0.16	1.05	3.06
	Female-headed	0.45	0.92	0.53	0.01	0.18	0.21	1.34	3.89
All households	Total	0.04	0.08	0.04	0.00	0.02	0.02	0.11	0.33
	Poor	0.04	0.07	0.04	0.00	0.01	0.02	0.11	0.31
	Nonpoor	0.04	0.08	0.05	0.00	0.02	0.02	0.12	0.34
	Male-headed	0.04	0.08	0.05	0.00	0.02	0.02	0.12	0.34
	Female-headed	0.03	0.07	0.04	0.00	0.01	0.02	0.10	0.30

Table A5.1: *(i) Continued.*

		Respect to original	Leader split	Small entrant	Leaders merge and small entrant	Leaders merge	Exit of largest	Equal market shares	Perfect competition
(E) International prices									
Only producers	Total	2.02	2.48	2.14	1.65	1.41	1.39	2.78	5.36
	Poor	2.52	3.09	2.67	2.06	1.76	1.73	3.47	6.67
	Nonpoor	1.77	2.17	1.88	1.45	1.24	1.22	2.44	4.69
	Male-headed	1.89	2.32	2.01	1.55	1.32	1.30	2.61	5.02
	Female-headed	2.41	2.95	2.55	1.96	1.68	1.66	3.31	6.37
All households	Total	0.20	0.25	0.21	0.16	0.14	0.14	0.28	0.53
	Poor	0.19	0.24	0.20	0.16	0.13	0.13	0.27	0.51
	Nonpoor	0.21	0.26	0.22	0.17	0.15	0.14	0.29	0.55
	Male-headed	0.21	0.26	0.22	0.17	0.15	0.14	0.29	0.55
	Female-headed	0.19	0.23	0.20	0.15	0.13	0.13	0.26	0.49

Table A5.1: *(i) Uganda, coffee (household income percentage changes).*

		Respect to original	Leader split	Small entrant	Leaders merge and small entrant	Leaders merge	Exit of largest	Equal market shares	Perfect competition
(A) Basic model									
Only producers	Total	0.00	0.09	0.01	0.06	0.08	0.10	0.81	1.59
	Poor	0.00	0.09	0.01	0.06	0.08	0.10	0.81	1.59
	Nonpoor	0.00	0.09	0.01	0.06	0.08	0.10	0.81	1.59
	Male-headed	0.00	0.09	0.01	0.06	0.08	0.10	0.87	1.70
	Female-headed	0.00	0.07	0.01	0.05	0.06	0.08	0.64	1.25
All households	Total	0.00	0.02	0.00	0.02	0.02	0.03	0.22	0.43
	Poor	0.00	0.02	0.00	0.01	0.02	0.02	0.17	0.33
	Nonpoor	0.00	0.03	0.00	0.02	0.02	0.03	0.26	0.51
	Male-headed	0.00	0.03	0.00	0.02	0.02	0.03	0.24	0.47
	Female-headed	0.00	0.02	0.00	0.01	0.01	0.02	0.16	0.30
(B) Complementary policies (farmers)									
Only producers	Total	0.16	0.25	0.17	0.10	0.08	0.06	0.97	1.77
	Poor	0.16	0.25	0.17	0.10	0.08	0.06	0.97	1.77
	Nonpoor	0.16	0.25	0.17	0.10	0.08	0.06	0.97	1.77
	Male-headed	0.17	0.26	0.19	0.11	0.09	0.07	1.04	1.89
	Female-headed	0.13	0.19	0.14	0.08	0.07	0.05	0.76	1.39
All households	Total	0.04	0.07	0.05	0.03	0.02	0.02	0.26	0.48
	Poor	0.03	0.05	0.04	0.02	0.02	0.01	0.20	0.37
	Nonpoor	0.05	0.08	0.06	0.03	0.03	0.02	0.31	0.56
	Male-headed	0.05	0.07	0.05	0.03	0.03	0.02	0.29	0.53
	Female-headed	0.03	0.05	0.03	0.02	0.02	0.01	0.19	0.34

Table A5.1: *(j) Continued.*

		Respect to original	Leader split	Small entrant	Leaders merge and small entrant	Leaders merge	Exit of largest	Equal market shares	Perfect competition
(C) Complementary policies (firms)									
Only producers	Total	0.25	0.34	0.26	0.19	0.17	0.15	1.05	1.85
	Poor	0.25	0.34	0.26	0.19	0.17	0.15	1.05	1.85
	Nonpoor	0.25	0.34	0.26	0.19	0.17	0.15	1.05	1.85
	Male-headed	0.27	0.36	0.28	0.20	0.18	0.16	1.12	1.97
	Female-headed	0.20	0.26	0.21	0.15	0.14	0.12	0.82	1.45
All households	Total	0.07	0.09	0.07	0.05	0.05	0.04	0.28	0.50
	Poor	0.05	0.07	0.05	0.04	0.04	0.03	0.22	0.38
	Nonpoor	0.08	0.11	0.08	0.06	0.05	0.05	0.33	0.59
	Male-headed	0.07	0.10	0.08	0.06	0.05	0.05	0.31	0.55
	Female-headed	0.05	0.06	0.05	0.04	0.03	0.03	0.20	0.35
(D) Complementary policies (farmers – firms)									
Only producers	Total	0.41	0.50	0.43	0.35	0.33	0.31	1.21	2.02
	Poor	0.41	0.50	0.43	0.35	0.33	0.31	1.21	2.02
	Nonpoor	0.41	0.50	0.43	0.35	0.33	0.31	1.21	2.02
	Male-headed	0.44	0.53	0.45	0.38	0.36	0.33	1.29	2.16
	Female-headed	0.32	0.39	0.33	0.28	0.26	0.25	0.95	1.59
All households	Total	0.11	0.13	0.11	0.10	0.09	0.08	0.33	0.55
	Poor	0.09	0.10	0.09	0.07	0.07	0.06	0.25	0.42
	Nonpoor	0.13	0.16	0.14	0.11	0.11	0.10	0.38	0.64
	Male-headed	0.12	0.15	0.13	0.11	0.10	0.09	0.36	0.60
	Female-headed	0.08	0.09	0.08	0.07	0.06	0.06	0.23	0.39

Table A5.1: *(j) Continued.*

		Respect to original	Leader split	Small entrant	Leaders merge and small entrant	Leaders merge	Exit of largest	Equal market shares	Perfect competition
(E) International prices									
Only producers	Total	2.12	2.21	2.14	2.06	2.03	2.01	2.93	3.92
	Poor	2.12	2.21	2.14	2.06	2.03	2.01	2.93	3.92
	Nonpoor	2.12	2.21	2.14	2.06	2.03	2.01	2.93	3.92
	Male-headed	2.26	2.36	2.28	2.20	2.16	2.14	3.12	4.18
	Female-headed	1.66	1.74	1.68	1.61	1.59	1.58	2.30	3.07
All households	Total	0.57	0.60	0.58	0.55	0.55	0.54	0.79	1.06
	Poor	0.44	0.46	0.44	0.43	0.42	0.42	0.61	0.81
	Nonpoor	0.67	0.70	0.68	0.65	0.64	0.64	0.93	1.24
	Male-headed	0.63	0.66	0.64	0.61	0.60	0.60	0.87	1.17
	Female-headed	0.40	0.42	0.41	0.39	0.39	0.38	0.56	0.75

Table A5.1: *(k) Malawi, tobacco (household income percentage changes).*

		Respect to original	Leader split	Small entrant	Leaders merge and small entrant	Leaders merge	Exit of largest	Equal market shares	Perfect competition
(A) Basic model									
Only producers	Total	0.00	1.45	0.04	1.16	1.36	1.59	5.68	12.24
	Poor	0.00	1.13	0.03	0.91	1.06	1.25	4.44	9.57
	Nonpoor	0.00	1.60	0.04	1.28	1.50	1.76	6.26	13.50
	Male-headed	0.00	1.47	0.04	1.18	1.38	1.61	5.75	12.40
	Female-headed	0.00	1.27	0.03	1.02	1.20	1.40	5.00	10.78
All households	Total	0.00	0.21	0.01	0.17	0.20	0.23	0.82	1.76
	Poor	0.00	0.12	0.00	0.09	0.11	0.13	0.46	0.99
	Nonpoor	0.00	0.28	0.01	0.23	0.26	0.31	1.10	2.38
	Male-headed	0.00	0.25	0.01	0.20	0.23	0.28	0.98	2.12
	Female-headed	0.00	0.08	0.00	0.06	0.07	0.08	0.30	0.64
(B) Complementary policies (farmers)									
Only producers	Total	0.42	1.85	0.47	0.73	0.94	1.17	6.07	12.78
	Poor	0.33	1.45	0.37	0.57	0.73	0.92	4.75	9.99
	Nonpoor	0.47	2.04	0.52	0.80	1.04	1.29	6.69	14.08
	Male-headed	0.43	1.87	0.48	0.74	0.95	1.19	6.15	12.94
	Female-headed	0.37	1.63	0.42	0.64	0.83	1.03	5.35	11.25
All households	Total	0.06	0.27	0.07	0.10	0.14	0.17	0.87	1.84
	Poor	0.03	0.15	0.04	0.06	0.08	0.10	0.49	1.04
	Nonpoor	0.08	0.36	0.09	0.14	0.18	0.23	1.18	2.48
	Male-headed	0.07	0.32	0.08	0.13	0.16	0.20	1.05	2.21
	Female-headed	0.02	0.10	0.02	0.04	0.05	0.06	0.32	0.67

Table A5.1: *(k) Continued.*

		Respect to original	Leader split	Small entrant	Leaders merge and small entrant	Leaders merge	Exit of largest	Equal market shares	Perfect competition
(C) Complementary policies (firms)									
Only producers	Total	0.70	2.08	0.77	0.43	0.66	0.89	6.26	12.98
	Poor	0.55	1.63	0.60	0.34	0.52	0.70	4.90	10.15
	Nonpoor	0.77	2.30	0.85	0.48	0.73	0.98	6.90	14.31
	Male-headed	0.71	2.11	0.78	0.44	0.67	0.90	6.34	13.14
	Female-headed	0.62	1.83	0.67	0.38	0.58	0.79	5.51	11.43
All households	Total	0.10	0.30	0.11	0.06	0.10	0.13	0.90	1.87
	Poor	0.06	0.17	0.06	0.04	0.05	0.07	0.51	1.05
	Nonpoor	0.14	0.40	0.15	0.08	0.13	0.17	1.22	2.52
	Male-headed	0.12	0.36	0.13	0.07	0.11	0.15	1.08	2.24
	Female-headed	0.04	0.11	0.04	0.02	0.03	0.05	0.33	0.68
(D) Complementary policies (farmers – firms)									
Only producers	Total	1.12	2.48	1.20	0.01	0.25	0.48	6.65	13.51
	Poor	0.88	1.94	0.94	0.00	0.19	0.37	5.20	10.56
	Nonpoor	1.24	2.74	1.32	0.01	0.27	0.52	7.33	14.89
	Male-headed	1.14	2.51	1.21	0.01	0.25	0.48	6.74	13.68
	Female-headed	0.99	2.19	1.06	0.01	0.22	0.42	5.86	11.89
All households	Total	0.16	0.36	0.17	0.00	0.04	0.07	0.96	1.94
	Poor	0.09	0.20	0.10	0.00	0.02	0.04	0.54	1.09
	Nonpoor	0.22	0.48	0.23	0.00	0.05	0.09	1.29	2.62
	Male-headed	0.19	0.43	0.21	0.00	0.04	0.08	1.15	2.33
	Female-headed	0.06	0.13	0.06	0.00	0.01	0.02	0.35	0.71

Table A5.1: *(k) Continued.*

		Respect to original	Leader split	Small entrant	Leaders merge and small entrant	Leaders merge	Exit of largest	Equal market shares	Perfect competition
(E) International prices									
Only producers	Total	6.03	7.43	6.22	4.88	4.49	4.26	11.64	19.78
	Poor	4.71	5.81	4.86	3.82	3.51	3.33	9.10	15.47
	Nonpoor	6.64	8.19	6.85	5.38	4.95	4.70	12.83	21.81
	Male-headed	6.10	7.52	6.30	4.94	4.55	4.32	11.79	20.04
	Female-headed	5.31	6.54	5.47	4.30	3.96	3.75	10.25	17.42
All households	Total	0.87	1.07	0.89	0.70	0.65	0.61	1.68	2.85
	Poor	0.49	0.60	0.50	0.40	0.36	0.35	0.94	1.60
	Nonpoor	1.17	1.44	1.21	0.95	0.87	0.83	2.26	3.84
	Male-headed	1.04	1.28	1.07	0.84	0.78	0.74	2.01	3.42
	Female-headed	0.31	0.39	0.32	0.25	0.23	0.22	0.61	1.03

Table A5.1: *(I) Zambia, tobacco (household income percentage changes).*

		Respect to original	Leader split	Small entrant	Leaders merge and small entrant	Leaders merge	Exit of largest	Equal market shares	Perfect competition
(A) Basic model									
Only producers	Total	0.00	3.25	0.74	1.16	2.48	4.69	7.23	21.75
	Poor	0.00	2.52	0.58	0.90	1.92	3.64	5.61	16.86
	Nonpoor	0.00	3.71	0.85	1.32	2.83	5.36	8.26	24.84
	Male-headed	0.00	3.37	0.77	1.20	2.56	4.86	7.49	22.53
	Female-headed	0.00	2.51	0.57	0.90	1.91	3.63	5.59	16.82
All households	Total	0.00	0.07	0.02	0.03	0.05	0.10	0.16	0.47
	Poor	0.00	0.05	0.01	0.02	0.04	0.07	0.11	0.32
	Nonpoor	0.00	0.09	0.02	0.03	0.07	0.13	0.20	0.59
	Male-headed	0.00	0.08	0.02	0.03	0.06	0.11	0.17	0.52
	Female-headed	0.00	0.04	0.01	0.01	0.03	0.05	0.08	0.25
(B) Complementary policies (farmers)									
Only producers	Total	0.50	3.76	1.26	0.65	1.99	4.19	7.68	22.43
	Poor	0.39	2.91	0.98	0.51	1.55	3.25	5.95	17.39
	Nonpoor	0.57	4.29	1.44	0.75	2.28	4.79	8.77	25.61
	Male-headed	0.52	3.89	1.31	0.68	2.07	4.34	7.95	23.23
	Female-headed	0.39	2.90	0.98	0.50	1.54	3.24	5.94	17.34
All households	Total	0.01	0.08	0.03	0.01	0.04	0.09	0.17	0.48
	Poor	0.01	0.05	0.02	0.01	0.03	0.06	0.11	0.33
	Nonpoor	0.01	0.10	0.03	0.02	0.05	0.11	0.21	0.61
	Male-headed	0.01	0.09	0.03	0.02	0.05	0.10	0.18	0.54
	Female-headed	0.01	0.04	0.01	0.01	0.02	0.05	0.09	0.26

Table A5.1: *(I) Continued.*

	Respect to original	Leader split	Small entrant	Leaders merge and small entrant	Leaders merge	Exit of largest	Equal market shares	Perfect competition
(C) Complementary policies (firms)								
Only producers								
Total	0.45	3.70	1.24	0.68	2.06	4.23	7.53	22.19
Poor	0.35	2.87	0.96	0.53	1.60	3.28	5.84	17.20
Nonpoor	0.52	4.22	1.42	0.78	2.35	4.83	8.60	25.33
Male-headed	0.47	3.83	1.29	0.71	2.13	4.38	7.80	22.98
Female-headed	0.35	2.86	0.96	0.53	1.59	3.27	5.82	17.16
All households								
Total	0.01	0.08	0.03	0.01	0.04	0.09	0.16	0.48
Poor	0.01	0.05	0.02	0.01	0.03	0.06	0.11	0.32
Nonpoor	0.01	0.10	0.03	0.02	0.06	0.11	0.20	0.60
Male-headed	0.01	0.09	0.03	0.02	0.05	0.10	0.18	0.53
Female-headed	0.01	0.04	0.01	0.01	0.02	0.05	0.09	0.26
(D) Complementary policies (farmers – firms)								
Only producers								
Total	0.95	4.20	1.76	0.18	1.58	3.73	7.98	22.86
Poor	0.74	3.26	1.36	0.14	1.23	2.89	6.18	17.73
Nonpoor	1.08	4.80	2.01	0.20	1.81	4.26	9.11	26.10
Male-headed	0.98	4.35	1.82	0.19	1.64	3.87	8.26	23.68
Female-headed	0.73	3.25	1.36	0.14	1.22	2.89	6.17	17.68
All households								
Total	0.02	0.09	0.04	0.00	0.03	0.08	0.17	0.49
Poor	0.01	0.06	0.03	0.00	0.02	0.05	0.12	0.33
Nonpoor	0.03	0.11	0.05	0.00	0.04	0.10	0.22	0.62
Male-headed	0.02	0.10	0.04	0.00	0.04	0.09	0.19	0.55
Female-headed	0.01	0.05	0.02	0.00	0.02	0.04	0.09	0.26

Table A5.1: *(l) Continued.*

		Respect to original	Leader split	Small entrant	Leaders merge and small entrant	Leaders merge	Exit of largest	Equal market shares	Perfect competition
(E) International prices									
Only producers	Total	5.42	8.98	6.49	4.27	2.49	0.30	12.57	29.48
	Poor	4.20	6.96	5.03	3.31	1.93	0.24	9.74	22.85
	Nonpoor	6.19	10.25	7.41	4.88	2.84	0.35	14.35	33.66
	Male-headed	5.61	9.30	6.73	4.42	2.58	0.32	13.02	30.53
	Female-headed	4.19	6.94	5.02	3.30	1.92	0.24	9.72	22.79
All households	Total	0.12	0.19	0.14	0.09	0.05	0.01	0.27	0.64
	Poor	0.08	0.13	0.09	0.06	0.04	0.00	0.18	0.43
	Nonpoor	0.15	0.24	0.18	0.12	0.07	0.01	0.34	0.80
	Male-headed	0.13	0.22	0.16	0.10	0.06	0.01	0.30	0.71
	Female-headed	0.06	0.10	0.08	0.05	0.03	0.00	0.15	0.34

Table A5.2: *Impact of supply chain changes on the outgrower contract model:*
(a) Zambia, cotton (household income percentage changes).

		Respect to original	Leader split	Small entrant	Leaders merge and small entrant	Leaders merge	Exit of largest	Equal market shares	Perfect competition
(A) Basic model									
Only producers	Total	0.00	2.26	0.14	1.57	1.89	3.22	6.46	18.41
	Poor	0.00	2.45	0.15	1.71	2.05	3.49	7.01	19.96
	Nonpoor	0.00	2.15	0.13	1.50	1.80	3.07	6.16	17.55
	Male-headed	0.00	2.27	0.14	1.58	1.90	3.23	6.49	18.48
	Female-headed	0.00	2.21	0.14	1.54	1.85	3.15	6.32	18.00
All households	Total	0.00	0.25	0.02	0.17	0.21	0.36	0.71	2.03
	Poor	0.00	0.22	0.01	0.15	0.18	0.31	0.62	1.77
	Nonpoor	0.00	0.27	0.02	0.19	0.23	0.39	0.79	2.24
	Male-headed	0.00	0.27	0.02	0.19	0.22	0.38	0.76	2.18
	Female-headed	0.00	0.18	0.01	0.12	0.15	0.25	0.51	1.44
(B) Complementary policies (farmers)									
Only producers	Total	0.36	2.60	0.51	1.21	1.53	2.84	6.79	18.95
	Poor	0.39	2.82	0.55	1.31	1.66	3.08	7.36	20.54
	Nonpoor	0.34	2.48	0.48	1.15	1.46	2.71	6.47	18.07
	Male-headed	0.36	2.61	0.51	1.21	1.54	2.85	6.82	19.02
	Female-headed	0.35	2.54	0.50	1.18	1.50	2.78	6.64	18.52
All households	Total	0.04	0.29	0.06	0.13	0.17	0.31	0.75	2.09
	Poor	0.03	0.25	0.05	0.12	0.15	0.27	0.65	1.82
	Nonpoor	0.04	0.32	0.06	0.15	0.19	0.35	0.83	2.31
	Male-headed	0.04	0.31	0.06	0.14	0.18	0.34	0.80	2.24
	Female-headed	0.03	0.20	0.04	0.09	0.12	0.22	0.53	1.48

Table A5.2: *(a) Continued.*

		Respect to original	Leader split	Small entrant	Leaders merge and small entrant	Leaders merge	Exit of largest	Equal market shares	Perfect competition
(C) Complementary policies (firms)									
Only producers	Total	0.54	2.78	0.71	1.01	1.38	2.64	6.93	19.09
	Poor	0.59	3.02	0.77	1.10	1.49	2.87	7.51	20.69
	Nonpoor	0.52	2.65	0.68	0.97	1.31	2.52	6.60	18.20
	Male-headed	0.54	2.79	0.72	1.02	1.38	2.65	6.95	19.16
	Female-headed	0.53	2.72	0.70	0.99	1.35	2.59	6.77	18.66
All households	Total	0.06	0.31	0.08	0.11	0.15	0.29	0.76	2.11
	Poor	0.05	0.27	0.07	0.10	0.13	0.25	0.67	1.84
	Nonpoor	0.07	0.34	0.09	0.12	0.17	0.32	0.84	2.32
	Male-headed	0.06	0.33	0.08	0.12	0.16	0.31	0.82	2.26
	Female-headed	0.04	0.22	0.06	0.08	0.11	0.21	0.54	1.50
(D) Complementary policies (farmers – firms)									
Only producers	Total	0.90	3.13	1.08	0.65	1.02	2.27	7.25	19.63
	Poor	0.97	3.40	1.17	0.70	1.11	2.46	7.86	21.28
	Nonpoor	0.86	2.99	1.03	0.62	0.98	2.17	6.91	18.71
	Male-headed	0.90	3.15	1.09	0.65	1.03	2.28	7.28	19.70
	Female-headed	0.88	3.06	1.06	0.63	1.00	2.22	7.09	19.18
All households	Total	0.10	0.35	0.12	0.07	0.11	0.25	0.80	2.17
	Poor	0.09	0.30	0.10	0.06	0.10	0.22	0.70	1.89
	Nonpoor	0.11	0.38	0.13	0.08	0.12	0.28	0.88	2.39
	Male-headed	0.11	0.37	0.13	0.08	0.12	0.27	0.86	2.32
	Female-headed	0.07	0.25	0.08	0.05	0.08	0.18	0.57	1.54

Table A5.2: (a) Continued.

	Respect to original	Leader split	Small entrant	Leaders merge and small entrant	Leaders merge	Exit of largest	Equal market shares	Perfect competition
(E) International prices								
Only producers								
Total	5.25	7.72	5.62	3.65	2.99	1.85	11.93	26.41
Poor	5.69	8.37	6.10	3.96	3.24	2.01	12.93	28.63
Nonpoor	5.01	7.36	5.36	3.48	2.85	1.77	11.37	25.18
Male-headed	5.27	7.75	5.64	3.66	3.00	1.86	11.97	26.51
Female-headed	5.13	7.54	5.50	3.57	2.92	1.81	11.66	25.82
All households								
Total	0.58	0.85	0.62	0.40	0.33	0.20	1.32	2.91
Poor	0.50	0.74	0.54	0.35	0.29	0.18	1.15	2.54
Nonpoor	0.64	0.94	0.68	0.44	0.36	0.23	1.45	3.21
Male-headed	0.62	0.91	0.66	0.43	0.35	0.22	1.41	3.12
Female-headed	0.41	0.60	0.44	0.29	0.23	0.15	0.93	2.07

Table A5.2: *(b) Benin, cotton (percentage) changes in household income.*

		Respect to original	Leader split	Small entrant	Leaders merge and small entrant	Leaders merge	Exit of largest	Equal market shares	Perfect competition
(A) Basic model									
Only producers	Total	0.00	3.80	0.04	0.33	0.41	5.53	18.12	32.13
	Poor	0.00	3.71	0.04	0.32	0.40	5.40	17.70	31.37
	Nonpoor	0.00	3.97	0.04	0.34	0.43	5.77	18.92	33.53
	Male-headed	0.00	2.45	0.03	0.21	0.26	3.56	11.68	20.71
	Female-headed	0.00	3.86	0.04	0.33	0.42	5.61	18.40	32.61
All households	Total	0.00	0.71	0.01	0.06	0.08	1.04	3.40	6.03
	Poor	0.00	0.90	0.01	0.08	0.10	1.31	4.28	7.59
	Nonpoor	0.00	0.53	0.01	0.05	0.06	0.77	2.52	4.46
	Male-headed	0.00	0.12	0.00	0.01	0.01	0.18	0.59	1.05
	Female-headed	0.00	0.82	0.01	0.07	0.09	1.19	3.91	6.92
(B) Complementary policies (farmers)									
Only producers	Total	0.47	4.23	0.52	0.14	0.05	4.98	18.54	32.83
	Poor	0.46	4.13	0.51	0.14	0.05	4.86	18.10	32.05
	Nonpoor	0.49	4.41	0.55	0.15	0.05	5.20	19.35	34.26
	Male-headed	0.30	2.73	0.34	0.09	0.03	3.21	11.95	21.16
	Female-headed	0.48	4.29	0.53	0.14	0.05	5.05	18.82	33.32
All households	Total	0.09	0.79	0.10	0.03	0.01	0.94	3.48	6.17
	Poor	0.11	1.00	0.12	0.03	0.01	1.18	4.38	7.76
	Nonpoor	0.07	0.59	0.07	0.02	0.01	0.69	2.57	4.56
	Male-headed	0.02	0.14	0.02	0.00	0.00	0.16	0.60	1.07
	Female-headed	0.10	0.91	0.11	0.03	0.01	1.07	3.99	7.07

Table A5.2: *(b) Continued.*

		Respect to original	Leader split	Small entrant	Leaders merge and small entrant	Leaders merge	Exit of largest	Equal market shares	Perfect competition
(C) Complementary policies (firms)									
Only producers	Total	0.47	4.17	0.53	0.13	0.03	4.86	18.34	32.41
	Poor	0.46	4.07	0.51	0.13	0.03	4.75	17.91	31.65
	Nonpoor	0.49	4.35	0.55	0.14	0.03	5.08	19.14	33.83
	Male-headed	0.30	2.69	0.34	0.09	0.02	3.13	11.82	20.90
	Female-headed	0.47	4.23	0.53	0.13	0.03	4.94	18.62	32.90
All households	Total	0.09	0.78	0.10	0.02	0.01	0.91	3.44	6.09
	Poor	0.11	0.99	0.12	0.03	0.01	1.15	4.33	7.66
	Nonpoor	0.06	0.58	0.07	0.02	0.00	0.68	2.55	4.50
	Male-headed	0.02	0.14	0.02	0.00	0.00	0.16	0.60	1.06
	Female-headed	0.10	0.90	0.11	0.03	0.01	1.05	3.95	6.99
(D) Complementary policies (farmers – firms)									
Only producers	Total	0.94	4.60	1.01	0.60	0.49	4.32	18.75	33.12
	Poor	0.92	4.50	0.99	0.59	0.48	4.21	18.31	32.34
	Nonpoor	0.98	4.80	1.05	0.63	0.51	4.50	19.57	34.56
	Male-headed	0.61	2.97	0.65	0.39	0.31	2.78	12.09	21.35
	Female-headed	0.96	4.67	1.02	0.61	0.49	4.38	19.03	33.61
All households	Total	0.18	0.86	0.19	0.11	0.09	0.81	3.52	6.22
	Poor	0.22	1.09	0.24	0.14	0.12	1.02	4.43	7.82
	Nonpoor	0.13	0.64	0.14	0.08	0.07	0.60	2.60	4.60
	Male-headed	0.03	0.15	0.03	0.02	0.02	0.14	0.61	1.08
	Female-headed	0.20	0.99	0.22	0.13	0.10	0.93	4.04	7.14

Table A5.2: *(b) Continued.*

	Respect to original	Leader split	Small entrant	Leaders merge and small entrant	Leaders merge	Exit of largest	Equal market shares	Perfect competition
(E) International prices								
Only producers								
Total	5.74	9.35	5.91	5.35	5.10	0.74	24.35	40.49
Poor	5.61	9.13	5.77	5.22	4.98	0.72	23.78	39.53
Nonpoor	5.99	9.76	6.17	5.58	5.32	0.77	25.42	42.26
Male-headed	3.70	6.03	3.81	3.45	3.29	0.47	15.70	26.10
Female-headed	5.83	9.49	6.00	5.43	5.18	0.75	24.72	41.10
All households								
Total	1.08	1.76	1.11	1.00	0.96	0.14	4.57	7.61
Poor	1.36	2.21	1.40	1.26	1.20	0.17	5.75	9.57
Nonpoor	0.80	1.30	0.82	0.74	0.71	0.10	3.38	5.62
Male-headed	0.19	0.30	0.19	0.17	0.17	0.02	0.79	1.32
Female-headed	1.24	2.02	1.27	1.15	1.10	0.16	5.25	8.73

Table A5.2: *(c) Burkina Faso, cotton (household income percentage changes).*

		Respect to original	Leader split	Small entrant	Leaders merge and small entrant	Leaders merge	Exit of largest	Equal market shares	Perfect competition
(A) Basic model									
Only producers	Total	0.00	6.51	0.38	0.35	1.26	−21.78	9.87	38.43
	Poor	0.00	6.25	0.36	0.34	1.20	−20.89	9.47	36.86
	Nonpoor	0.00	6.68	0.39	0.36	1.29	−22.33	10.12	39.41
	Male-headed	0.00	6.61	0.38	0.36	1.28	−22.12	10.03	39.03
	Female-headed	0.00	2.08	0.12	0.11	0.40	6.96	3.16	12.29
All households	Total	0.00	0.15	0.01	0.01	0.03	0.52	0.23	0.91
	Poor	0.00	0.12	0.01	0.01	0.02	0.39	0.18	0.70
	Nonpoor	0.00	0.19	0.01	0.01	0.04	0.63	0.29	1.11
	Male-headed	0.00	0.16	0.01	0.01	0.03	0.55	0.25	0.96
	Female-headed	0.00	0.02	0.00	0.00	0.00	0.06	0.03	0.10
(B) Complementary policies (farmers)									
Only producers	Total	0.37	6.94	0.03	0.69	1.64	−20.97	10.45	39.54
	Poor	0.36	6.66	0.03	0.67	1.57	−20.12	10.03	37.93
	Nonpoor	0.38	7.12	0.03	0.71	1.68	−21.51	10.72	40.55
	Male-headed	0.38	7.05	0.03	0.70	1.66	−21.30	10.62	40.16
	Female-headed	0.12	2.22	0.01	0.22	0.52	6.70	3.34	12.64
All households	Total	0.01	0.16	0.00	0.02	0.04	0.50	0.25	0.94
	Poor	0.01	0.13	0.00	0.01	0.03	0.38	0.19	0.72
	Nonpoor	0.01	0.20	0.00	0.02	0.05	0.61	0.30	1.14
	Male-headed	0.01	0.17	0.00	0.02	0.04	0.53	0.26	0.99
	Female-headed	0.00	0.02	0.00	0.00	0.00	0.06	0.03	0.11

Table A5.2: *(c) Continued.*

		Respect to original	Leader split	Small entrant	Leaders merge and small entrant	Leaders merge	Exit of largest	Equal market shares	Perfect competition
(C) Complementary policies (firms)									
Only producers	Total	0.34	7.15	0.06	0.60	1.57	−20.35	10.82	39.82
	Poor	0.33	6.85	0.06	0.58	1.50	−19.52	10.38	38.19
	Nonpoor	0.35	7.33	0.06	0.62	1.61	−20.86	11.10	40.83
	Male-headed	0.35	7.26	0.06	0.61	1.59	−20.67	10.99	40.44
	Female-headed	0.11	2.28	0.02	0.19	0.50	6.51	3.46	12.73
All households	Total	0.01	0.17	0.00	0.01	0.04	0.48	0.26	0.94
	Poor	0.01	0.13	0.00	0.01	0.03	0.37	0.20	0.72
	Nonpoor	0.01	0.21	0.00	0.02	0.05	0.59	0.31	1.15
	Male-headed	0.01	0.18	0.00	0.02	0.04	0.51	0.27	1.00
	Female-headed	0.00	0.02	0.00	0.00	0.00	0.06	0.03	0.11
(D) Complementary policies (farmers – firms)									
Only producers	Total	0.74	7.58	0.32	0.97	1.96	−19.56	11.40	40.93
	Poor	0.71	7.27	0.31	0.93	1.88	−18.76	10.93	39.26
	Nonpoor	0.76	7.77	0.33	0.99	2.01	−20.05	11.69	41.97
	Male-headed	0.75	7.70	0.33	0.98	1.99	−19.86	11.57	41.57
	Female-headed	0.24	2.42	0.10	0.31	0.63	6.25	3.64	13.08
All households	Total	0.02	0.18	0.01	0.02	0.05	0.46	0.27	0.97
	Poor	0.01	0.14	0.01	0.02	0.04	0.35	0.21	0.74
	Nonpoor	0.02	0.22	0.01	0.03	0.06	0.56	0.33	1.18
	Male-headed	0.02	0.19	0.01	0.02	0.05	0.49	0.29	1.03
	Female-headed	0.00	0.02	0.00	0.00	0.01	0.05	0.03	0.11

Table A5.2: *(c) Continued.*

		Respect to original	Leader split	Small entrant	Leaders merge and small entrant	Leaders merge	Exit of largest	Equal market shares	Perfect competition
(E) International prices									
Only producers	Total	7.95	16.30	7.81	7.88	8.50	−10.95	21.78	55.87
	Poor	7.63	15.63	7.49	7.56	8.15	−10.50	20.89	53.59
	Nonpoor	8.16	16.71	8.01	8.08	8.72	−11.23	22.33	57.28
	Male-headed	8.08	16.55	7.93	8.01	8.63	−11.12	22.12	56.74
	Female-headed	2.54	5.21	2.50	2.52	2.72	3.50	6.96	17.86
All households	Total	0.19	0.39	0.18	0.19	0.20	0.26	0.52	1.32
	Poor	0.14	0.29	0.14	0.14	0.15	0.20	0.39	1.01
	Nonpoor	0.23	0.47	0.23	0.23	0.25	0.32	0.63	1.61
	Male-headed	0.20	0.41	0.20	0.20	0.21	0.27	0.55	1.40
	Female-headed	0.02	0.04	0.02	0.02	0.02	0.03	0.06	0.15

Table A5.2: *(d) Côte d'Ivoire, cotton (household income percentage changes).*

		Respect to original	Leader split	Small entrant	Leaders merge and small entrant	Leaders merge	Exit of largest	Equal market shares	Perfect competition
(A) Basic model									
Only producers	Total	0.00	4.34	0.19	2.50	2.96	6.19	12.33	33.41
	Poor	0.00	4.17	0.18	2.41	2.85	5.96	11.86	32.15
	Nonpoor	0.00	4.40	0.19	2.54	3.00	6.28	12.52	33.93
	Male-headed	0.00	4.30	0.19	2.48	2.93	6.13	12.22	33.11
	Female-headed	0.00	5.67	0.24	3.27	3.87	8.09	16.11	43.66
All households	Total	0.00	0.35	0.02	0.20	0.24	0.50	1.00	2.71
	Poor	0.00	0.19	0.01	0.11	0.13	0.27	0.54	1.46
	Nonpoor	0.00	0.53	0.02	0.31	0.36	0.76	1.51	4.08
	Male-headed	0.00	0.41	0.02	0.24	0.28	0.58	1.16	3.16
	Female-headed	0.00	0.08	0.00	0.04	0.05	0.11	0.22	0.59
(B) Complementary policies (farmers)									
Only producers	Total	0.70	5.01	0.91	1.79	2.28	5.45	12.98	34.46
	Poor	0.67	4.82	0.87	1.72	2.19	5.25	12.49	33.16
	Nonpoor	0.71	5.09	0.92	1.82	2.31	5.54	13.18	34.99
	Male-headed	0.69	4.97	0.90	1.77	2.26	5.40	12.86	34.15
	Female-headed	0.91	6.55	1.19	2.34	2.97	7.12	16.96	45.02
All households	Total	0.06	0.41	0.07	0.15	0.18	0.44	1.05	2.80
	Poor	0.03	0.22	0.04	0.08	0.10	0.24	0.57	1.50
	Nonpoor	0.09	0.61	0.11	0.22	0.28	0.67	1.59	4.21
	Male-headed	0.07	0.47	0.09	0.17	0.21	0.51	1.23	3.25
	Female-headed	0.01	0.09	0.02	0.03	0.04	0.10	0.23	0.61

Table A5.2: *(d) Continued.*

	Respect to original	Leader split	Small entrant	Leaders merge and small entrant	Leaders merge	Exit of largest	Equal market shares	Perfect competition
(C) Complementary policies (firms)								
Only producers								
Total	1.20	5.47	1.45	1.29	1.84	4.91	13.39	34.91
Poor	1.15	5.27	1.39	1.24	1.77	4.73	12.88	33.59
Nonpoor	1.22	5.56	1.47	1.30	1.87	4.99	13.60	35.45
Male-headed	1.19	5.42	1.43	1.27	1.82	4.87	13.27	34.59
Female-headed	1.56	7.15	1.89	1.68	2.40	6.42	17.49	45.61
All households								
Total	0.10	0.44	0.12	0.10	0.15	0.40	1.09	2.84
Poor	0.05	0.24	0.06	0.06	0.08	0.21	0.58	1.52
Nonpoor	0.15	0.67	0.18	0.16	0.22	0.60	1.64	4.27
Male-headed	0.11	0.52	0.14	0.12	0.17	0.46	1.26	3.30
Female-headed	0.02	0.10	0.03	0.02	0.03	0.09	0.24	0.61
(D) Complementary policies (farmers – firms)								
Only producers								
Total	1.89	6.14	2.17	0.58	1.16	4.18	14.03	35.95
Poor	1.82	5.91	2.08	0.56	1.12	4.03	13.50	34.60
Nonpoor	1.92	6.24	2.20	0.59	1.18	4.25	14.25	36.51
Male-headed	1.88	6.09	2.15	0.57	1.15	4.15	13.91	35.63
Female-headed	2.47	8.03	2.83	0.76	1.52	5.47	18.33	46.98
All households								
Total	0.15	0.50	0.18	0.05	0.09	0.34	1.14	2.92
Poor	0.08	0.27	0.09	0.03	0.05	0.18	0.61	1.57
Nonpoor	0.23	0.75	0.26	0.07	0.14	0.51	1.71	4.39
Male-headed	0.18	0.58	0.20	0.05	0.11	0.40	1.32	3.39
Female-headed	0.03	0.11	0.04	0.01	0.02	0.07	0.25	0.63

Table A5.2: *(d) Continued.*

		Respect to original	Leader split	Small entrant	Leaders merge and small entrant	Leaders merge	Exit of largest	Equal market shares	Perfect competition
(E) International prices									
Only producers	Total	10.98	15.63	11.60	8.36	7.26	4.50	23.76	49.62
	Poor	10.57	15.04	11.16	8.05	6.98	4.33	22.86	47.75
	Nonpoor	11.15	15.87	11.78	8.49	7.37	4.57	24.12	50.39
	Male-headed	10.88	15.49	11.50	8.29	7.19	4.46	23.54	49.18
	Female-headed	14.35	20.43	15.16	10.93	9.48	5.88	31.04	64.84
All households	Total	0.89	1.27	0.94	0.68	0.59	0.37	1.93	4.03
	Poor	0.48	0.68	0.51	0.36	0.32	0.20	1.04	2.16
	Nonpoor	1.34	1.91	1.42	1.02	0.89	0.55	2.90	6.07
	Male-headed	1.04	1.48	1.10	0.79	0.69	0.43	2.24	4.69
	Female-headed	0.19	0.28	0.20	0.15	0.13	0.08	0.42	0.87

Supply Chains in Sub-Saharan Africa

Table A5.2: *(e) Malawi, cotton (household income percentage changes).*

		Respect to original	Three firms	Four firms	Small entrant with half of the benefits
(A) Basic model					
Only producers	Total	0.00	0.86	1.50	0.15
	Poor	0.00	0.68	1.20	0.12
	Nonpoor	0.00	0.98	1.71	0.17
	Male-headed	0.00	0.87	1.52	0.15
	Female-headed	0.00	0.77	1.35	0.13
All households	Total	0.00	0.03	0.05	0.00
	Poor	0.00	0.02	0.03	0.00
	Nonpoor	0.00	0.03	0.06	0.01
	Male-headed	0.00	0.03	0.05	0.01
	Female-headed	0.00	0.01	0.02	0.00
(B) Complementary policies (farmers)					
Only producers	Total	0.19	1.06	1.72	0.35
	Poor	0.15	0.85	1.37	0.28
	Nonpoor	0.22	1.21	1.96	0.40
	Male-headed	0.19	1.08	1.74	0.36
	Female-headed	0.17	0.96	1.55	0.32
All households	Total	0.01	0.03	0.05	0.01
	Poor	0.00	0.02	0.04	0.01
	Nonpoor	0.01	0.04	0.06	0.01
	Male-headed	0.01	0.04	0.06	0.01
	Female-headed	0.00	0.01	0.02	0.00
(C) Complementary policies (firms)					
Only producers	Total	0.32	1.22	1.89	0.47
	Poor	0.25	0.97	1.51	0.37
	Nonpoor	0.36	1.39	2.15	0.53
	Male-headed	0.32	1.23	1.91	0.47
	Female-headed	0.29	1.10	1.71	0.42
All households	Total	0.01	0.04	0.06	0.01
	Poor	0.01	0.03	0.04	0.01
	Nonpoor	0.01	0.05	0.07	0.02
	Male-headed	0.01	0.04	0.07	0.02
	Female-headed	0.00	0.02	0.02	0.01

Table A5.2: *(e) Continued.*

		Respect to original	Three firms	Four firms	Small entrant with half of the benefits
(D) Complementary policies (farmers – firms)					
Only producers	Total	0.51	1.42	2.11	0.67
	Poor	0.40	1.13	1.68	0.53
	Nonpoor	0.58	1.62	2.40	0.76
	Male-headed	0.51	1.44	2.13	0.68
	Female-headed	0.46	1.28	1.90	0.60
All households	Total	0.02	0.04	0.06	0.02
	Poor	0.01	0.03	0.05	0.01
	Nonpoor	0.02	0.05	0.08	0.02
	Male-headed	0.02	0.05	0.08	0.02
	Female-headed	0.01	0.02	0.03	0.01
(E) International prices					
Only producers	Total	3.01	4.29	5.19	3.18
	Poor	2.40	3.42	4.14	2.54
	Nonpoor	3.42	4.88	5.91	3.62
	Male-headed	3.04	4.34	5.26	3.22
	Female-headed	2.71	3.87	4.69	2.87
All households	Total	0.09	0.13	0.16	0.10
	Poor	0.07	0.10	0.12	0.07
	Nonpoor	0.11	0.16	0.19	0.12
	Male-headed	0.11	0.16	0.19	0.12
	Female-headed	0.04	0.05	0.07	0.04

Table A5.2: *(f) Côte d'Ivoire, cocoa (household income percentage changes).*

		Respect to original	Leader split	Small entrant	Leaders merge and small entrant	Leaders merge	Exit of largest	Equal market shares	Perfect competition
(A) Basic model									
Only producers	Total	0.00	1.16	0.17	0.66	0.88	1.32	10.23	21.18
	Poor	0.00	1.17	0.17	0.66	0.89	1.33	10.30	21.31
	Nonpoor	0.00	1.16	0.17	0.65	0.87	1.31	10.16	21.03
	Male-headed	0.00	1.18	0.17	0.66	0.89	1.33	10.33	21.39
	Female-headed	0.00	0.95	0.14	0.54	0.72	1.08	8.36	17.30
All households	Total	0.00	0.35	0.05	0.19	0.26	0.39	3.03	6.28
	Poor	0.00	0.37	0.05	0.21	0.28	0.41	3.21	6.65
	Nonpoor	0.00	0.32	0.05	0.18	0.24	0.37	2.84	5.87
	Male-headed	0.00	0.40	0.06	0.22	0.30	0.45	3.51	7.27
	Female-headed	0.00	0.08	0.01	0.05	0.06	0.09	0.73	1.51
(B) Complementary policies (farmers)									
Only producers	Total	0.94	2.11	1.13	0.29	0.06	0.37	11.14	22.34
	Poor	0.95	2.12	1.13	0.30	0.06	0.37	11.20	22.48
	Nonpoor	0.94	2.09	1.12	0.29	0.06	0.37	11.05	22.17
	Male-headed	0.95	2.13	1.14	0.30	0.06	0.38	11.24	22.56
	Female-headed	0.77	1.72	0.92	0.24	0.05	0.30	9.10	18.25
All households	Total	0.28	0.63	0.33	0.09	0.02	0.11	3.30	6.62
	Poor	0.30	0.66	0.35	0.09	0.02	0.12	3.50	7.02
	Nonpoor	0.26	0.59	0.31	0.08	0.02	0.10	3.09	6.19
	Male-headed	0.32	0.72	0.39	0.10	0.02	0.13	3.82	7.66
	Female-headed	0.07	0.15	0.08	0.02	0.00	0.03	0.79	1.59

Table A5.2: *(f) Continued.*

		Respect to original	Leader split	Small entrant	Leaders merge and small entrant	Leaders merge	Exit of largest	Equal market shares	Perfect competition
(C) Complementary policies (firms)									
Only producers	Total	1.22	2.38	1.41	0.58	0.34	0.08	11.26	22.44
	Poor	1.23	2.39	1.42	0.59	0.34	0.08	11.33	22.57
	Nonpoor	1.21	2.36	1.40	0.58	0.34	0.08	11.18	22.27
	Male-headed	1.23	2.40	1.43	0.59	0.34	0.08	11.37	22.66
	Female-headed	1.00	1.94	1.15	0.48	0.28	0.07	9.20	18.32
All households	Total	0.36	0.71	0.42	0.17	0.10	0.02	3.34	6.65
	Poor	0.38	0.75	0.44	0.18	0.11	0.03	3.54	7.05
	Nonpoor	0.34	0.66	0.39	0.16	0.09	0.02	3.12	6.22
	Male-headed	0.42	0.82	0.48	0.20	0.12	0.03	3.86	7.70
	Female-headed	0.09	0.17	0.10	0.04	0.02	0.01	0.80	1.60
(D) Complementary policies (farmers – firms)									
Only producers	Total	2.16	3.32	2.36	1.53	1.27	0.86	12.16	23.59
	Poor	2.18	3.34	2.38	1.54	1.28	0.86	12.23	23.74
	Nonpoor	2.15	3.29	2.34	1.51	1.26	0.85	12.07	23.42
	Male-headed	2.18	3.35	2.38	1.54	1.29	0.87	12.28	23.82
	Female-headed	1.77	2.71	1.93	1.25	1.04	0.70	9.93	19.27
All households	Total	0.64	0.98	0.70	0.45	0.38	0.25	3.60	6.99
	Poor	0.68	1.04	0.74	0.48	0.40	0.27	3.82	7.41
	Nonpoor	0.60	0.92	0.65	0.42	0.35	0.24	3.37	6.54
	Male-headed	0.74	1.14	0.81	0.52	0.44	0.29	4.17	8.09
	Female-headed	0.15	0.24	0.17	0.11	0.09	0.06	0.87	1.68

Table A5.2: (f) *Continued.*

	Respect to original	Leader split	Small entrant	Leaders merge and small entrant	Leaders merge	Exit of largest	Equal market shares	Perfect competition
(E) International prices								
Only producers								
Total	11.59	12.83	11.88	10.95	10.59	10.19	21.81	35.37
Poor	11.66	12.91	11.96	11.01	10.65	10.25	21.95	35.58
Nonpoor	11.50	12.74	11.79	10.87	10.51	10.11	21.65	35.10
Male-headed	11.70	12.96	12.00	11.05	10.69	10.29	22.02	35.71
Female-headed	9.47	10.48	9.70	8.94	8.65	8.32	17.81	28.89
All households								
Total	3.44	3.80	3.52	3.25	3.14	3.02	6.47	10.49
Poor	3.64	4.03	3.73	3.44	3.33	3.20	6.85	11.11
Nonpoor	3.21	3.56	3.29	3.04	2.94	2.83	6.05	9.81
Male-headed	3.98	4.40	4.08	3.76	3.63	3.50	7.48	12.13
Female-headed	0.83	0.92	0.85	0.78	0.76	0.73	1.56	2.52

Table A5.2: *(g) Ghana, cocoa (household income percentage changes).*

		Respect to original	Leader split	Small entrant	Leaders merge and small entrant	Leaders merge	Exit of largest	Equal market shares	Perfect competition
(A) Basic model									
Only producers	Total	0.00	1.06	0.05	0.24	0.30	1.31	6.93	11.49
	Poor	0.00	1.01	0.04	0.23	0.29	1.25	6.62	10.98
	Nonpoor	0.00	1.12	0.05	0.25	0.32	1.38	7.32	12.14
	Male-headed	0.00	1.09	0.05	0.24	0.31	1.35	7.14	11.84
	Female-headed	0.00	0.95	0.04	0.21	0.27	1.17	6.21	10.30
All households	Total	0.00	0.17	0.01	0.04	0.05	0.22	1.15	1.90
	Poor	0.00	0.17	0.01	0.04	0.05	0.21	1.13	1.87
	Nonpoor	0.00	0.18	0.01	0.04	0.05	0.22	1.17	1.94
	Male-headed	0.00	0.20	0.01	0.04	0.06	0.25	1.32	2.18
	Female-headed	0.00	0.12	0.01	0.03	0.03	0.14	0.76	1.27
(B) Complementary policies (farmers)									
Only producers	Total	0.41	1.46	0.46	0.18	0.10	0.88	7.33	11.99
	Poor	0.39	1.39	0.44	0.17	0.10	0.84	7.00	11.46
	Nonpoor	0.44	1.54	0.49	0.19	0.11	0.93	7.74	12.67
	Male-headed	0.42	1.50	0.48	0.18	0.11	0.91	7.55	12.36
	Female-headed	0.37	1.31	0.41	0.16	0.09	0.79	6.57	10.75
All households	Total	0.07	0.24	0.08	0.03	0.02	0.15	1.21	1.98
	Poor	0.07	0.24	0.08	0.03	0.02	0.14	1.19	1.95
	Nonpoor	0.07	0.25	0.08	0.03	0.02	0.15	1.24	2.02
	Male-headed	0.08	0.28	0.09	0.03	0.02	0.17	1.39	2.28
	Female-headed	0.05	0.16	0.05	0.02	0.01	0.10	0.81	1.32

Table A5.2: (g) Continued.

		Respect to original	Leader split	Small entrant	Leaders merge and small entrant	Leaders merge	Exit of largest	Equal market shares	Perfect competition
(C) Complementary policies (firms)									
Only producers	Total	0.63	1.66	0.68	0.39	0.31	0.64	7.45	12.10
	Poor	0.60	1.58	0.65	0.38	0.30	0.61	7.11	11.56
	Nonpoor	0.66	1.75	0.72	0.42	0.33	0.67	7.87	12.78
	Male-headed	0.65	1.71	0.70	0.41	0.32	0.66	7.67	12.47
	Female-headed	0.56	1.48	0.61	0.35	0.28	0.57	6.68	10.85
All households	Total	0.10	0.27	0.11	0.07	0.05	0.11	1.23	2.00
	Poor	0.10	0.27	0.11	0.06	0.05	0.10	1.21	1.97
	Nonpoor	0.11	0.28	0.12	0.07	0.05	0.11	1.26	2.04
	Male-headed	0.12	0.31	0.13	0.07	0.06	0.12	1.41	2.30
	Female-headed	0.07	0.18	0.08	0.04	0.03	0.07	0.82	1.33
(D) Complementary policies (farmers – firms)									
Only producers	Total	1.04	2.06	1.10	0.81	0.72	0.21	7.84	12.60
	Poor	0.99	1.97	1.05	0.77	0.69	0.20	7.49	12.04
	Nonpoor	1.10	2.18	1.16	0.85	0.76	0.23	8.28	13.31
	Male-headed	1.07	2.12	1.13	0.83	0.74	0.22	8.08	12.99
	Female-headed	0.93	1.85	0.98	0.72	0.65	0.19	7.03	11.30
All households	Total	0.17	0.34	0.18	0.13	0.12	0.04	1.30	2.09
	Poor	0.17	0.34	0.18	0.13	0.12	0.03	1.28	2.05
	Nonpoor	0.18	0.35	0.19	0.14	0.12	0.04	1.32	2.12
	Male-headed	0.20	0.39	0.21	0.15	0.14	0.04	1.49	2.39
	Female-headed	0.11	0.23	0.12	0.09	0.08	0.02	0.86	1.39

Table A5.2: *(g) Continued.*

		Respect to original	Leader split	Small entrant	Leaders merge and small entrant	Leaders merge	Exit of largest	Equal market shares	Perfect competition
(E) International prices									
Only producers	Total	5.58	6.61	5.69	5.34	5.20	4.35	12.62	18.23
	Poor	5.33	6.31	5.44	5.10	4.96	4.15	12.05	17.41
	Nonpoor	5.90	6.98	6.01	5.64	5.49	4.59	13.33	19.25
	Male-headed	5.76	6.81	5.87	5.50	5.36	4.48	13.00	18.78
	Female-headed	5.01	5.93	5.10	4.79	4.66	3.90	11.31	16.34
All households	Total	0.92	1.09	0.94	0.88	0.86	0.72	2.09	3.02
	Poor	0.91	1.08	0.93	0.87	0.85	0.71	2.06	2.97
	Nonpoor	0.94	1.11	0.96	0.90	0.88	0.73	2.13	3.07
	Male-headed	1.06	1.26	1.08	1.01	0.99	0.83	2.40	3.46
	Female-headed	0.62	0.73	0.63	0.59	0.57	0.48	1.39	2.01

Table A5.2: *(h) Côte d'Ivoire, coffee (household income percentage changes).*

		Respect to original	Leader split	Small entrant	Leaders merge and small entrant	Leaders merge	Exit of largest	Equal market shares	Perfect competition
(A) Basic model									
Only producers	Total	0.00	0.60	0.09	0.34	0.45	0.68	5.27	10.90
	Poor	0.00	0.69	0.10	0.39	0.52	0.78	6.08	12.59
	Nonpoor	0.00	0.44	0.07	0.25	0.33	0.50	3.86	7.98
	Male-headed	0.00	0.61	0.09	0.34	0.46	0.69	5.37	11.11
	Female-headed	0.00	0.37	0.05	0.21	0.28	0.41	3.21	6.65
All households	Total	0.00	0.14	0.02	0.08	0.10	0.16	1.21	2.50
	Poor	0.00	0.19	0.03	0.11	0.15	0.22	1.69	3.51
	Nonpoor	0.00	0.08	0.01	0.04	0.06	0.09	0.67	1.40
	Male-headed	0.00	0.16	0.02	0.09	0.12	0.18	1.41	2.93
	Female-headed	0.00	0.02	0.00	0.01	0.02	0.03	0.20	0.42
(B) Complementary policies (farmers)									
Only producers	Total	0.49	1.09	0.58	0.15	0.03	0.19	5.73	11.50
	Poor	0.56	1.25	0.67	0.17	0.03	0.22	6.62	13.27
	Nonpoor	0.36	0.80	0.42	0.11	0.02	0.14	4.20	8.42
	Male-headed	0.50	1.11	0.59	0.15	0.03	0.20	5.84	11.72
	Female-headed	0.30	0.66	0.35	0.09	0.02	0.12	3.50	7.02
All households	Total	0.11	0.25	0.13	0.03	0.01	0.04	1.31	2.63
	Poor	0.16	0.35	0.19	0.05	0.01	0.06	1.84	3.70
	Nonpoor	0.06	0.14	0.07	0.02	0.00	0.02	0.73	1.47
	Male-headed	0.13	0.29	0.16	0.04	0.01	0.05	1.54	3.09
	Female-headed	0.02	0.04	0.02	0.01	0.00	0.01	0.22	0.44

Table A5.2: *(h) Continued.*

		Respect to original	Leader split	Small entrant	Leaders merge and small entrant	Leaders merge	Exit of largest	Equal market shares	Perfect competition
(C) Complementary policies (firms)									
Only producers	Total	0.63	1.22	0.73	0.30	0.17	0.04	5.79	11.55
	Poor	0.73	1.41	0.84	0.35	0.20	0.05	6.69	13.33
	Nonpoor	0.46	0.90	0.53	0.22	0.13	0.03	4.24	8.45
	Male-headed	0.64	1.25	0.74	0.31	0.18	0.04	5.91	11.77
	Female-headed	0.38	0.75	0.44	0.18	0.11	0.03	3.54	7.05
All households	Total	0.14	0.28	0.17	0.07	0.04	0.01	1.33	2.64
	Poor	0.20	0.39	0.23	0.10	0.06	0.01	1.86	3.71
	Nonpoor	0.08	0.16	0.09	0.04	0.02	0.01	0.74	1.48
	Male-headed	0.17	0.33	0.20	0.08	0.05	0.01	1.56	3.10
	Female-headed	0.02	0.05	0.03	0.01	0.01	0.00	0.22	0.44
(D) Complementary policies (farmers – firms)									
Only producers	Total	1.11	1.71	1.21	0.79	0.65	0.44	6.26	12.14
	Poor	1.28	1.97	1.40	0.91	0.76	0.51	7.22	14.01
	Nonpoor	0.81	1.25	0.89	0.57	0.48	0.32	4.58	8.89
	Male-headed	1.13	1.74	1.24	0.80	0.67	0.45	6.38	12.37
	Female-headed	0.68	1.04	0.74	0.48	0.40	0.27	3.82	7.41
All households	Total	0.25	0.39	0.28	0.18	0.15	0.10	1.43	2.78
	Poor	0.36	0.55	0.39	0.25	0.21	0.14	2.01	3.90
	Nonpoor	0.14	0.22	0.16	0.10	0.08	0.06	0.80	1.56
	Male-headed	0.30	0.46	0.33	0.21	0.18	0.12	1.68	3.26
	Female-headed	0.04	0.07	0.05	0.03	0.03	0.02	0.24	0.47

Table A5.2: *(h) Continued.*

		Respect to original	Leader split	Small entrant	Leaders merge and small entrant	Leaders merge	Exit of largest	Equal market shares	Perfect competition
(E) International prices									
Only producers	Total	5.96	6.60	6.11	5.63	5.45	5.24	11.22	18.20
	Poor	6.88	7.62	7.06	6.50	6.29	6.05	12.96	21.01
	Nonpoor	4.37	4.84	4.48	4.13	3.99	3.84	8.22	13.33
	Male-headed	6.08	6.73	6.23	5.74	5.55	5.34	11.44	18.55
	Female-headed	3.64	4.03	3.73	3.44	3.32	3.20	6.85	11.11
All households	Total	1.37	1.51	1.40	1.29	1.25	1.20	2.57	4.17
	Poor	1.92	2.12	1.97	1.81	1.75	1.69	3.61	5.85
	Nonpoor	0.76	0.85	0.78	0.72	0.70	0.67	1.44	2.33
	Male-headed	1.60	1.77	1.64	1.51	1.46	1.41	3.01	4.89
	Female-headed	0.23	0.25	0.23	0.22	0.21	0.20	0.43	0.70

Table A5.2: *(i) Rwanda, coffee (household income percentage changes).*

		Respect to original	Leader split	Small entrant	Leaders merge and small entrant	Leaders merge	Exit of largest	Equal market shares	Perfect competition
(A) Basic model									
Only producers	Total	0.00	0.32	0.02	0.35	0.41	0.44	0.66	2.70
	Poor	0.00	0.40	0.03	0.44	0.51	0.55	0.82	3.37
	Nonpoor	0.00	0.28	0.02	0.31	0.36	0.39	0.57	2.37
	Male-headed	0.00	0.30	0.02	0.33	0.39	0.41	0.61	2.53
	Female-headed	0.00	0.38	0.02	0.42	0.49	0.52	0.78	3.21
All households	Total	0.00	0.03	0.00	0.04	0.04	0.04	0.07	0.27
	Poor	0.00	0.03	0.00	0.03	0.04	0.04	0.06	0.26
	Nonpoor	0.00	0.03	0.00	0.04	0.04	0.05	0.07	0.28
	Male-headed	0.00	0.03	0.00	0.04	0.04	0.05	0.07	0.28
	Female-headed	0.00	0.03	0.00	0.03	0.04	0.04	0.06	0.25
(B) Complementary policies (farmers)									
Only producers	Total	0.14	0.46	0.16	0.21	0.28	0.31	0.79	2.88
	Poor	0.17	0.57	0.20	0.27	0.35	0.38	0.99	3.59
	Nonpoor	0.12	0.40	0.14	0.19	0.24	0.27	0.69	2.52
	Male-headed	0.13	0.43	0.15	0.20	0.26	0.29	0.74	2.70
	Female-headed	0.16	0.55	0.19	0.25	0.33	0.36	0.94	3.42
All households	Total	0.01	0.05	0.02	0.02	0.03	0.03	0.08	0.29
	Poor	0.01	0.04	0.02	0.02	0.03	0.03	0.08	0.27
	Nonpoor	0.01	0.05	0.02	0.02	0.03	0.03	0.08	0.30
	Male-headed	0.01	0.05	0.02	0.02	0.03	0.03	0.08	0.30
	Female-headed	0.01	0.04	0.01	0.02	0.03	0.03	0.07	0.26

Table A5.2: *(i) Continued.*

		Respect to original	Leader split	Small entrant	Leaders merge and small entrant	Leaders merge	Exit of largest	Equal market shares	Perfect competition
(C) Complementary policies (firms)									
Only producers	Total	0.19	0.52	0.22	0.15	0.22	0.25	0.84	2.94
	Poor	0.24	0.64	0.27	0.19	0.28	0.31	1.05	3.66
	Nonpoor	0.17	0.45	0.19	0.13	0.20	0.22	0.74	2.57
	Male-headed	0.18	0.48	0.21	0.14	0.21	0.24	0.79	2.75
	Female-headed	0.23	0.61	0.26	0.18	0.27	0.30	1.00	3.49
All households	Total	0.02	0.05	0.02	0.02	0.02	0.03	0.08	0.29
	Poor	0.02	0.05	0.02	0.01	0.02	0.02	0.08	0.28
	Nonpoor	0.02	0.05	0.02	0.02	0.02	0.03	0.09	0.30
	Male-headed	0.02	0.05	0.02	0.02	0.02	0.03	0.09	0.30
	Female-headed	0.02	0.05	0.02	0.01	0.02	0.02	0.08	0.27
(D) Complementary policies (farmers – firms)									
Only producers	Total	0.33	0.65	0.36	0.02	0.09	0.12	0.98	3.11
	Poor	0.41	0.82	0.45	0.02	0.11	0.15	1.22	3.88
	Nonpoor	0.29	0.57	0.31	0.01	0.08	0.10	0.86	2.73
	Male-headed	0.31	0.61	0.34	0.01	0.09	0.11	0.92	2.92
	Female-headed	0.39	0.78	0.43	0.02	0.11	0.14	1.16	3.70
All households	Total	0.03	0.07	0.04	0.00	0.01	0.01	0.10	0.31
	Poor	0.03	0.06	0.03	0.00	0.01	0.01	0.09	0.30
	Nonpoor	0.03	0.07	0.04	0.00	0.01	0.01	0.10	0.32
	Male-headed	0.03	0.07	0.04	0.00	0.01	0.01	0.10	0.32
	Female-headed	0.03	0.06	0.03	0.00	0.01	0.01	0.09	0.29

Table A5.2: *(i) Continued.*

	Respect to original	Leader split	Small entrant	Leaders merge and small entrant	Leaders merge	Exit of largest	Equal market shares	Perfect competition
(E) International prices								
Only producers Total	1.82	2.20	1.89	1.46	1.33	1.30	2.51	5.04
Poor	2.27	2.74	2.35	1.82	1.65	1.62	3.13	6.28
Nonpoor	1.59	1.93	1.65	1.28	1.16	1.14	2.20	4.42
Male-headed	1.70	2.06	1.77	1.37	1.24	1.22	2.35	4.72
Female-headed	2.17	2.62	2.25	1.74	1.58	1.55	2.99	6.00
All households Total	0.18	0.22	0.19	0.15	0.13	0.13	0.25	0.50
Poor	0.17	0.21	0.18	0.14	0.13	0.12	0.24	0.48
Nonpoor	0.19	0.23	0.20	0.15	0.14	0.13	0.26	0.52
Male-headed	0.19	0.23	0.20	0.15	0.14	0.13	0.26	0.52
Female-headed	0.17	0.20	0.17	0.13	0.12	0.12	0.23	0.46

Table A5.2: *(i) Uganda, coffee (household income percentage changes).*

		Respect to original	Leader split	Small entrant	Leaders merge and small entrant	Leaders merge	Exit of largest	Equal market shares	Perfect competition
(A) Basic model									
Only producers	Total	0.00	0.09	0.01	0.06	0.07	0.10	0.77	1.54
	Poor	0.00	0.09	0.01	0.06	0.07	0.10	0.77	1.54
	Nonpoor	0.00	0.09	0.01	0.06	0.07	0.10	0.77	1.54
	Male-headed	0.00	0.09	0.01	0.06	0.08	0.11	0.82	1.65
	Female-headed	0.00	0.07	0.01	0.05	0.06	0.08	0.60	1.21
All households	Total	0.00	0.02	0.00	0.02	0.02	0.03	0.21	0.42
	Poor	0.00	0.02	0.00	0.01	0.01	0.02	0.16	0.32
	Nonpoor	0.00	0.03	0.00	0.02	0.02	0.03	0.24	0.49
	Male-headed	0.00	0.03	0.00	0.02	0.02	0.03	0.23	0.46
	Female-headed	0.00	0.02	0.00	0.01	0.01	0.02	0.15	0.29
(B) Complementary policies (farmers)									
Only producers	Total	0.16	0.25	0.17	0.10	0.09	0.06	0.93	1.72
	Poor	0.16	0.25	0.17	0.10	0.09	0.06	0.93	1.72
	Nonpoor	0.16	0.25	0.17	0.10	0.09	0.06	0.93	1.72
	Male-headed	0.17	0.27	0.18	0.11	0.09	0.06	0.99	1.84
	Female-headed	0.13	0.20	0.13	0.08	0.07	0.05	0.73	1.35
All households	Total	0.04	0.07	0.05	0.03	0.02	0.02	0.25	0.46
	Poor	0.03	0.05	0.03	0.02	0.02	0.01	0.19	0.36
	Nonpoor	0.05	0.08	0.05	0.03	0.03	0.02	0.29	0.55
	Male-headed	0.05	0.07	0.05	0.03	0.03	0.02	0.28	0.51
	Female-headed	0.03	0.05	0.03	0.02	0.02	0.01	0.18	0.33

Table A5.2: *(j) Continued.*

		Respect to original	Leader split	Small entrant	Leaders merge and small entrant	Leaders merge	Exit of largest	Equal market shares	Perfect competition
(C) Complementary policies (firms)									
Only producers	Total	0.21	0.30	0.22	0.15	0.14	0.11	0.97	1.76
	Poor	0.21	0.30	0.22	0.15	0.14	0.11	0.97	1.76
	Nonpoor	0.21	0.30	0.22	0.15	0.14	0.11	0.97	1.76
	Male-headed	0.22	0.32	0.23	0.16	0.15	0.12	1.03	1.88
	Female-headed	0.17	0.23	0.17	0.12	0.11	0.09	0.76	1.38
All households	Total	0.06	0.08	0.06	0.04	0.04	0.03	0.26	0.47
	Poor	0.04	0.06	0.05	0.03	0.03	0.02	0.20	0.37
	Nonpoor	0.07	0.09	0.07	0.05	0.04	0.04	0.31	0.56
	Male-headed	0.06	0.09	0.07	0.05	0.04	0.03	0.29	0.52
	Female-headed	0.04	0.06	0.04	0.03	0.03	0.02	0.18	0.34
(D) Complementary policies (farmers – firms)									
Only producers	Total	0.37	0.46	0.38	0.31	0.30	0.27	1.12	1.94
	Poor	0.37	0.46	0.38	0.31	0.30	0.27	1.12	1.94
	Nonpoor	0.37	0.46	0.38	0.31	0.30	0.27	1.12	1.94
	Male-headed	0.39	0.49	0.41	0.33	0.32	0.29	1.20	2.07
	Female-headed	0.29	0.36	0.30	0.24	0.23	0.21	0.88	1.52
All households	Total	0.10	0.12	0.10	0.08	0.08	0.07	0.30	0.52
	Poor	0.08	0.09	0.08	0.06	0.06	0.06	0.23	0.40
	Nonpoor	0.12	0.15	0.11	0.10	0.09	0.09	0.36	0.62
	Male-headed	0.11	0.14	0.11	0.09	0.09	0.08	0.34	0.58
	Female-headed	0.07	0.09	0.07	0.06	0.06	0.05	0.21	0.37

Table A5.2: *(j) Continued.*

		Respect to original	Leader split	Small entrant	Leaders merge and small entrant	Leaders merge	Exit of largest	Equal market shares	Perfect competition
(E) International prices									
Only producers	Total	1.93	2.02	1.94	1.87	1.84	1.82	2.71	3.68
	Poor	1.93	2.02	1.94	1.87	1.84	1.82	2.71	3.68
	Nonpoor	1.93	2.02	1.94	1.87	1.84	1.82	2.71	3.68
	Male-headed	2.06	2.16	2.07	1.99	1.97	1.94	2.89	3.93
	Female-headed	1.51	1.59	1.52	1.46	1.45	1.43	2.12	2.89
All households	Total	0.52	0.55	0.52	0.50	0.50	0.49	0.73	0.99
	Poor	0.40	0.42	0.40	0.39	0.38	0.38	0.56	0.76
	Nonpoor	0.61	0.64	0.62	0.59	0.59	0.58	0.86	1.17
	Male-headed	0.57	0.60	0.58	0.56	0.55	0.54	0.81	1.10
	Female-headed	0.37	0.39	0.37	0.36	0.35	0.35	0.52	0.70

Table A5.2: (k) Malawi, tobacco (household income percentage changes).

		Respect to original	Leader split	Small entrant	Leaders merge and small entrant	Leaders merge	Exit of largest	Equal market shares	Perfect competition
(A) Basic model									
Only producers	Total	0.00	0.80	0.02	1.20	1.30	1.67	4.87	11.56
	Poor	0.00	0.63	0.01	0.94	1.01	1.31	3.81	9.04
	Nonpoor	0.00	0.88	0.02	1.33	1.43	1.84	5.37	12.74
	Male-headed	0.00	0.81	0.02	1.22	1.31	1.69	4.94	11.71
	Female-headed	0.00	0.70	0.02	1.06	1.14	1.47	4.29	10.18
All households	Total	0.00	0.12	0.00	0.17	0.19	0.24	0.70	1.66
	Poor	0.00	0.06	0.00	0.10	0.11	0.14	0.39	0.94
	Nonpoor	0.00	0.16	0.00	0.23	0.25	0.32	0.95	2.24
	Male-headed	0.00	0.14	0.00	0.21	0.22	0.29	0.84	2.00
	Female-headed	0.00	0.04	0.00	0.06	0.07	0.09	0.25	0.60
(B) Complementary policies (farmers)									
Only producers	Total	0.40	1.20	0.42	0.80	0.90	1.27	5.26	12.09
	Poor	0.31	0.94	0.33	0.63	0.70	0.99	4.12	9.45
	Nonpoor	0.44	1.32	0.47	0.88	0.99	1.40	5.80	13.33
	Male-headed	0.40	1.22	0.43	0.81	0.91	1.29	5.33	12.24
	Female-headed	0.35	1.06	0.37	0.70	0.79	1.12	4.64	10.64
All households	Total	0.06	0.17	0.06	0.12	0.13	0.18	0.76	1.74
	Poor	0.03	0.10	0.03	0.06	0.07	0.10	0.43	0.98
	Nonpoor	0.08	0.23	0.08	0.16	0.17	0.25	1.02	2.35
	Male-headed	0.07	0.21	0.07	0.14	0.16	0.22	0.91	2.09
	Female-headed	0.02	0.06	0.02	0.04	0.05	0.07	0.27	0.63

Table A5.2: *(k) Continued.*

		Respect to original	Leader split	Small entrant	Leaders merge and small entrant	Leaders merge	Exit of largest	Equal market shares	Perfect competition
(C) Complementary policies (firms)									
Only producers	Total	0.55	1.35	0.58	0.63	0.75	1.10	5.36	12.17
	Poor	0.43	1.05	0.45	0.50	0.58	0.86	4.19	9.52
	Nonpoor	0.60	1.49	0.64	0.70	0.82	1.22	5.91	13.42
	Male-headed	0.55	1.37	0.59	0.64	0.76	1.12	5.43	12.33
	Female-headed	0.48	1.19	0.51	0.56	0.66	0.97	4.72	10.72
All households	Total	0.08	0.19	0.08	0.09	0.11	0.16	0.77	1.75
	Poor	0.04	0.11	0.05	0.05	0.06	0.09	0.43	0.99
	Nonpoor	0.11	0.26	0.11	0.12	0.14	0.21	1.04	2.36
	Male-headed	0.09	0.23	0.10	0.11	0.13	0.19	0.93	2.10
	Female-headed	0.03	0.07	0.03	0.03	0.04	0.06	0.28	0.64
(D) Complementary policies (farmers – firms)									
Only producers	Total	0.94	1.75	0.98	0.23	0.35	0.70	5.75	12.70
	Poor	0.74	1.37	0.77	0.18	0.27	0.55	4.50	9.93
	Nonpoor	1.04	1.92	1.08	0.26	0.39	0.77	6.34	14.00
	Male-headed	0.95	1.77	1.00	0.24	0.36	0.71	5.83	12.87
	Female-headed	0.83	1.54	0.87	0.20	0.31	0.62	5.07	11.19
All households	Total	0.14	0.25	0.14	0.03	0.05	0.10	0.83	1.83
	Poor	0.08	0.14	0.08	0.02	0.03	0.06	0.47	1.03
	Nonpoor	0.18	0.34	0.19	0.05	0.07	0.14	1.12	2.47
	Male-headed	0.16	0.30	0.17	0.04	0.06	0.12	0.99	2.20
	Female-headed	0.05	0.09	0.05	0.01	0.02	0.04	0.30	0.66

Table A5.2: *(k) Continued.*

		Respect to original	Leader split	Small entrant	Leaders merge and small entrant	Leaders merge	Exit of largest	Equal market shares	Perfect competition
(E) International prices									
Only producers	Total	5.30	6.66	5.43	4.11	3.88	3.56	10.38	18.51
	Poor	4.15	5.21	4.24	3.21	3.04	2.79	8.12	14.48
	Nonpoor	5.84	7.35	5.98	4.53	4.28	3.93	11.45	20.41
	Male-headed	5.37	6.75	5.50	4.16	3.93	3.61	10.52	18.76
	Female-headed	4.67	5.87	4.78	3.62	3.42	3.14	9.14	16.30
All households	Total	0.76	0.96	0.78	0.59	0.56	0.51	1.49	2.66
	Poor	0.43	0.54	0.44	0.33	0.31	0.29	0.84	1.50
	Nonpoor	1.03	1.29	1.05	0.80	0.75	0.69	2.02	3.59
	Male-headed	0.92	1.15	0.94	0.71	0.67	0.62	1.79	3.20
	Female-headed	0.28	0.35	0.28	0.21	0.20	0.19	0.54	0.97

Table A5.2: *(I) Zambia, tobacco (household income percentage changes).*

		Respect to original	Leader split	Small entrant	Leaders merge and small entrant	Leaders merge	Exit of largest	Equal market shares	Perfect competition
(A) Basic model									
Only producers	Total	0.00	2.93	0.37	0.94	1.53	4.50	6.48	20.99
	Poor	0.00	2.27	0.29	0.73	1.19	3.49	5.03	16.27
	Nonpoor	0.00	3.35	0.42	1.07	1.75	5.14	7.40	23.97
	Male-headed	0.00	3.04	0.38	0.97	1.58	4.66	6.72	21.74
	Female-headed	0.00	2.27	0.29	0.73	1.18	3.48	5.01	16.23
All households	Total	0.00	0.06	0.01	0.02	0.03	0.10	0.14	0.45
	Poor	0.00	0.04	0.01	0.01	0.02	0.07	0.09	0.31
	Nonpoor	0.00	0.08	0.01	0.03	0.04	0.12	0.18	0.57
	Male-headed	0.00	0.07	0.01	0.02	0.04	0.11	0.16	0.50
	Female-headed	0.00	0.03	0.00	0.01	0.02	0.05	0.07	0.24
(B) Complementary policies (farmers)									
Only producers	Total	0.48	3.41	0.86	0.46	1.07	4.01	6.93	21.67
	Poor	0.37	2.64	0.67	0.36	0.83	3.11	5.37	16.80
	Nonpoor	0.54	3.89	0.99	0.53	1.22	4.57	7.91	24.74
	Male-headed	0.49	3.53	0.90	0.48	1.11	4.15	7.18	22.44
	Female-headed	0.37	2.64	0.67	0.36	0.83	3.10	5.36	16.75
All households	Total	0.01	0.07	0.02	0.01	0.02	0.09	0.15	0.47
	Poor	0.01	0.05	0.01	0.01	0.02	0.06	0.10	0.32
	Nonpoor	0.01	0.09	0.02	0.01	0.03	0.11	0.19	0.59
	Male-headed	0.01	0.08	0.02	0.01	0.03	0.10	0.17	0.52
	Female-headed	0.01	0.04	0.01	0.01	0.01	0.05	0.08	0.25

Table A5.2: *(l) Continued.*

	Respect to original	Leader split	Small entrant	Leaders merge and small entrant	Leaders merge	Exit of largest	Equal market shares	Perfect competition
(C) Complementary policies (firms)								
Only producers								
Total	0.32	3.24	0.72	0.61	1.25	4.13	6.70	21.31
Poor	0.25	2.51	0.56	0.47	0.97	3.20	5.20	16.52
Nonpoor	0.36	3.69	0.83	0.70	1.43	4.71	7.65	24.33
Male-headed	0.33	3.35	0.75	0.63	1.29	4.27	6.94	22.07
Female-headed	0.25	2.50	0.56	0.47	0.97	3.19	5.18	16.47
All households								
Total	0.01	0.07	0.02	0.01	0.03	0.09	0.14	0.46
Poor	0.00	0.05	0.01	0.01	0.02	0.06	0.10	0.31
Nonpoor	0.01	0.09	0.02	0.02	0.03	0.11	0.18	0.58
Male-headed	0.01	0.08	0.02	0.01	0.03	0.10	0.16	0.51
Female-headed	0.00	0.04	0.01	0.01	0.01	0.05	0.08	0.25
(D) Complementary policies (farmers – firms)								
Only producers								
Total	0.79	3.71	1.22	0.13	0.79	3.63	7.15	21.98
Poor	0.62	2.88	0.94	0.10	0.62	2.82	5.54	17.04
Nonpoor	0.91	4.24	1.39	0.15	0.91	4.15	8.16	25.10
Male-headed	0.82	3.84	1.26	0.14	0.82	3.76	7.40	22.77
Female-headed	0.61	2.87	0.94	0.10	0.61	2.81	5.53	17.00
All households								
Total	0.02	0.08	0.03	0.00	0.02	0.08	0.15	0.47
Poor	0.01	0.05	0.02	0.00	0.01	0.05	0.10	0.32
Nonpoor	0.02	0.10	0.03	0.00	0.02	0.10	0.19	0.60
Male-headed	0.02	0.09	0.03	0.00	0.02	0.09	0.17	0.53
Female-headed	0.01	0.04	0.01	0.00	0.01	0.04	0.08	0.25

Table A5.2: *(I) Continued.*

	Respect to original	Leader split	Small entrant	Leaders merge and small entrant	Leaders merge	Exit of largest	Equal market shares	Perfect competition
(E) International prices								
Only producers								
Total	4.79	7.97	5.43	3.79	2.79	0.07	11.41	28.12
Poor	3.71	6.17	4.21	2.94	2.17	0.05	8.85	21.80
Nonpoor	5.46	9.09	6.20	4.32	3.19	0.08	13.03	32.11
Male-headed	4.96	8.25	5.62	3.92	2.89	0.07	11.82	29.13
Female-headed	3.70	6.16	4.20	2.93	2.16	0.05	8.82	21.74
All households								
Total	0.10	0.17	0.12	0.08	0.06	0.00	0.25	0.61
Poor	0.07	0.12	0.08	0.06	0.04	0.00	0.17	0.41
Nonpoor	0.13	0.22	0.15	0.10	0.08	0.00	0.31	0.76
Male-headed	0.11	0.19	0.13	0.09	0.07	0.00	0.27	0.68
Female-headed	0.06	0.09	0.06	0.04	0.03	0.00	0.13	0.32

References

Abbott, P. (2007). Distortions to agricultural incentives in Côte d'Ivoire. Agricultural Distortions Working Paper 46. World Bank.

Balat, J., and G. Porto (2007). Globalization and complementary policies: poverty impacts in rural Zambia. In *Globalization and Poverty* (ed. A. Harrison). University of Chicago Press for the NBER.

Balat, J., and G. Porto (2008). Changes in the structure of the value chain in agriculture in Zambia: impacts on farm income. Mimeo, World Bank.

Barnum, H., and L. Squire (1979). A model of an agricultural household: theory and evidence. World Bank Occasional Paper 27.

Barrett, C., and P. A. Dorosh (1996). Farmers' welfare and changing food prices: nonparametric evidence from rice in Madagascar. *American Journal of Agricultural Economics* 78, 656-669.

Benjamin, D. (1992). Household composition, labor markets, and labor demand: testing for separation in agricultural household models. *Econometrica* 60(2), 287-322.

Benjamin, D., and A. Deaton (1993). Household welfare and the pricing of cocoa and coffee in Côte d'Ivoire: lessons from the living standards surveys. *The World Bank Economic Review* 7, 293-318.

Brambilla, I., and G. Porto (2011). Market structure, outgrower contracts and farm output. Evidence from cotton reforms in Zambia. Oxford Economic Papers, forthcoming.

Brooks, J., A. Croppenstedt, and E. Aggrey-Fynn (2007). Distortions to agricultural incentives in Ghana. Agricultural Distortions Working Paper 47. World Bank.

Budd, J. W. (1993). Changing food prices and rural welfare: a nonparametric examination of the Côte d'Ivoire. *Economic Development and Cultural Change* 41, 587-603.

Cadot, O., L. Dutoit, and J. de Melo (2009). The elimination of Madagascar's Vanilla Marketing Board, 10 years on. *Journal of African Economies* 18(3), 388-430.

Cheyns, E., H. A. Mrema, and B. Sallée (2006). *Socio-Economic Study of the Ugandan Coffee Chain.* Centre de Coopération Internationale en Recherche Agronomique pour le Développement.

De Janvry, A., M. Fafchamps, and E. Sadoulet (1991). Peasant household behaviour with missing markets: some paradoxes explained. *Economic Journal* 101, 1400-1417.

Deaton, A. (1989a). Rice prices and income distribution in Thailand: a non-parametric analysis. *Economic Journal* 99(395), 1-37.

Deaton, A. (1989b). Household survey data and pricing policies in developing countries. *The World Bank Economic Review* 3, 183-210.

Deaton, A. (1997). *The Analysis of Household Surveys: A Microeconometric Approach to Development Policy.* Johns Hopkins University Press for the World Bank.

Deininger, K., and P. Olinto (2000). Why liberalization alone has not improved agricultural productivity in Zambia: the role of asset ownership and working capital constraints. World Bank Working Paper 2302.

Ennis, H. (2009). Agriculture, value chains, and income distribution in rural Africa. Mimeo, Universidad Carlos III Madrid.

Eswaran, M., and A. Kotwal (1986). Access to capital and agrarian production organization. *Economic Journal* **96**, 482–498.

FAO (1993). *Agricultural Extension and Farm Women in the 1980s*. Rome: FAO.

FAO (2003). *Issues in the Global Tobacco Economy: Selected Case Studies*. Rome: FAO.

Friedman, J., and J. Levinsohn (2002). The distributional impacts of Indonesia's financial crisis on household welfare: a "rapid response" methodology. *World Bank Economic Review* **16**, 397–423.

Gergely, N. (2009). The cotton sector in Benin. Africa Region Working Paper Series 125. World Bank.

Gittinger, J. P., S. Chernick, N. R. Horenstein, and K. Saito (1990). *Household Food Security and the Role of Women*. World Bank.

Glover, D. J. (1984). Contract farming and smallholder outgrower schemes in less-developed countries. *World Development* **12**(11–12), 1143–1157.

Glover, D. J. (1990). Contract farming and outgrower schemes in East and Southern Africa. *Journal of Agricultural Economics* **41**(3), 303–315.

Goldberg, P., and N. Pavcnik (2004). Trade, inequality, and poverty: what do we know? Evidence from recent trade liberalization episodes in developing countries. *Brookings Trade Forum* **2004**, 223–269.

Goldberg, P., and N. Pavcnik (2007). Distributional effects of globalization in developing countries. *Journal of Economic Literature* **45**(1), 39–82.

Habyalimana, S. (2007). Access to finance through value chains: lessons from Rwanda. AEGIS European Conference on African Studies, July 11–14, 2007, Leiden, The Netherlands.

Hanson, S. (2008). C-4 cotton reform and production update. GAIN Report SG8020. USDA Foreign Agricultural Service.

Heltberg, R., and F. Tarp (2002). Agriculture supply response and poverty in Mozambique. *Food Policy* **27**(2), 103–24.

Hertel, T., and A. L. Winters (eds) (2006). *Poverty Impacts of the Doha Development Agenda*. Palgrave–McMillan for the World Bank.

Hoekman, B., and M. Olarreaga (eds) (2007). *Global Trade and Poor Nations: Poverty Impacts and Policy Implications of Liberalization*. Brookings Institution Press.

Horenstein, N. R. (1989). *Women and Food Security in Kenya*. World Bank.

Horn, H., and J. Levinsohn (2001). Merger policies and trade liberalisation. *Economic Journal* **111**, 244–277.

International Coffee Organization (ICO). Country profiles. URL: www.ico.org.

Ivanic, M., and W. Martin (2008). Implications of higher global food prices for poverty in low-income countries. World Bank Policy Research Working Paper Series 4594.

Jaffe, S. M. (2003). Malawi's tobacco sector: standing on one strong leg is better than on none. Africa Region Working Paper Series 55. World Bank.

Jiggins, J. (1989a). How poor women earn income in sub-Saharan Africa and what works against them. *World Development* **17**(7), 953–963.

Jiggins, J. (1989b). Agricultural technology: impact, issues and action. In *The Women and International Development Annual* (ed. R. S. Gallin, M. Aronoff, and A. Ferguson), Volume 1, Part 1, Chapter 1. Boulder, CO: Westview Press.

Key, N., E. Sadoulet, and A. De Janvry (2000). Transactions costs and agricultural household supply response. *American Journal of Agricultural Economics* **82**, 245–259.

Koyi, G. (2005). The textiles and clothing industry in Zambia. Paper prepared for the Conference on the Future of African Textiles Industry, Cape Town, October 10–12, 2005.

Kranton, R., and A. Swamy (2008). Contracts, hold-up, and exports: textiles and opium in colonial India. *American Economic Review* **98**(3), 967–989.

Laven, A. (2007). *Marketing Reforms in Ghana's Cocoa Sector.* Overseas Development Department.

Likulunga, M. (2005). The status of contract farming and contractual arrangements in Zambian agriculture and agribusiness. Report prepared for the Food, Agriculture and Natural Resources Policy Analysis Network (FARNPAN).

Lopez, R., J. Nash, and J. Stanton (1995). Adjustment and poverty in Mexican agriculture: how farmers' wealth affects supply response. World Bank Policy Research Working Paper 1494.

Losch, B. (2002). Global restructuring and liberalization: Côte d'Ivoire and the end of the international cocoa market? *Journal of Agrarian Change* 2(2), 206-227.

Loveridge, S., J. B. Nyarwaya, and E. Shingiro (2003). Decaffeinated? Situation, trends and prospects for smallholder coffee production in Rwanda. Rwanda Food Security Research Project/MINAGRI. URL: http://aec.msu.edu/fs2/rwanda/index.htm.

Ludmer, S. (2010). A model of supply chains in export agriculture. Mimeo, Universidad Nacional de La Plata, Argentina.

Lundstedt, H., and S. Pärssinen (2009). Cocoa is Ghana, Ghana is cocoa: evaluating reforms of the Ghanaian cocoa sector. Masters Thesis, Lund University.

Masiga, M., A. Ruhweza, and YOMA Consultants (2007). *Commodity Revenue Management: Coffee and Cotton in Uganda.* International Institute for Sustainable Development.

McKay, A., O. Morrissey, and C. Vaillant (1997). Trade liberalization and agricultural supply response: issues and some lessons. *European Journal of Development Research* 9(2), 129-147.

McMillan, M., D. Rodrik, and K. H. Welch (2003). When economic reform goes wrong: cashews in Mozambique. *Brookings Trade Forum* **2003**, 97-151.

Nicita, A. (2009). The price effect of tariff liberalization: measuring the impact on household welfare. *Journal of Development Economics* **89**(1), 19-27

Olawoye, J. E. (1989). Women in extension. In *Extension for Development: Concepts and Issues* (ed. W. M. Rivera and T. O. Ogunfiditimi), Chapter 14. Ibadan: Lidato Press.

Pagan, A., and A. Ullah (1999). *Nonparametric Econometrics.* Cambridge University Press.

Porter, G., and K. Phillips-Howard (1997). Comparing contracts: an evaluation of contract farming schemes in Africa. *World Development* 25(2), 227-238.

Porto, G. (2005). Informal export barriers and poverty. *Journal of International Economics* **66**, 447-470.

Porto, G. (2006). Using survey data to assess the distributional effects of trade policy. *Journal of International Economics* **70**, 140-160.

Porto, G. (2007). Globalization and poverty in Latin America: some channels and some evidence. *The World Economy* 30(9), 1430-1456.

Porto, G. (2010). Commodity prices: impact and adjustment. Mimeo, Universidad Nacional de La Plata, Argentina.

Porto, G. (2011). On trade, poverty, and prices in developing countries. PREM Note, World Bank, forthcoming.

Poulton, C., J. Kydd, and D. Kabambe (2007). Case study on Malawi tobacco. All-Africa Review of Experiences with Commercial Agriculture. World Bank.

RATES (2003). Cotton-textile-apparel value chain report Malawi.

Ravallion, M. (1990). Rural welfare effects of food price changes under induced wage responses: theory and evidence for Bangladesh. *Oxford Economic Papers* **42**, 574-585.

Sahn, D., and A. Sarris (1991). Structural adjustment and the welfare of rural smallholders: a comparative analysis from sub-Saharan Africa. *World Bank Economic Review* **5**, 259-289.

Saito, K., and C. J. Weidemann (1990). *Agricultural Extension for Women Farmers in Africa*. World Bank.

Saizonou, J. (2008). The Interprofessional Cotton Association in Benin. URL: www.inter-reseaux.org/ IMG/pdf/Fiche_AIC_premiere_version_english.pdf.

Salop, S. (1979). Monopolistic competition with outside goods. *Bell Journal of Economics* **10**(1), 141–156.

Sexton, R., I. Sheldon, S. McCorriston, and H. Wang (2007). Agricultural trade liberalization and economic development: the role of downstream market power. *Agricultural Economics* **36**, 253–270.

Sheldon, I. (2006). Market structure, industrial concentration, and price transmission. Mimeo, Ohio State University.

Singh, I., L. Squire, and J. Strauss (eds) (1986). *Agricultural Household Models: Extensions, Applications and Policy*. Baltimore, MD: Johns Hopkins Press for the World Bank.

Stokey, N., and R. E. Lucas (1989). *Recursive Methods in Economic Dynamics*. Cambridge, MA: Harvard University Press.

Sundaram, R. K. (1996). *A First Course in Optimization Theory*. Cambridge University Press.

Syverson, C. (2004). Market structure and productivity: a concrete example. *Journal of Political Economy* **112**(6), 1181–1222.

Taylor, E., and H. Adelman (2003). Agricultural household models: genesis, evolution and extensions. *Review of Economics of the Household* **1**(1), 33–58.

Tchale, H., and J. Keyser (2009). *Malawi Country Economic Memorandum. Seizing Opportunities for Growth Through Trade. Volume II: Background Papers. Quantitative Value Chain Analysis*. World Bank.

Tchale, H., and J. Keyser (2010). Quantitative value chain analysis: an application to Malawi. Policy Research Working Paper 5242, World Bank.

Trivedi, P., and T. Akiyama (1992). A framework for evaluating the impact of pricing policies for cocoa and coffee in Côte d'Ivoire. *The World Bank Economic Review* **6**(2), 307–330.

Tschirley, D., and S. Kabwe (2007). Cotton in Zambia: 2007 assessment of its organization, performance, current policy initiatives, and challenges for the future. Food Security Collaborative Working Papers 54485.

Tschirley, D., and S. Kabwe (2009). The cotton sector of Zambia. Africa Region Working Paper Series 124, World Bank.

Tschirley, D., C. Poulton, and P. Labaste (2009). *Organization and Performance of Cotton Sectors in Africa: Learning from Reform Experience*. World Bank.

van Donge, J. (2002). Disordering the market: the liberalisation of burley tobacco in Malawi in the 1990s. *The Journal of Southern African Studies* **28**(1), 89–115.

Vargas Hill, R. (2010). Liberalisation and producer price risk: examining subjective expectations in the Ugandan coffee market. *Journal of African Economies* **19**(4), 433–458.

Vigneri, M., and P. Santos (2007). *Ghana and the Cocoa Marketing Dilemma: What Has Liberalization without Price Competition Achieved?* Overseas Development Institute.

Warning, M., and N. Key (2002). The social performance and distributional consequences of contract farming: an equilibrium analysis of the Arachide de Bouche program in Senegal. *World Development* **30**(2), 255–263.

Wilcox, J. M., and P. Abbott (2004). Market power and structural adjustment: the case of West African cocoa market liberalization. American Agricultural Economics Association Annual Meeting.

Winters, A., N. McCulloch, and A. McKay (2004). Trade liberalization and poverty: the evidence so far. *Journal of Economic Literature* **42**, 72–115.

Wodon, Q., C. Tsimpo, P. Backiny-Yetna, G. Joseph, F. Adoho, and H. Coulombe (2008). Potential impact of higher food prices on poverty: summary estimates for a dozen West and Central African countries. World Bank Policy Research Working Paper Series 4745.

World Bank (2005). *Diagnostic Trade Integration Study of Benin.* World Bank.

World Bank (2008). Pathways to greater efficiency in the Malawi tobacco industry. Poverty Reduction and Economic Management, AFTP1. World Bank, Africa Region.

World Trade Organization (2004a). *Burkina Faso Trade Policy Review.* Geneva: World Trade Organization.

World Trade Organization (2004b). *Rwanda Trade Policy Review.* Geneva: World Trade Organization.

Yartey, C. (2008). Tackling Burkina Faso's cotton crisis. IMF Survey Magazine. URL: www.imf.org/external/pubs/ft/survey/so/2008/CAR022508B.htm.